LIVE LONGER, FEEL YOUNGER

LIVE LONGER, FEEL YOUNGER

The complete guide to enjoying a fun, fit and healthy later life

DIANA MORAN

CONTENTS

PART 1
LOOKING YOUNGER ALL THE TIME

PART 2
MAXIMIZING YOUR HEALTH

PART 3
A NEW YOU

This edition first published in the UK in 2005 by
Hamlyn, a division of Octopus Publishing Group Limited.
Exclusively for Marks and Spencer p.l.c.

www.marksandspencer.com

Copyright © Octopus Publishing Group Limited 2005

ISBN 0 600 61358 5

Printed and bound in China

RECIPE NOTES

Both metric and imperial measurements are given for the recipes. Use one set of measures only, not a mixture of both.

Ovens should be preheated to the specified temperature. If using a fan-assisted oven, follow the manufacturer's instructions for adjusting the time and temperature. Grills should also be preheated.

This book includes dishes made with nuts and nut derivatives. It is advisable for those with known allergic reactions to nuts and nut derivatives and those who may be potentially vulnerable to these allergies, such as pregnant and nursing mothers, invalids, the elderly, babies and children, to avoid dishes made with nuts and nut oils. It is also prudent to check the labels of preprepared ingredients for the possible inclusion of nut derivatives.

The Department of Health advises that eggs should not be consumed raw. This book contains some dishes made with raw or lightly cooked eggs. It is prudent for more vulnerable people, such as pregnant and nursing mothers, invalids, the elderly, babies and young children, to avoid uncooked or lightly cooked dishes made with eggs.

Meat and poultry should be cooked thoroughly. To test if poultry is cooked, pierce the flesh through the thickest part with a skewer or fork - the juices should run clear, never pink or red.

Fresh herbs should be used unless otherwise stated. If unavailable use dried herbs as an alternative but halve the quantities stated.

All the recipes in this book have been analysed by a professional nutritionist. The analysis refers to each serving.

INTRODUCTION

If you are a feisty fifty or a super sixty-year-old then rejoice. We live in a stimulating, albeit uncertain time in history, and there's never been a better time to be mature. Thanks to medical advances, we no longer live under the threat of death or serious disease, and gone too are the social and economic restrictions of past generations. Education, careers, travel and new experiences are available for all. Far from this being a time of life to think about switching off and slowing down, it's an age of endless opportunities, a time to pursue lifelong interests, to re-educate yourself, or even to have the courage to start out on a second career or a new relationship.

AGE IS BUT A NUMBER

Every day, whether we like it or not, we get that little bit older. In fact, the whole world is getting older, life expectancy is increasing and the birth rate is slowing down. Baby Boomers – people born during or immediately after World War 2 (myself included) – have finally grown up, and generally speaking are healthier, more knowledgeable, and possess more disposable income than previous generations. As the cliché goes, it is not how old you are but more importantly how old you feel.

Ageing is inevitable and there's nothing we can do about it. Or is there? We can't determine how long we will live for, but we do have some control over the quality of our lives. Take advantage of your predicted longevity by looking after yourself, your family, your relationships, your looks, and your health. Adopting this approach will be a major step towards enabling you to pursue your ambitions, dreams and hopes. As the old Arabian proverb says, 'He who has health has hope, and he who has hope has everything.'

REDRESSING YOUTH CULTURE

In many Western societies, youth culture is a powerful force. Many people approaching maturity are in danger of being written off as too old, not useful, or no longer interesting. This encourages many women (and increasingly men) to undergo cosmetic surgery and spend vast amounts on products and treatments hoping to hold back the years. It also engenders a feeling that life is over and there is little left to achieve now.

In continental Europe, however, many older people remain the traditional head of the family, held in respect by its junior members. Some still live in and run the family house, actively looking after children, providing meals and giving youngsters the wisdom of their advice. Many of these women are powerful, admired, and to some extent iconic, with youngsters seeking to emulate them.

Throughout history we've seen examples of self-confident, beautiful mature women, often a force to be reckoned with. Ordinary women today, not just queens and heads of states, deserve that same respect. There are many successful and financially sound and prominent career women in business, politics, teaching, the media, and law. We should all be working to redress the balance and regain that respect.

THE LOST GENERATION

So where does our generation fit into today's society? For the first half of our lives we conformed to the dictates of our parents and grandparents. Grown up, and finally rid of the constraints imposed on us during childhood, we now find ourselves living in a time where the emphasis has shifted from reverence of age to the worship of youth. We realise that our children now have the top spot, not us, and we may feel cheated out of the respect that age, up until now, has deserved. It is crucial that we don't become despondent in the face of this.

Now is the time to move forward, not backwards, and to cut a new and exciting path for ourselves and future generations. A recent survey in the UK showed there were more people aged over 60 than 16 year olds, and the numbers are increasing. In the UK women outnumber men and have a life expectancy of 79 years. With the menopause occurring on average at 52, that means some 30 postmenopausal years to enjoy. The whole world is getting older and our generation will have a major influence on political agenda, particularly on issues fundamental to us, such as governmental policy affecting work, health, housing and pensions.

NEW HORIZONS

Many mature women today are experienced and financially better off than previous generations, possessing skills and confidence acquired through education and years of hard work. Retired, successful women have more time and money, which makes it possible to indulge fancies and fantasies only previously dreamed of. Retirement no longer signifies a time for reflecting on the past, but instead must be viewed as an opportunity to experiment, experience and explore new horizons. Could this be a time to re-apply your skills by teaching them to youngsters and giving back to society a little of what brought you happiness or financial gain? Society needs leaders and role models in order to make revolutionary changes and a difference; it takes stamina, determination and a positive mental attitude.

THE IMPORTANCE OF HEALTH

If you want to make a difference to the world, you'll need to keep fit and be in touch. If we are living longer we need to work harder at maintaining physical and mental independence in order to live our lives to the full.

A great many people age well and have strong bodies in middle and later years. Health is a bit like an insurance policy. If you invested during your youth there will be more to draw upon in times of trouble, but it's never too late to

start. With the onset of aches and pains it's all too easy to blame them on the passing years and to make the mistake of disguising physical or mental problems as 'just old age'. Ageing and inactivity is not the same thing, and today the trouble is that we increasingly use our brains instead of our brawn, to the detriment of our health.

Health wise, we are moving very fast from one physical extreme to another and alarm bells are ringing. By ridding ourselves of problems brought on by physical hard work in the past, we are creating other serious medical conditions through not being active enough. Our cars, washing machines and computers have freed us from physical stress and strain, but too much sitting around, or peering at television and computer screens, is inevitably unhealthy. Heart disease, stiff joints, osteoporosis and obesity are just a few examples of health-related problems which we can bring upon ourselves through lack of physical activity.

ABOUT THIS BOOK

This book contains everything you need to know about making the most of this period of your life, ensuring you feel your best, look your best, and continue to do so. It is packed with vital information on health issues, plenty of sensible advice about relationships and attitudes, exercises to try, fantastic recipes for health-giving foods, massage techniques and great ways to relax.

Part 1 is all about looking good and shaping up. With radiant hair and skin, and a more slender toned shape, you will feel better about yourself, giving your confidence and self-respect a boost. And don't forget the health benefits you will enjoy with gentle exercise and an improved eating regime.

Part 2 is all about maximizing your health now and in the future – how to minimize the effects of the menopause, lay the foundations for strong bones to protect against osteoporosis, lifestyle choices to ensure your heart stays healthy, and all-important breast care.

Part 3 discovers a new you. There is sensible and inspiring advice for dealing with life's challenges, a chapter

with positive approaches to making life seem a little rosier, and some brain boosters for keeping your memory in great shape.

It is easy to slip into a rut and start to feel useless, so why not take control of your life and implement some positive changes? Spending just a little time on yourself each day and addressing the less successful aspects of your life can pay great dividends. But don't put it off by thinking you will start in the new year, or after your holiday. Start right now and you could already be feeling the benefits this time next week.

RISING TO THE CHALLENGE

There are many simple, practical ways to improve your quality of life and natural ways to help you live longer and look younger. This book will show you which exercises and activities are beneficial to your overall health, and how massage can help lessen stresses and strains. Being physically fit adds a quality and buzz to life, obesity restricts it. But total fitness is not just about being physically fit – we need to aim to be medically, nutritionally, mentally, emotionally and socially fit too.

Learn to be vigilant about bodily changes as being alert could prevent the onset of serious illnesses. Remember to make sure you are receiving the medical checks which may help you avoid health problems. This book gives you the lowdown on foods with anti-ageing properties and shows you how to recognise foods which do more harm than good. Equipped with this information, you can make the food choices which are right for you.

This book will also show how simple facial exercise and massage plus natural ingredients can help relieve tension, make you look more beautiful and put a smile on your face.

Common everyday problems can cause distress and worry so discover simple ways to share your feelings, cope with your emotions and improve relationships. Finally, armed with the latest information and an optimistic attitude, check out how your skills or talents could be used to help others as well as yourself.

ON A PERSONAL NOTE

I consider myself fortunate to have borne children, two sons now aged 41 and 44. As a young wife I was often rebellious: juggling a home, young family and a career, which was somewhat frowned upon then. In today's society, a young woman takes it for granted that she will both hold down a career and raise a family. Although we live in turbulent times I still love the challenge life has to offer and don't intend to waste a minute of it. Like many of you, I now find myself single again with my family grown and flown, but I'm independent, physically, mentally and sexually active and still hope to fulfil some of my lifelong ambitions. Being alone (but rarely lonely) there are great opportunities to travel, meet new friends, reacquaint myself with old ones and, on a whim, change direction without upsetting anybody. I've more time for my garden, oil painting and messing about in boats.

I'm also lucky to have young children around me again, having been blessed with four grandchildren whose boundless energy is an inspiration. They make me acutely aware of time passing, and of human fragility. This was also highlighted for me 16 years ago when I had breast cancer. Cancer made me realise that none of us is invincible, but it also taught me to appreciate my life and live it to the full. When I was a girl my granny told me, 'Live for the day, but keep a cautious eye on the future.' It was, and still is, wise advice.

Personally, I feel comfortable with my maturity, regard this period of life as a bonus, and have finally come around to accepting myself for who I am. Being over 50 and female is challenging and I'm planning positively for my future, as I'm sure many of you are. However, I'm aware that during any period of change, negativity can strike and I hope this book will provide encouragement at those difficult moments. You should relish your individualism, be open-minded and eager to embrace all the opportunities that life still has to offer. You will find that the knowledge, wisdom and experience acquired through life's journey now equips you to embrace life like never before.

PART 1
LOOKING YOUNGER
ALL THE TIME

CHAPTER 1
INSTANT BEAUTY BOOSTERS   14

During the menopause, your skin and hair may lose their vitality and healthy glow, mainly due to changes in hormone levels. It is therefore important that you eat a good diet and boost your circulation by massage and exercise. This chapter contains all the information you need to help you to keep your skin and hair looking healthy and radiant, including beauty routines, massages and facial exercises.

CHAPTER 2
LOOSEN UP AND SHAPE UP   38

This chapter focuses on Pilates – an excellent form of exercise as it can be adapted for all levels of fitness, age and body type. It can help to relieve tension and reduce muscle and joint stiffness as well as aches and pains, particularly of the back. By following the exercises presented here, you can improve your coordination, flexibility and fluidity of movement, and also increase your overall sense of wellbeing.

CHAPTER 3
HEALTHY EATING
FOR A LONGER LIFE   68

What you eat is very important, especially when your body is undergoing changes as it will during the menopause. This chapter looks at how you can obtain the optimum nutrients so that your body works as well as it possibly can, ensuring that you both look and feel healthy. An easy-to-follow three-day detox plan will also help you to recover from the build-up of toxins that can lead to a feeling of illness or lethargy.

CHAPTER 1
INSTANT BEAUTY BOOSTERS

During the menopause, your skin is likely to become drier and flakier, wrinkles or sunspots more pronounced and your hair greyer, drier and more brittle. Therefore, you need to take special care of your skin and hair, reducing the amount of toxins you are exposed to, and using facial treatments and massage to improve your skin and combat the effects of ageing.

WHAT YOUR SKIN AND HAIR NEED

A poor complexion and lacklustre hair may be due to toxic overload, from smoking, alcohol, stress and/or sunlight. If toxins are wreaking havoc on the rest of the body, nutrients are diverted away from the skin and hair.

NEEDS

SKIN

Antioxidants These are the most vital way to protect your skin against free-radical attack (see page 70). Aim for 6–10 servings of fresh fruit or vegetables a day for best results. This will also supply vitamin C, which helps build collagen and vitamin A, and encourages the growth of new skin cells.

Essential fatty acids (EFAs) As well as keeping red blood cells healthy, which boosts circulation, EFAs also help fight dry skin. Good sources are oily fish, nuts and seeds – aim for one serving a day.

Sulphur This helps the body form new collagen. It is found in eggs, onions and garlic. Aim for one serving a day.

HAIR

B vitamins Hair doesn't grow unless adequate levels of B vitamins are found in the body. They are found in whole grains, dairy products and leafy green vegetables. Aim for at least three servings a day.

Essential fatty acids (EFAs) Like skin, a lack of EFAs results in dry hair. Have at least one serving (see above) daily.

Protein If you don't get enough protein in your diet, your hair actually grows with a lifted cuticle. This not only increases the risk of dehydration, but it also makes hair look dull because light can't reflect from it. Aim for two servings of protein-rich foods (like eggs, fish, dairy products, nuts, pulses or meat) each day.

Vitamin H (biotin) Found in eggs, fish, milk, nuts and pulses, this nutrient actually helps hair (and nails) grow. Aim for one serving of biotin-rich foods a day.

DOESN'T NEED

Sugar As well as being a major source of free radicals, sugar also attacks the skin. It attaches to proteins in collagen, causing them to become stiff and inflexible, which eventually leads to wrinkling.

Salty foods These are high in iodine, which can encourage spots to break out.

Too much vitamin A While this nutrient may help skin, high quantities of foods that are heavy in vitamin A, like liver, can actually trigger hair loss; instead, get your vitamin A through foods containing beta-carotene (like carrots, pumpkin, sweet potatoes), since such foods do not cause the same reaction.

A DAY'S DIET AT-A-GLANCE

Skin and hair need slightly different things to thrive (see chart opposite), but the following diet will aid both (see also Chapter 3 for general dietary advice).

07:30 **Take supplements** One multivitamin and mineral supplement, plus 1,000 mg of methyl sulphonyl methane (which converts to sulphur in the body) and 500 mg of evening primrose oil. Drink the supplements with at least one glass of water; aim to drink another eight throughout the day.

08:00 **Breakfast** Have a bowl of bran or wheat cereal with skimmed milk, 2 tablespoons of blueberries and 2 tablespoons of raspberries, plus drink a glass of orange juice.

11:30 **Mid-morning snack** Have a piece of fruit and a handful of nuts or a low-fat yogurt.

13:00 **Lunch** Take another 500 mg of evening primrose oil. Have a sandwich made with two slices of wholegrain bread filled with 50 g (2 oz) of fish, chicken or low-fat cheese. Top with a mix of lettuce or alfalfa sprouts, chopped onion, tomato, avocado and cucumber. Serve with a cup of tomato, carrot or vegetable soup.

15:30 **Mid-afternoon snack** Have another piece of fruit.

20:00 **Evening meal** Take another 500 mg of evening primrose oil. Eat a 75 g (3 oz) serving of lean protein. Serve with 50 g (2 oz) of brown rice, wholewheat pasta, jacket potato, new potatoes or wholegrain bread. Add 2 tablespoons of a green vegetable and 2 tablespoons of another vegetable.

HINT FOR HEALTH

Alcohol can rob your skin of the vitamins and minerals it needs, so don't overindulge, and have a few days a week where you drink water or fruit and vegetable juice (see pages 88–93) instead of having an alcoholic drink.

CARING FOR YOUR SKIN

Like a plant, the skin on the face needs one thing more than any other to flourish – water. Dehydration in other organs of the body, which is, by the way, composed of two-thirds water, can cause many unseen problems. And dehydrated skin manifests itself to the world as wrinkles, bags and bulges. Just as a balloon needs air to keep its membrane taut and bouncy and its shape regular, so the skin needs water to fill it out. Deprive either of the material that keeps it 'buoyant' and they collapse downwards and inwards. Unlike the sudden collapse of a balloon, however, dehydration of the skin happens slowly over a long period of time.

'Most people, without knowing it, are chronically dehydrated.'

EFFECTS OF AGEING

Dehydration is a part of the natural ageing process. With age, the skin thins, with the effect that more moisture can evaporate through it. Already bearing the thinnest skin on the body, the face loses proportionately more moisture than its depth dictates because it is also the most exposed part of the body. This thinning process is seen to accelerate at the time of the menopause.

As we age, we also perspire less and produce less sebum. While sweat and oil do not sound like a great recipe for beauty, they are great guardians of moisture. Facial oil prevents water escaping from the skin by providing a surface seal.

MOISTURIZERS

Most women respond by using moisturizers in an effort to refresh their thirsty skin. Yet, despite their name, these do not primarily put moisture into the skin. The epidermis can absorb relatively little moisture and even this limited capacity for absorption declines with age. Moisturizers are a sort of sebum-and-sweat substitute designed to stop water escaping from the surface.

However sophisticated the technology behind modern moisturizing products, all efforts are focused on the external symptom rather than the internal cause of dehydration. Yet it is deep within the dermis where water is really needed. The greatest benefits to the skin therefore come from consuming enough water regularly rather than applying it, by whatever means, to your face.

USE IT OR LOSE IT

In the course of a normal day, the average body loses at least 1.5 litres (2½ pints) of water through the skin, lungs, gut and kidneys. It has to do this to eliminate toxins from the body. At the same time as it is expelling water, the body also needs to produce a third of a litre (half a pint) of water to burn glucose sugar for energy. Consequently, the average person needs to take in at least 2 litres (3½ pints) of water a day to function optimally.

Few people drink anything like that quantity of water. A lot of liquid is drunk as coffee, tea, beer, cola and other saccharin-sweetened fizzy drinks. All these drinks are diuretics, so much of the liquid taken in is excreted within an hour or two. Most people, without knowing it, are therefore chronically dehydrated. Fatigue, headaches, indigestion and joint pain are the most common symptoms of dehydration, though we usually attribute them to other causes.

BOTTLED OR TAP?

In principle, there is good reason to swap tap water for a bottled alternative. Hundreds of chemical contaminants have been identified in tap water, the most common being nitrates, lead, aluminium and pesticides. Yet bottled water is not always the pure and simple substance it sounds. Bottled water can be classified as table water, spring water or natural mineral water. Only the last is guaranteed to be from an unpolluted underground source and is untreated. On the analysis label, look for a high calcium-to-sodium ratio. If you buy bottled water, choose glass bottles, as chemicals from plastic bottles can leak into the water when left in sunlight.

FILTERING WATER

Most jug water filters remove metals, chlorine and water hardness, but also some naturally occurring minerals, such as calcium. Filters also remove the chlorine put in tap water to destroy bacteria, so never keep water standing in the jug for more than a day, or refrigerate it. Change the filter regularly, or the harmful residues caught inside the filter can start to leach back into the jug.

BENEFITS OF MORE WATER

- If you increase your water intake, then the water supply to the dermal cells, which is needed to plump the cells out, is increased.

- In people with dry-to-normal skin, the sebaceous glands are stimulated into producing more oil, which traps in more moisture (but it will not make oily skin more oily).

- The kidneys are flushed out more effectively, so fewer toxins travel to the skin's surface.

- Muscles in the face and elsewhere become more powerful and flexible.

- Connective tissues become less rigid, so the gelatin in which it is grounded becomes more flexible and facial expressions become less fixed.

See also ►
Eight-step beauty plan, pages 22–23

SKIN TREATMENTS

Today there are numerous cosmetic options on offer if you are unhappy with the way you look. It is important to understand what is involved before you undertake any procedure, as they all have advantages and disadvantages.

PROCEDURE	WHAT HAPPENS	ADVANTAGES	DISADVANTAGES
Facelift	The skin is cut and lifted, then draped back over the face and the excess skin cut off. The muscles can be lifted and tightened at the same time. Parts of certain muscles can also be removed altogether to prevent further furrowing and creasing of the face.	Improves the shape of the face and removes surface lines. Once the bruising and scarring have faded, the improvement is immediately visible and will last 6–10 years. Where certain facial areas are particularly affected, a smaller operation can be performed – most typically a browlift or eyelift.	If the procedure is repeated, facial mobility is reduced, so the face is less expressive. Carries a small risk of nerve damage, which may be permanent. Results in a mask-like effect if the skin is stretched taut when lifted. The surface area of the skin is reduced, so it may be less efficient at circulating essential nutrients and air.
Laser treatment	Epidermis and part of the dermis are removed with a high-powered beam of energy.	Can be very closely targeted to individual wrinkles and the depth of the ablation can be accurately controlled with the use of magnifying instruments. Works well on fine wrinkles such as crow's feet and upper-lip wrinkles.	Skin is painful, swollen and covered in a crust for up to 10 days and pink for three to six months before it resumes its natural colour. Risk of irregular pigmentation, especially if skin is regularly exposed to the sun. Not very effective on deep furrows such as those between the eyebrows or at the sides of the mouth. Sensitivity to cosmetics may be increased. Demarcation line may be visible if not expertly done.
Dermabrasion	The epidermis and top part of the dermis is removed, along with fine lines and wrinkles. The skin regrows thicker, with new collagen and elastin.	Can be effective on deep upper-lip wrinkles.	Same disadvantages as laser treatment, with added disadvantage that dermabrasion produces more bleeding and the new look of the skin lasts only a matter of months.

PROCEDURE	WHAT HAPPENS	ADVANTAGES	DISADVANTAGES
Chemical peeling	An abrasive acid paste, applied to the face, removes the epidermis. New skin regrows as after dermabrasion.	Can be done with different pastes and to varying depths according to severity of wrinkles. Lightest and most popular is the alpha-hydroxy (fruit) acid peel, which is very quick and less painful, but the results are less dramatic. A phenol peel is more effective, but this often reduces the skin's pigmentation.	Paste has to be applied about three times over 24 hours. Removal of the paste is very painful. Skin is red, flaky and swollen for up to a month after a light peel, several months after a deep one. Destroys surface pigment cells, so exposure to the sun can cause pigmentation problems. Not good for neck, which heals poorly.
Collagen implantation	Animal collagen is injected into the wrinkles. The lines are filled out immediately and the body's own production of natural collagen is stimulated over the subsequent months.	There is no scarring and the improvement is immediate, though red spots may be visible for a few hours after the treatment.	Lasts a few months at most. Often requires a course of up to three injections. Possibility of allergic reaction. Need to avoid using facial muscles for around four hours after treatment is completed.
Fat implantation	Fat is removed from stomach or thigh under local anaesthetic. Blood and excess fluid is removed and fat cells injected. Collagen grows around the new fat.	Good for deep wrinkles. No risk of allergic reaction.	A lot of fat cells need to be implanted, making the face red and lumpy for several weeks or even some months. More expensive than silicone or collagen implantation, though a lot of the fat will disappear.
Silicone injection	Silicone is injected deep into wrinkles. The body produces collagen that surrounds the silicone, filling out the wrinkle.	Effect is permanent as silicone remains in tissue. Good for forehead and mouth furrows.	Risk of silicone migrating to other parts of the body, so many practitioners no longer offer the treatment, which has been outlawed in the USA.
Botox 'hibernation'	Botulinum toxin is injected into the muscle to paralyse it so that creases cannot deepen. Most often used to treat frowning muscles.	Very effective for treatment of forehead lines.	Limits expression in face. Only lasts three to four months.

EIGHT-STEP BEAUTY PLAN

Carry out the following regime just once and notice the instant improvement in the look of your skin and hair; then use the elements marked with an asterisk (*) nightly to fight beauty problems for good.

1 CONDITION THE HAIR

Shampoo your hair and towel dry it so that it is just damp. Apply an intensive conditioning treatment, or mix up your own with half a cup of warm (not hot) olive oil and 10 drops of lavender essential oil. Apply this to the hair using gentle massage movements to stimulate the scalp. Tie a plastic carrier bag around your hair (keeping your face well clear) to increase penetration. Leave on while you carry out your facial.

2 *THE 'LION'

This yoga move tones your facial muscles while simultaneously reducing muscle tension that can hinder circulation. Sit comfortably on the floor or a chair, resting your palms on your legs. Inhale, then exhale slowly while opening your eyes and mouth as widely as possible. Very slowly, stick your tongue out and down as far as it will go (without straining), and you will feel the muscles around your face tighten. Now stiffen your arms and fingers. Hold this position for as long as you can comfortably, then slowly relax.

3 *CLEANSE THE SKIN

Cleanse the skin with your normal cleanser or mix up a natural cleanser using 1 tablespoonful of natural yogurt and 1 teaspoonful of lemon juice. Dab this off the skin with a tissue, then rinse with cool water.

4 EXFOLIATE THE SKIN

Use a gentle store-bought exfoliator, or add enough water to 1 teaspoon of sugar to make it into a smooth paste – not too thick and scratchy nor too liquid.

5 STEAM THE SKIN

Steaming helps release any toxins and impurities that may be just under the skin's surface, blocking circulation. Fill a bowl with boiling water, then gently place your face about 10 cm (4 in) from the surface for 2–3 minutes.

6 *SPLASH THE SKIN

Quickly splash the skin 20 to 30 times with cold water, then pat dry with a towel. On a night when you have not steamed the skin, you can use iced water to rapidly boost the blood flow to the area, but it is best avoided on steam nights, since the dramatic change in temperature can overstress the skin and lead to broken veins.

7 *ADD MOISTURE

On ordinary nights, use your normal moisturizer and the same moves, but on this programme you are going to use essential oils because these can create rapid improvements to the skin's surface. Apply 2 drops of oil (use camomile for dry skins, rose for oily skins and carrotseed for mature skins) to a carrier oil. Grapeseed is fine enough for use on the face and is an antioxidant in its own right. Apply the moisturizer, massaging the skin as you do so.

- Start at your chin, gently smoothing the skin upwards with the pads of your fingers; don't tug the skin, just smooth it. Now drum your fingers lightly again, moving upwards up the jaw line. Repeat 5 times.

- Repeat these moves over your cheeks. Now quickly pat the cheeks and jaw 5–10 times; start lightly but then get firmer.

- Stroke up around the temples and up the forehead. Repeat the drumming.

- When you get to the middle of the forehead, alternately use the index finger of each hand to brush rapidly upwards from the middle of your brows to the hairline; this should feel like a smooth, rolling movement.

- Dab a little oil along the socket bone below your eye (oils should never go directly on the eye area), and massage this in well, using gentle upward strokes. Finish by lightly drumming your fingers along the socket bone. Repeat the process under your other eye.

8 RINSE AND DRY YOUR HAIR

Rinse the conditioning treatment out of your hair (it may take a couple of shampoos to remove it completely) and apply conditioner. Rinse again and towel dry. Ideally, leave your hair to dry naturally, but if you have to blow-dry, use only a warm setting.

DRY OR AGEING SKIN OILS

Apricot oil is easily absorbed into the skin and has a softening effect. It has a mild fragrance and is calming for irritated skin.

Avocado oil is made from the dried flesh of the fruit, so is rich in nutrients, including vitamins D, E and B5, and can help restore damaged skin tissue.

Macadamia oil is made up of 40 per cent saturated acids, but is quite easily absorbed. It has a soft, silky feel and traps in a lot of moisture.

Wheatgerm oil is a dark yellow, sticky oil with a prominent smell that needs to be blended with a less potent oil. It is rich in minerals and vitamin E, so is good for ageing skin. But it oxidizes quickly and may need more vitamin E added to stop it going rancid.

HAIRCARE

Your hair reflects the state of your inner health and wellbeing. An unhealthy diet and lifestyle, tiredness and stress all take their toll on your hair, and good haircare involves nourishing it and treating it well, as well as finding a hairstyle that suits both you and your lifestyle.

TOP TIPS FOR BEAUTIFUL HAIR

- **Get rid of** split ends by having your hair trimmed regularly.
- **Always use** a good-quality hairbrush, as poor-quality brushes will scratch the scalp and damage the hair shaft.
- **Brush** your hair before you wash it to massage the scalp and help loosen dead skin cells.
- **Do not overheat** your hair when blow-drying. Use a medium setting, and finish with a blast of cold air to close the cuticles – when they lie flat, the hair reflects the light and looks healthier.
- **Avoid overdrying** your hair with heated rollers, straighteners or curling tongs.
- **Try to avoid** non-organic dyes if you colour your hair, especially peroxides.
- **Consider letting** your natural greying/silver hair colour come through or having a shorter cut to remove damaged, discoloured and mistreated hair.
- **Condition** your hair naturally using egg yolks for normal to dry hair and egg whites or a strong herbal infusion of camomile for oily or balanced hair.

YOUR DIET AND YOUR HAIR

Like the rest of your body, your scalp and hair require a balanced diet with sufficient minerals and vitamins. While you can't actually improve the health of the hair you have already, as these cells are dead, you can improve the underlying, unseen parts – the roots.

If you have dull or dry hair, then perhaps you are not drinking enough water so that your body is permanently dehydrated (see page 19), or perhaps you are not eating enough essential fatty acids, which aid the production of sebum and therefore naturally lubricate the hair. To increase your intake of essential fatty acids eat more nuts, sunflower seeds and sesame seeds (also see page 73).

AROMATHERAPY HAIR TREATMENT

Use essential oils to give your hair a deep-cleansing treatment. Make up a treatment oil suitable for your hair by adding the following essential oils to 50 ml (2 fl oz) of vegetable oil:

- **Greasy hair:** add 10 drops of cedarwood essence, 10 drops of lavender and 5 drops of grapefruit.

- **Dry and damaged hair:** add 10 drops of rosewood, 10 drops of lavender and 5 drops of sandalwood essence.

Massage your chosen treatment into your hair, then wrap a towel around your head and leave on for as long as possible (even overnight) before rinsing it out.

AGEING HAIR

As we get older, strands of hair can lose their natural pigment and go white, blending with natural hair colour to give the appearance of grey hair. This white/grey hair has a different texture and may be thinner. Fortunately, there are strategies for dealing with grey, coarse and thinning hair.

However, do not feel that you have to colour your hair – some women look stunning with naturally greying hair. Instead, experiment with different haircuts and styles rather than sticking to the style that you have always had.

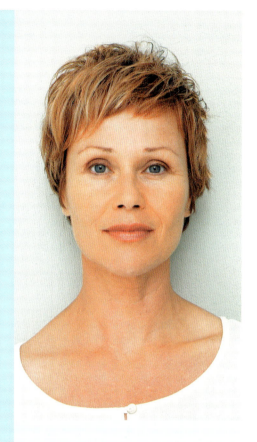

- **A little grey hair** Use a gentle temporary or semi-permanent colour close to your natural hair colour to highlight the grey. Easily applied at home, this type of colourant lasts for six to eight washes, although you need to be aware of colour build-up. Or visit your hairdresser for highlights or lowlights, whereby colour is applied to isolated strands to hide some of the grey while lifting the rest. Try a longer-lasting (12–24 washes) semi-permanent colour on 'salt and pepper' hair.

- **Lots of grey hair** Completely grey or white hair can be very attractive, but if you prefer colour, a permanent tint provides effective coverage, although it needs touching up at the roots every four to six weeks. Choose a shade close to your natural hair colour and one that suits your skin tone (which pales as you get older) to avoid a harsh look and make root regrowth less obvious. Specially designed 'colour-protect' shampoos and conditioners make colours last longer.

- **Brittle/coarse hair** White/grey hair is brittle and coarse and requires feeding with deep conditioners, anti-frizz products and leave-in lotions. Heat damages hair, so avoid hairdryers and heated styling equipment and wear a hat in the sun. A change of hairstyle may become necessary when the amount of grey/white hair renders the texture so different that your normal style is unmanageable.

- **Thinning hair** Thinning is another inevitability as we age, and hair loss is a possibility during the menopause (for which HRT might help). Combat the possible causes of excessive thinning – stress, poor diet and poor circulation (head massage and exercise can help here) – and avoid harsh hair products and brushing your hair when wet and fragile. A good haircut can give hair the impression of being thicker, as can volumizing shampoos and styling products.

HINT FOR HEALTH

Regular exercise is just as important for the state of your hair – it promotes good circulation of the blood to the scalp, so that vital nutrients get to the roots of the hair.

See also ▶

What your skin and hair need, pages 16–17
Eight-step beauty plan, pages 22–23
Healthy eating for a longer life, Chapter 3

EXERCISING YOUR FACIAL MUSCLES

As we age, muscle starts to shrink as its fibres lose protein. While the number of fibres remains the same, their diameter decreases, so muscle thins out. Muscle also becomes drier, and so loses fluid bulk. But it does not lose length, and may even become longer as a result of being stretched, giving rise to the droopy look seen in old age. The process happens so slowly that it is imperceptible, until you compare your face to that of a 25-year-old. Exercising the facial muscles can help to minimize these effects.

See also ▶

Self-massage for sleep, pages 294–295

HORMONAL CHANGES

Another consequence of muscle shrinkage is that it is accompanied by a drop in the production of steroid hormones from the adrenal and sex glands. These are responsible for, among other things, smooth, supple skin. Exercise can also help slow down the decline in hormone levels.

OTHER BENEFITS OF EXERCISE

The muscles under the skin are not the only things to benefit from exercise. A facial workout also seems to have an effect on the adjoining connective tissue. By increasing the supply of oxygen and nutrients to the tissue, exercise is thought to stimulate cell growth in the elastic fibres that naturally atrophy with age. This contrasts with the top layer of skin, which the years thin, however many well-marketed lotions and potions you use.

LOSS OF FATTY TISSUE

Another diminishing asset on the ageing face is fat. In the space where fat once sat, wrinkles congregate. This is most noticeable where the skin is thinnest, such as around the eyes. When that area loses some of the little fatty tissue it has, the eyes take on a more hollow appearance, often exaggerated by circles of darkening skin. So, as fat stores atrophy all over the face, it takes on a more gaunt look.

One option is to increase your calorie intake and accept the indignity of a wobbly pair of hips. A more attractive solution is to fill the facial skin out again with muscle by doing exercises (see pages 28–33).

WHISTLESTOP

As we age, the muscles around the mouth can lose their tone and become saggy. This exercise will banish droopy mouths and can also help to lessen the appearance of unsightly vertical lines running down from the nose to the upper lip. You can whistle whatever tune you like!

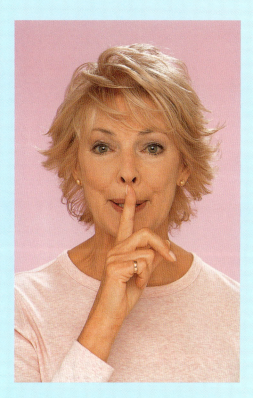

1 Keep your shoulders down and relaxed, and sit up tall and straight. Breathe in and stretch out your top lip and pull it taut over your top teeth. Locate the muscles at the corner of your mouth, pull them up and feel your cheek muscles working as you breathe out.

2 Place your index finger in the middle of your upper lip (keeping it taut) and breathe in. Now you are in the correct position to whistle without forming horrid vertical lines.

3 Pull up the corners of your mouth hard, bring your bottom jaw up and forwards. With lower teeth showing, whistle through your teeth as you breathe out for a count of 5. Make as much noise as you can while keeping your upper lip stretched over your teeth. Do not purse your lips.

THE JOKER

'Smile and the world smiles with you'. This smiling exercise will re-define your cheeks, brighten up your face and lift the corners of your lips. Although it is similar to the Whistlestop exercise (see page 27), try not to confuse these movements because there is a subtle difference.

1 Keep your shoulders down and relaxed and sit up straight. Look ahead and keep your chin parallel to the floor.

2 Breathe in, part your lips and pull both top and bottom lips back as far as possible. Keep the lips tight with both the top and the bottom teeth showing in a wide, exaggerated smile.

3 Narrow your lips and breathe out, keeping them mean and taut and pulling up the corners of your mouth in a joker-like smile. Feel your cheek and mouth muscles working, too. Hold for a count of 5 and then relax.

CROW'S FEET

Squinting gives us crow's feet – lines that resemble a bird's claw. During this exercise, you use your forefinger, placed strategically on your eye socket bone, to hold both skin and muscle in position to offer some resistance, making the muscle work that little bit harder.

1 Keep your shoulders relaxed and down and look straight ahead. Place the pads of your forefingers on the skin and bone at the outside corners of your eyes.

2 Pull back your fingers ever so slightly to create some resistance, but take care not to stretch the skin as you do so. Breathe in.

3 As you breathe out squint up the entire eye, pushing hard against the resistance, and hold for a count of 5. Feel the muscles at the sides of your eyes quivering and working.

UPPERS

Tired-looking eyes can result from a lack of sleep, illness, eyestrain, tension and emotional upsets. They are one of the first facial areas to show signs of ageing. Uppers is a simple movement, your eyes will immediately look and feel much brighter – and younger.

1 Place your forefingers, horizontally, on the centre of your brow bones, under your eyebrows but above the eye sockets. Place your thumbs in front of your ears, holding the skin and muscle firmly in place, but do not stretch or pull the skin.

2 Bring your upper eyelids down to the lower lids, and close your eyes. Get ready to work the muscles above the eye and breathe normally.

3 Now, continuously open and shut your eyes very quickly with a fluttering movement; do this at least 20 times. (Be forewarned that this fast flutter creates a 1920s black-and-white film effect.) Feel the muscle working against the resistance of your fingers. Relax.

DOWNERS

Lines under the eyes are signs of overtiredness, eyestrain or overindulgence in caffeine, alcohol or drugs. If the exercise is done correctly there is only a small movement seen under the eye – like a cat narrowing its eyes – so first you need to locate, observe and practise.

1 Keep your shoulders relaxed and down, and look straight ahead at the mirror – in this way so you can observe the smallest of movements involved.

2 Place your forefingers horizontally under the centre of your eyes, and put your thumbs in front of your ears. Feel the top of your cheekbones, and hold the muscle and skin firmly in place to offer resistance. Take care not to drag or stretch the delicate skin under the eye. Breathe in.

3 As you breathe out, contract and squeeze up the tiny muscle under your lower eyelids. Don't screw up your eyes completely – just pull up the lower lids using the muscle under the eyes. (Be careful not to push up the skin and muscle with your fingers.) Hold for a count of 5.

FIVE STEPS TO YOUTHFUL RADIANCE

1 Sit in the correct posture. Place your hands vertically on the centre of your forehead so that your forefingers touch the hairline. Gently slide your right fingers up and your left fingers down your forehead from the eyebrows up into the hairline. Then, reverse the brisk but delicate sawing movement, moving your right fingers down and your left up. Work your fingers out to your right temple, back to the centre and then repeat on the left side. Repeat these movements twice. Place your hands in your lap, with your palms uppermost and your thumbs and middle fingers touching.

2 Breathe deeply and relax your neck and shoulders. Now, bring your hands up, with the palms facing downwards and your fingers horizontally on top of each other, and place them on the bridge of your nose. Slide your fingers backwards and forwards, gently working up over the nose and forehead into the hairline and back down again. Repeat twice.

Tension surfaces on your face as frown lines, but other tell-tale signs are rigid jaws, staring eyes and pursed lips. Facial massage is a wonderful way of releasing tension and reducing stress, leaving your face looking relaxed and younger. Light massage of your facial muscles stimulates the circulation and makes your complexion glow. To avoid damaging or stretching your skin, apply some moisturizer, your favourite aromatherapy blend or some vegetable oil to your forehead and use only light, feathery touches. Take your time, relax and enjoy the pampering sensation, and hopefully, when you've finished, you will experience a feeling of calm and wellbeing.

3 Now, slant your hands and incline them to the right. With backwards and forwards movements, work diagonally over and up into the hairline at your right temple and back to the centre. Repeat twice, then do this 3 times on the left side. When you have finished, place your hands gently in your lap as before. Breathe deeply and relax your shoulders.

4 Bring your hands to your face and lightly place both forefingers horizontally on your nose. Use a light, feathery touch to stroke from the nose to the hairline with alternate forefingers, one after the other in a circular motion. Use delicate strokes, and move up over your nose, forehead and into your hairline 10 times to help you relax. Then rest your hands in your lap as before.

5 Finally, bring your hands up and place all your fingertips lightly at the centre of the forehead at the hairline. Trace the hairline out across your forehead, down the sides of your face and past your ears. Sweep them round to your chin, up over your nose and back to your forehead. Repeat this 5 times. Place your hands in your lap and breathe deeply, relax and enjoy a moment of tranquillity.

CARING FOR YOUR HANDS AND NAILS

As we get older, our skin becomes thinner, drier and more fragile thanks to a loss of collagen and elasticity and the skin's diminished ability to retain moisture. This ageing of the skin is particularly evident on the backs of hands where the skin is naturally very thin. Add to this the daily exposure of hands (generally unprotected by clothing) to cold weather, the sun, pollution, detergents and too much hot water, all of which are responsible over time for damaging skin and weakening fingernails, and you'll appreciate the importance of taking care of your hands.

A QUICK FIX FOR DRY HANDS

For an easy do-it-yourself solution for dry hands, spread moisturizing cream or petroleum jelly liberally over your hands. Put on cotton gloves, then snug-fitting latex surgical gloves. Leave the gloves in place for at least 2 hours, but preferably overnight. In the morning, remove the gloves and you will have beautifully smooth and supple, moisturized hands. Repeat the treatment as and when required.

HANDY PROTECTION

Dry skin and ageing go hand in hand (excuse the pun!), so avoid washing your hands too often and using ordinary soap, both of which remove the skin's natural oils. Use a mild cream cleanser instead and always apply moisturizer after washing your hands – keep a tube, pot or bottle of hand cream by every sink in the house, as well as in your handbag, beside the bed and in your desk drawer, to make it easier to apply wherever and whenever you need to.

Try to wear gloves for protection whenever possible, for example when gardening or doing housework, or smooth a barrier cream over your hands first. Always wear rubber gloves for washing up, and wear warm gloves in cold weather to protect your hands.

SUN CARE

Although we are all now well aware of the need to protect ourselves from the sun by using creams and lotions with a high sun protection factor (SPF), we often forget to look after our hands. Age spots (or 'liver spots') tend to appear on the backs of hands as we get older and are a direct result of exposure to the sun.

To prevent age spots worsening, or new ones from appearing, stay out of the sun as much as you possibly can and always use a sunscreen or moisturizer with an SPF of at least 15 on the backs of your hands whenever they will be exposed – even when simply going about your day-to-day activities outdoors. Skincare products containing vitamin A derivatives (for example, tretinoin or retinol) or mulberry extract may help fade age spots.

COSMETIC SOLUTIONS

The various options for improving hands showing signs of wear and tear entail visiting the beauty salon or even a plastic surgeon. A paraffin wax treatment is an enjoyable rehydrating solution for dry hands. Laser and ultrasound treatment can help fade patches of abnormal pigmentation on the backs of hands, while glycolic treatment involves using natural fruit acids to remove dead skin cells. A more drastic step is to have lipostructure, whereby fat is removed from the stomach and inserted into the backs of the hands to plump out the skin.

NAILCARE

Nails also show signs of ageing, and ridging and splitting of nails from the tip are quite common. To keep your nails healthy, make sure you include plenty of iron, zinc and vitamins A and D in your diet (see pages 70–71 and 78–79), wear gloves to protect your hands when doing domestic chores and give your nails regular manicures (see box, right).

There are plenty of chemically based commercial products for nailcare. If you prefer homemade treatments, dried dill and horsetail are particularly good for strengthening weak nails. Make an infusion of either herb by pouring 150 ml (¼ pint) of boiling water on to 2 tablespoons of chopped horsetail or dill. Leave to cool, then strain into a bottle. Use the infusion warm and soak the nails for 10 minutes every other day. On alternate days, soak your nails in warm olive oil for 5 minutes. Almond oil is also good for keeping nails strong.

MANICURES

Hand treatments should not be regarded only as a beauty salon pampering treat. Regular manicures, which you can do yourself at home, help keep nails healthy. Soak your fingernails in warm water before trimming so as to soften them and make them easier to cut. Use nail clippers rather than nail scissors if they are quite long and a large emery board rather than a metal file for shaping, as the latter can weaken and burn the nail. Don't rub back and forth, but use the emery board repeatedly in the same direction. Use orange sticks rather than metal implements for cleaning the nails and pushing back the cuticles.

FOOTCARE

Healthy feet are essential for mobility and balance, and good footcare is essential for healthy feet. Unfortunately, our feet are invariably forgotten in day-to-day bodycare until they start to give us trouble. It is generally neglect and badly fitting shoes rather than any inherent condition that cause problems, and women are four times more likely than men to experience foot problems – high heels are partly to blame. Regular skincare, exercise, massage and foot baths can all help make life easier for your feet.

POOR OLD SOLES

It has been calculated that, on average, we take 8,000–10,000 steps a day. This adds up to about 185,000 km (115,000 miles) over a lifetime – enough to circle the earth four times! No wonder then that to some extent our feet wear out – the ball of the foot, for example, gets thinner with age and can be a painful pressure point. Aids such as plantar cushions can help with painful areas of your feet.

PUT YOUR FEET FIRST

The skin on our feet ages in the same way that it does elsewhere on the body – it becomes drier and thinner, and loses some of its elasticity. Healing therefore takes longer, so any common foot problems such as warts, calluses or corns may trouble you more and for longer than they did previously.

Aim to pay your feet regular attention every day. When you are having a shower, remove the hard skin around your heels and toes using a pumice stone or a foot file. Every night, take time to rub a rich moisturizing cream into your feet to keep the skin soft and supple. However, avoid moisturizing between the toes as these are moist areas in which fungus can thrive.

If, despite these daily efforts to improve their condition, your feet are still looking and feeling in poor shape, try this intensive treatment. Apply a generous layer of heavy moisturizer or petroleum jelly and wrap each foot in kitchen clingfilm. This is so that the plastic will trap your body heat, thereby increasing the moisturizer's penetration of the skin. Wrap a warm towel around your plastic-encased feet, put your feet up and relax for 15–20 minutes. Alternatively, and even more beneficial, put on a pair of woollen socks over the plastic and wear them in bed overnight. In the morning, your feet will be soft and smooth.

TREAT YOUR FEET

Walking is the best exercise for your feet. It also contributes to your general health by improving circulation, controlling weight (see page 74) and promoting general wellbeing. After overdoing it on your feet, however, you may be in need of some – or indeed all – of the following food pick-me-ups:

- **Foot massage** After a long, tiring day, try to spend 10 minutes lying down with your feet higher than your head. Using a massage oil or soothing foot massage cream, gently massage your feet to relieve stiffness, then gently massage each leg from the foot to the knee, working upwards to improve circulation.

- **Aromatherapy foot massage** Essential oils like lime, marigold or comfrey essence combined with sweet almond oil make a pleasant massage oil that will help reduce swollen, tired feet. Marigold and cypress essences are effective for combating smelly feet (see page 287).

- **Foot baths** Revitalize tired feet and ease uncomfortable aches and pains with a foot bath. Choose one of the herbal or essential oil soaks below to soothe and tone your feet. Sit comfortably with both feet immersed in the water and simply relax or read for 20–30 minutes Pat them dry, then apply a cooling and reviving moisturizer or foot lotion, containing ingredients such as peppermint, aloe vera and comfrey, or gently massage your feet using a relaxing oil.

SENSIBLE SHOE SHOPPING

Getting older and putting on weight (or losing it) can cause your feet to become bigger, wider or smaller. Make sure you 'test fit' new shoes and remember that shoes that feel tight in the shop will be even worse after a day on your feet. Always measure both feet, and if your feet are different sizes, buy shoes for the larger one.

SOOTHING FOOT BATH RECIPES

Herbal soak: Add 1 tablespoon of chopped fresh rosemary or mint or juniper berries to 2.5 litres (4 pints) of boiling water. Leave to stand for 15 minutes, then strain and use while still warm.

Peppermint soak: Add 6 drops of peppermint essence to a bowl of warm water and mix well.

Sea salt and lavender soak: Add a cup of sea salt and a few drops of lavender oil to a bowl of warm water and mix well.

CHAPTER 2
LOOSEN UP AND SHAPE UP

Pilates is ideal for adults at any level of fitness and will help you to improve your posture, strength and flexibility, boost your energy and decrease your stress levels. It will also give you an extraordinary sense of wellbeing. These exercises have been specially adapted to minimize any unnecessary strain on the back and joints, and include advice for anyone with injuries.

GETTING STARTED

You will need an area where you can lie down with enough room to move freely without restriction. Lying on a mat or folded towel will help to support the body. You may also wish to support your neck with a towel or cushion, particularly if you have a history of neck pain or stiffness. The area you choose to exercise in should be free of distractions, such as a telephone or television. The temperature of the room is also important – it is better to be too warm than too cold when exercising.

IF IN DOUBT...

It is a good idea to consult your medical practitioner before embarking on any new exercise programme. You should always do this if you are receiving treatment for a medical condition, or if you are taking any form of medication.

CLOTHING

Wear comfortable, loose-fitting clothing that doesn't restrict your movement. It is preferable to work with bare feet, as this will improve the sensory feedback of the feet in weight-bearing postures.

MUSIC

Some people prefer to exercise to music. Music can help to develop a sense of rhythm and create a certain atmosphere. The choice of music is entirely your own – just be aware of its influence, as it can make all the difference to your focus and the outcome of your training.

BREATHING

The breathing pattern used in these exercises is known as thoracic or rib breathing (see page 46). The aim is to keep your abdominal and spinal muscles engaged and your shoulders relaxed while your ribcage expands as you inhale. As you exhale, the ribcage contracts down towards the waist, again involving the spinal muscles and also the pelvic floor muscles. The breathing also allows you to achieve a rhythm with the exercise. If you have any respiratory conditions, such as asthma, however, it is better to breathe naturally.

FLUIDS

It is important to drink plenty of water during and after exercise, particularly in hot climates. Still water is preferable to carbonated fluids as these will not hydrate you as effectively.

CREATING A ROUTINE

Structure the programme so that it fits in with the other activities in your life. If you break your routine, try to get back into a pattern as soon as possible. If you work long hours, and particularly if you are sitting for prolonged periods, try to get up and walk around every 30 minutes, or do a few gentle stretches for areas that are prone to tightness or pain, for example the lumbar spine or shoulders. Develop a knowledge of how your body works during exercise, focus on specific muscles and movement patterns, and then begin to integrate your understanding into everyday activities. For example, correct your posture while sitting at your desk and lengthen your spine as you walk.

PAIN

If you suffer pain during exercise it could be that your body is at risk of damage or injury. You may be able to relieve symptoms if you exercise within a smaller range or use an alternative movement pattern, but if the pain is persistent, discuss it with your medical practitioner.

AGE AND FITNESS

Your age and level of fitness are not issues, as there are ways to modify the workout to fit your individual physicality and goals. Take responsibility for yourself as you exercise and do not force yourself beyond your limits – you know your body better than anyone else and, with practice, you can refine your knowledge of your strengths and limitations and progress appropriately. However, if you experience any discomfort or have difficulty with a particular movement or exercise, consult your medical practitioner. Seek medical advice if you experience any of the following:

- Pain
- Faintness
- Bleeding
- Rapid pulse on resting
- Dizziness
- Back pain
- Shortness of breath
- Palpitations
- Difficulty in walking

'Develop a knowledge of how your body works during exercise, focus on specific muscles and movement patterns and then begin to integrate your understanding into everyday activities.'

See also ▶
Warm-up exercises, pages 42–45
The principles of Pilates, pages 46–47
The feel-good factor, Chapter 9

WARM-UP EXERCISES

Before you start working on any specific area of the body to tone, shape or strengthen it, it is vital to warm up first. Warm-ups prevent possible strains and injury, which are much more likely when your muscles are exerted from cold. These first few exercises loosen the shoulders, hips and ribs as well as the all-important spinal column.

ROLL DOWN

The roll down will help you to feel your body in alignment and is a good way to wake your body in the morning. Always start with a roll down before you exercise.

Care Do not strain to reach the floor if this is not comfortable.

Repetitions 3 times

1 Stand with your feet hip-width apart, toes facing forwards, your shoulders relaxed, your head in line with your spine and your stomach muscles held in lightly to prevent any arching in your back.

2 Drop your head down towards your chest and, very slowly, let the curve continue into your shoulders and your back.

3 Bend your knees as you continue the curve into the waist, letting your arms drop in front of you.

4 Bend over, extend your arms down and rest your hands on the floor or let them dangle. Stay for a few seconds and let the weight of your head stretch out your spine. Very slowly, roll the body back up.

Care Keep good posture (see page 47) throughout the exercise.

Repetitions 3 circles in each direction

SHOULDER CIRCLES

The shoulders are often a site of tension, which means they become tense and hunched up. These exercises will help you to focus on and relax these muscles, so that they become less tight and your posture will also improve.

1 Stand with a good posture, your shoulders dropped and relaxed. Start to rotate the shoulders forwards. If you are doing it correctly, your arms will have turned so that your palms are facing towards you.

2 Continue the circle so that your shoulders lift up towards your ears, then pull them down and back so that your shoulder blades squeeze together. Make sure that at this point you avoid arching the small of the back.

3 Finally, drop your shoulders right down. If you feel any tension in your neck, drop your head forwards on to your chest to relax the muscles.

LEG SWINGS

This exercise is particularly good for warming up the hip socket, but you can shape and tone your leg muscles throughout the day simply by stretching out the muscles of your legs and buttocks while you are walking or exercising.

Care Engage your stomach muscles to prevent your back from arching.

Repetitions 16 times for each leg, raising the leg a little higher each time

1&2 Stand with a good posture, one hand resting on a suitable support such as a chair back or table. Take your outside leg forwards slightly and then back in a gentle swing, keeping your upper body still and upright throughout.

3&4 With each repetition, bring your leg slightly higher off the ground. Then, change sides so that your other hand is resting on the support and repeat the whole exercise with the other leg.

PLIÉS

Care Take care not to arch your back as you bend your knees.

Repetitions As stated for each step

Pliés are a good way to improve your posture as well as exercising your leg, buttock, back and stomach muscles. Remember not to strain the muscles though – build up your body tone gradually.

1 Stand tall with your feet slightly apart and toes facing forwards.

2 Bend your knees without lifting your heels. Feel your stomach muscles pushing back towards your spine. Do this 8 times.

3 Turn your feet out in a V shape. Keep your knees over your feet at all times – don't let them roll in as this could damage them.

4 Bend your knees – feel your thigh muscles turn out and buttock muscles pull under. Bend 3 times, keeping heels on the floor.

5 With your feet about 45 cm (18 in) apart, turn your legs out from the hip sockets so that your knees are over your feet.

6 Bend as in previous pliés, keeping your heels firmly on the ground, with your thigh muscles turning out. Do 4 slow pliés.

THE PRINCIPLES OF PILATES

There are six fundamental principles of Pilates that you should focus on: breathing, concentration, control, centring, precision and flow. Bear in mind that it takes time to develop these and to lengthen and strengthen muscles, but as you practise the exercises, you will become more aware of what they are doing, so be patient and you'll see fantastic results.

CORE STABILIZATION

Core stabilization is the key to Pilates. You need to strengthen your 'centre', your trunk, in order to move most efficiently. The deep abdominal and spinal muscles are worked effectively together to stabilize the spine and maintain lower-back control.

LATERAL BREATHING

In Pilates, 'lateral' breathing is used, which means that the ribcage is expanded sideways with each breath, with air entering the sides and back of the ribcage. This works the muscles between the ribs, facilitating their expansion and making the upper body more flexible.

Place your hands on either side of your ribcage. Breathe in slowly and gently through your nose, allowing your ribs to expand outwards laterally into your hands as you try to fill the sides and back of your ribcage with air. Don't force the movement, your ribcage may move only slightly at first. Exhale slowly through the mouth keeping your lips and jaw relaxed – you don't want pursed lips or clenched jaws.

DRAWING IN THE ABDOMINALS

When we breathe laterally in Pilates, we also incorporate the abdominal muscles and pelvic floor in our movements for greater core stability.

Lie on your back, with your knees bent at a 90-degree angle and your feet and knees hip-width apart. Rest your arms by your sides. Inhale gently through the nose, taking the breath in laterally, filling the sides and back of your ribcage with air. Pause momentarily.

As you start to exhale slowly through the mouth, gently engage your pelvic floor, and as you breathe out, feel your lower stomach start to sink down towards the floor. As you continue to exhale, allow your stomach to sink down a little further by drawing in your lower stomach muscles. Your stomach will hollow out. Don't brace your stomach muscles, just let them sink gently downwards, and make sure you don't move your spine. Pause momentarily.

Gently inhale through your nose into the sides and back of your ribcage. Pause momentarily, then repeat the exhalation as above.

GOOD POSTURE

- **Stand** with your feet hip-width apart, so that they are facing forwards and parallel.
- **Balance** the weight evenly between the ball of your big toe, the outside edge of your foot and the heel.
- **Keep** your knees in a soft, unlocked position.
- **Gently draw in** your abdominal muscles and let your tailbone (coccyx) drop down.
- **Stand up tall**, so that there is plenty of space between your hips and your ribcage, making sure the ribs don't poke out.
- **Relax** your shoulders and let your arms fall over the middle of your hips. Palms should face your sides and not face backwards behind you.
- **Lengthen** the back of the neck. Imagine there is a rope attached to the crown of your head being very gently drawn up towards the ceiling.

NEUTRAL SPINE

This describes the natural curves of your back and is usually the best position for your spine, as it places the least stress on the spine and therefore protects the back. It is unique to the individual, so finding the position that is right for you may take a little practice.

If you lie on the floor and tilt your pelvis up (by rocking your pubic bone up towards the ceiling) you will lose the natural curve in your back as your spine flattens into the floor and your tailbone lifts off it. If you tilt your pelvis the other way (by rocking your pubic bone down to the floor), your back overarches. The neutral spine position lies between these two positions. When you are 'in neutral' your tailbone remains on the floor and lengthens away, and your pubic bone and two hipbones are level with one another. In most cases there should be just enough room for someone to slide a flat hand in the slight gap behind your waist and the floor.

You should exercise in neutral spine when you are standing, sitting or lying down with your feet on the floor. If your feet are lifted off the mat then you can come out of neutral spine and allow your lower back to press into the floor for additional support.

PILATES TO TONE, SHAPE AND STRENGTHEN

Follow the exercises in the order they are given and aim to practise them two or three times a week. Always follow the advice given in the care boxes. When you practise, aim initially to perform a movement safely and correctly, assessing yourself as you go. As your practice develops, refer back to the principles of Pilates (see pages 46–47) and try to include them in your movements.

SMALL HIP ROLL

This exercise strengthens and lengthens the abdominal muscles and releases tension in the back and neck. If your back is very stiff, don't take the knees as far over. Keep the movement very small at first.

Care This exercise is safe for most back injuries, but always check with a doctor if you suffer from any kind of back problem.

Repetitions 10 each side, alternating sides

1 Lie on your back with your knees bent at a 90-degree angle and feet together. Place your hands on your hips. Keep the back and the neck long.

2 **Inhale**, rolling the knees to one side, while pressing your opposite hand gently down on the hip to keep your hips and buttocks glued to the floor. You will not be able to go very far.

3 **Exhale**, drawing in the abdominals to return the knees to the centre. Imagine that your thighs are made of lead so that you really have to use your abdominal muscles to pull your knees back to the centre each time.

4 **Inhale** and roll the knees over to the other side, while pressing down on the hip with the opposite hand.

5 **Exhale**, drawing in the abdominals again to return the knees to the centre.

PELVIC TILT

This strengthens the abdominal muscles, increases spinal flexibility, mobilizes the shoulders and relieves most minor backache and stiffness. If the exercise feels tough, or you feel any tension in your back, shoulders, chest or neck, just come up halfway until you grow stronger and more flexible. If you have shoulder problems, raise your arms to the ceiling rather than overhead, or just keep them on the floor.

Care Proceed only under supervision if you have any back injuries or any disc problems.

Repetitions 6

1 Lie on your back on a mat with your knees bent at a 90-degree angle, feet parallel to each other and hip-width apart. Your arms should reach long by your sides with your palms face down. Draw your chin down slightly to ensure that the back of your neck is long. **Inhale**.

2 **Exhale**, drawing in your abdominal muscles as you peel your spine off the mat one vertebra at a time so that your hips curl up towards the ceiling. Press down through your feet as you start to lift off, curling up as far as your body can comfortably go with the abdominals still engaged.

3 **Inhale**, holding your body perfectly still, and raise your arms up to the ceiling and then over towards your head until they are in line with your ears.

4 **Exhale**, drawing in your abdominal muscles as you use them to roll down through your spine, lowering one vertebra at a time, leaving your arms behind you. Imagine your spine softening and almost melting into the mat as you roll down.

5 **Inhale**, lowering your arms to your sides. Repeat steps 2–5 for the required number of repetitions.

HIP ROLL

This strengthens the abdominal muscles, stretches the lower back and releases tension in the upper spine. It is great for stiff shoulders, backs or necks. If you feel tension in your lower back, don't take your knees over so far.

Care Omit this exercise if you have a bad neck or back injury.

Repetitions 10 each side, alternating sides

1 Lie on a mat on your back with your knees bent at a 90-degree angle and your feet slightly wider than hip-width apart. Your neck is long and your spine relaxed. Place your arms straight out to the sides, in line with your shoulders, with palms facing down. **Inhale**.

2 **Exhale**, drawing in the abdominal muscles, as you roll your knees towards the floor; the soles of your feet will come off the mat. As you perform this move, let your head roll in the opposite direction to your knees so that you feel a stretch through your body. **Inhale** and rest in this position.

3 **Exhale**, drawing in your abdominal muscles, and roll your knees all the way over to the other side. Again, let your head roll in the opposite direction. Imagine your lower abdominal muscles sinking down through your spine towards the floor. **Inhale** and rest in this position. Then, alternate smoothly from side to side.

Care Proceed only under supervision if you have a back or neck injury.

Repetitions 6

CHEST LIFT

This strengthens the abdominal muscles for a firmer, flatter stomach, and highlights the neutral spine position (see page 47). If your abdominal muscles start to quiver or pop out as you roll up, don't come up so high for the moment.

1 Lie on your back on a mat with your knees bent, your feet and knees hip-width apart. Bend your arms to fold your hands behind your head, your fingers interlaced and your elbows out to the side. Check that you are in neutral spine position (see page 47). **Inhale**.

2 **Exhale**, drawing in your abdominal muscles, to roll your head and shoulders off the mat. As you roll up, slide your shoulder blades down into your back to keep the tops of your shoulders away from your ears. Keep your chin pointing towards your chest with only a small space in between. Imagine you are gently holding a peach under your chin. **Inhale** and remain perfectly still in this lifted position.

3 **Exhale**, drawing in the abdominal muscles, to roll your head and shoulders back on to the mat.

OBLIQUE REACHES

This exercise strengthens the abdominal muscles and trims the waist. If you can't maintain neutral spine (see page 47), and find that you are tucking under and pressing your lower back into the mat, don't come up so high.

Care Proceed only under supervision if you have a neck or back injury.

Repetitions 6 each side

1 Lie on your back with your knees bent, and your feet hip-width apart. Bend one arm to fold one hand behind your head. The other hand should rest on the opposite hipbone. **Inhale**.

2 **Exhale**, drawing in the abdominal muscles to cross your arm over your body, stretching towards the outside of your opposite knee, palm down. Stay in neutral position (see page 47), rotating your lower ribcage over to the side rather than just twisting the shoulders. Imagine there is an egg lying under your waist in the curve of your back. As you twist over, be careful not to flatten your lower back and crush it.

3 **Inhale** and roll back down to the step 1 position, keeping the stomach muscles engaged. Repeat steps 2–3 for the required number of repetitions.

Care Proceed with caution if you are prone to shoulder dislocation.

Repetitions 6

CHEST OPENER

This stretch counteracts rounded shoulders, releases neck and shoulder tension, relieves stiffness in the upper and mid-back and strengthens and tones the chest and arms. If your shoulders are very tight, just open the arms halfway.

1 Lie on a mat on your back with your knees bent at a 90-degree angle, feet hip-width apart, in neutral spine (see page 47), with your neck and shoulders relaxed. Lift both arms to the ceiling, shoulder-width apart, palms facing. Keep the arms straight without locking elbows. Your hands should be level with your elbows.

2 **Inhale** as you slowly open your arms straight out to the sides without bending them. Slide your shoulder blades down into your back as your arms open. Imagine you are painting the arc of a rainbow, beginning at the centre and working your way outwards to each end.

3 **Exhale**, drawing in the abdominal muscles, to return your arms to the start position, using your chest muscles to perform the movement.

ARM SPLITS

This strengthens and tones the back, chest and arm muscles, releases tension in the neck, shoulders and upper back and stretches the chest muscles. If the movement is uncomfortable, just take your arms halfway at first.

Care If you have a recent shoulder injury, check with your doctor first, and go slowly and carefully.

Repetitions 6 each way

1 Lie on your back with your knees bent at a 90-degree angle and your feet hip-width apart. Reach your arms up to the ceiling. Your arms should be straight without locking your elbows, with your palms facing away from you. **Inhale**.

2 **Exhale**, draw in the abdominal muscles and split one arm in each direction, your upper arm moving towards ear level while you take your lower arm to hip level. Slide your shoulder blades down into your back.

3 **Inhale** to return your arms to the start position.

4 **Exhale**, drawing in the abdominal muscles, and split the arms in the opposite direction.

5 **Inhale** to return your arms to the ceiling.

SINGLE LEG CIRCLES

This all-round exercise increases strength and flexibility in the hips, lengthens the backs of the thighs, strengthens the inner thighs, stretches and strengthens the outer thighs and firms the buttocks. If you have a tight lower back and hamstrings, holding the position may feel a little uncomfortable. If you are unable to keep both your hips down on the mat while extending your leg to the ceiling, bend your knee slightly until you are able to straighten the leg out comfortably.

Care Proceed only under supervision if you have a back injury. If you experience any clicking in your hip, try reducing the size of the circle.

Repetitions 5 circles in each direction with one leg; 5 circles in each direction with the other leg

1 Lie on your back on a mat with your knees bent at a 90-degree angle with your feet hip-width apart. Place your arms by your sides, pressing your palms down into the mat for support. Ensure that the back of your neck is lengthened and your shoulders are down and relaxed. Lift one slightly bent leg up to the ceiling, turning out the leg by engaging the lower buttock muscles to rotate the thigh outwards in the hip socket. Point your toe. Your other leg remains bent with the foot firmly planted on the mat.

2 **Inhale** as you cross your leg over your body without letting your hips lift off the mat.

3 **Exhale**, drawing in your abdominal muscles, as you sweep your leg in a circle down towards the centre of your body.

4 Keep **exhaling** as you continue the circle round to the other side of your body.

5 Circle your leg back up to its start position in the centre, still **exhaling**. Imagine you are painting a small circle in the air, using your big toe as the paintbrush. Control the movement with your abdominal muscles so that your torso and your bent leg stay completely still throughout.

6 Reverse the circle by **inhaling** to take your leg over to the side away from your body. **Exhale** as you take the leg down, around and back to the centre.

SINGLE LEG STRETCH

This exercise tones the abdominal muscles, trims the waist and encourages good body alignment. If you find it difficult to keep your back flat on the mat, try straightening your leg towards the ceiling instead. As your strength improves, bring your leg to a lower angle. If your knee aches, hold under the knee and take the exercise at a slower pace.

Care Proceed only under supervision if you have a back injury. Proceed with caution if you have weak knees.

Repetitions 6 each side, alternating the legs

1 Lie on a mat on your back with your knees bent and shins parallel to the mat. Place your hands either side of your right knee. Your knees should be positioned quite close together.

2 **Inhale**, then **exhale**, drawing in the abdominal muscles as you straighten one leg at a 45-degree angle. Your torso and your other leg, supported by your two hands, shouldn't move. **Inhale**.

3 **Exhale** and draw in the abdominal muscles as you switch legs, bending your straight leg in, switching your hands over to that leg, while straightening your other leg out to 45 degrees. Continue to switch legs on each out-breath for the required number of repetitions. Between exhalations, you should take the tiniest of in-breaths, almost a 'sniff'. The focus should be on the out-breath as you bend one leg in and straighten the other leg.

Care Proceed only under supervision if you have any kind of back injury. Proceed with caution if you have any stiffness in the lower back.

Repetitions 3

SPINE STRETCH FORWARDS

This works the abdominal muscles, is a great stretch for the lower back, improves spinal flexibility, stretches the backs of the legs and improves your sitting posture.

1 To help you maintain a straight back, sit on a cushion or a folded towel. Sit up tall with your legs straight, hip-width apart, and your feet flexed so that your toes point to the ceiling. Lift your arms parallel to your legs at shoulder height, ensuring that the shoulder blades are relaxed down into your back. **Inhale**.

2 **Exhale**, drawing in the abdominal muscles, and round your spine forwards one vertebra at a time. Keep rolling forwards until your spine forms a letter C-shaped curve – imagine your back is against a wall, lower your head, then peel your upper back off the wall, followed by your mid-back and then lower back. Your head should end up just above your arms, following the line of the C-shaped curve.

3 **Inhale**, then **exhale**, drawing in your abdominal muscles as you reverse the movement. Roll back up your imaginary wall to your tall sitting position, one vertebra at a time, moving your lower back, then your mid-back, followed by your upper back and finally your head. Keep pulling your abdominal muscles in until you are sitting up really tall. Focus on lifting up out of your hips with a straight back.

OUTER THIGH LIFT

This exercise tones the outer thigh muscles to reduce saddlebags and create slimmer thighs, strengthens the buttock muscles and stretches the leg muscles all the way from your bottom right down to your ankles.

Care Don't allow your hip to roll forwards as you lift your top leg to hip height.

Repetitions 6 each side

1 Lie on your side with one hip on top of the other. Your ear, middle of shoulder, hip and ankle should all be in a straight line, feet pointing down. Your upper arm rests on the floor, the lower arm stretches out above your head, palm up, your head resting on a folded towel. Bend your lower leg forwards. Reach your upper leg away from you, without moving your hips, and flex your foot. Turn the upper thigh inwards in the hip socket so that the leg is slightly internally rotated, without moving the hip. **Inhale**.

2 **Exhale**, drawing in the abdominal muscles to keep your body stable, and squeeze your buttock muscles gently together. Stretch the upper leg away from you, as you lift it level with the hip. Lengthen your waist and really reach your upper leg away from you, keeping the internal rotation, pushing through the heel of your foot as you lift. Imagine you are trying to touch the wall opposite you with your heel.

3 **Inhale** and lower your leg to the start position.

Care Don't allow your hips to roll forwards or backwards.

Repetitions 4

INNER THIGH LIFT

This strengthens and firms the inner thigh muscles. Place a folded towel between your head and your arm for comfort. Bend your top leg and rest it on two cushions to stabilize your hips. If it is difficult to keep your back and hips stable, or your top leg straight, place your back against a wall.

1 Lie on your side with one hip carefully stacked on top of the other. Your ear, the middle of your shoulder, your hip and ankle should all be in a straight line. Your feet are pointing down. Your upper arm rests on the floor in front of you, your lower arm stretches out above your head, palm up, your head resting on a folded towel. Bring your top leg in front with the knee bent and rest it on two cushions, keeping one hip stacked on top of the other. Your lower leg remains straight underneath it. **Inhale.**

2 **Exhale**, drawing in the abdominal muscles, and stretch your lower leg away from you, with your foot flexed, as you slowly lift the heel about 15 cm (6 in) off the mat. Make sure you keep your lower knee facing forwards throughout and that your hips don't move. Imagine that you are trying to touch the wall opposite you with your heel.

3 **Inhale** as you lower your leg to the mat.

DOUBLE LEG LIFT

This exercise strengthens the abdominals, trims the waist and firms the inner thighs. Place a folded towel between your head and your arm. If you find it hard to stop your hips from rolling, lie on your side with your back against a wall.

Care Proceed only under supervision if you have a back injury.

Repetitions 6 on each side

1 Lie on a mat on your side with one hip carefully stacked on top of the other. Your ear, the middle of your shoulder, your hip and ankle should all be in a straight line. Your feet are pointing down. Your upper arm rests on the floor in front of you, your lower arm stretches out above your head, palm up, your head resting on a folded towel on your arm. Now take your legs slightly further forwards. **Inhale**.

2 **Exhale**, drawing in the abdominal muscles to stabilize your body, and lift both straight legs off the mat – about 10 cm (4 in). Squeeze your inner thighs together as you lift, and stretch your legs away from you. Imagine your inner thighs have been stuck together with glue so they move as a single unit. Hold for a count of 3.

3 **Inhale** as you slowly lower both legs down.

Care You should feel no strain in your lower back. Proceed only under supervision if you have any lower back injury.

Repetitions 6 on each leg

HAMSTRING LIFT

This exercise lifts and tones the buttocks, strengthens the hamstring muscles in the backs of the thighs and stretches the legs for a more streamlined appearance.

1 Lie on a mat on your front with your legs stretched away from you, feet together. Bend your elbows and place your hands one on top of the other under your forehead. Press your pubic bone gently towards the mat to lengthen your lower back. **Inhale**.

2 **Exhale**, drawing in the abdominal muscles, and lift one leg off the mat, stretching the leg along its length from where it meets the buttock all the way down to the heel. Hold for a count of 6. Imagine your leg is like a piece of sticky toffee, growing thinner and thinner as you stretch it in opposite directions.

3 **Inhale** and lower your leg.

HAMSTRING STRETCH

This exercise lengthens the hamstring muscles in the backs of the thighs and helps to release a tight lower back. If you have fairly flexible hamstrings, you can stretch the leg that is not supported by your hands away from you along the mat so that the leg lies straight rather than bent.

Care If this position feels uncomfortable, use a belt or a dressing gown cord to support your foot.

Repetitions Once each side

1 Lie on your back on a mat with your knees bent and your feet hip-width apart. Raise one leg and place your hands behind your thigh to support it. **Inhale**, making sure your tailbone (at the base of your spine) is down on the mat.

2 **Exhale**, drawing in the abdominal muscles, as you stretch your raised leg up towards the ceiling using your hands to support your leg as it extends. Flex the foot. Hold this for about 30 seconds. Repeat on the other leg.

Care If you have problem knees and this position causes discomfort, omit this exercise for the moment.

Repetitions Once on each leg

BUTTOCK STRETCH

This exercise stretches the buttock muscles and helps to release a tight lower back. If this feels relatively easy and you would like to increase the stretch, hold both hands behind the thigh of the leg bent at right angles and bring your knee in a little further towards the chest, still keeping the tailbone down. Hold for 30 seconds each side.

1 Lie down on a mat on your back with one knee bent at a 90-degree angle. Cross your other leg over and place the ankle just above the knee. Hold this ankle while keeping your head and shoulders on the floor. **Inhale**.

2 **Exhale**, drawing in your abdominal muscles, as you pull your top ankle up towards you a little. You will feel a stretch in the buttock of the leg being held at the ankle. Hold this position for about 30 seconds.

CHAPTER 3
HEALTHY EATING
FOR A LONGER LIFE

This chapter highlights which foods are good for you, what to eat to help combat ageing and what you should avoid if you are worried about weight gain, as well as providing recipes for healthy and delicious juices. It also presents The three-day detox plan to kickstart the elimination of toxins from your body, with suggestions for mimimizing the effects of everyday toxins.

HOW TO COMBAT AGEING

Researchers now agree that destructive molecules known as free radicals are responsible for many of the age-related degenerative conditions in the human body – for example, wrinkles, memory loss, arthritis, atherosclerosis (which causes heart disease) and cancer-causing mutations in cells. The good news is that you can limit the damage inflicted by free radicals and therefore affect the rate at which you age by making changes to your diet and lifestyle to reduce the levels of free radicals in your bloodstream.

HOMOCYSTEINE

As we get older, our bodies produce more of an amino acid called homocysteine, which comes from eating animal protein (meat, milk, cheese and eggs). Raised homocysteine levels are thought to clog arteries and increase blood clotting, and may actually be more harmful than cholesterol, resulting in heart disease, leg ulcers and deep vein thrombosis. Increased intake of folic acid and vitamins B6 and B12 can reduce homocysteine levels.

WHAT ARE FREE RADICALS?

Free radicals are electrochemically unstable molecules, generated within our bodies by normal metabolic functions such as breathing, digesting food and fighting infections, as well as by factors such as certain foods (for example, heated fats), overeating, smoking, stress, sunburn and pollution. In large quantities, free radicals can damage DNA, accelerate ageing and contribute to a wide range of disorders.

ARM YOURSELF WITH ANTIOXIDANTS

Antioxidants are nutrients that seek out and neutralize the cell-damaging free radicals, blocking their path of destruction. In this way, they can help ward off cancer, heart disease, high blood pressure, stroke, Alzheimer's disease, cataracts and other age-related illnesses and conditions, hence their renown as anti-ageing nutrients.

The key antioxidants are beta-carotene (which the body converts into vitamin A), vitamins C and E and the minerals selenium and zinc (see pages 78–79). Manganese and copper, some B complex vitamins and certain enzymes and amino acids also have antioxidant properties. Many antioxidants work together, enhancing each other's action, which is why a varied diet that includes different antioxidants is so important.

ANTIOXIDANT FOODS

In order to slow down the signs of ageing you need to include plenty of antioxidant foods in your diet. Since nutrients can be destroyed in cooking, uncooked fresh fruit and vegetables are the best sources of antioxidants. Particularly good ones include: apples, avocados, bananas, berries (blackberries, blackcurrants, blueberries, raspberries,

redcurrants, strawberries), brazil nuts, broccoli, carrots, cherries, citrus fruits, garlic, hazelnuts, kiwifruit, peas, plums, prunes, raisins, red grapes, red peppers, spinach, strawberries, tomatoes and watermelon.

FEED UP ON FIBRE

Dietary fibre is the part of fruit, vegetables and whole grains that our bodies cannot digest but that is essential as it ensures a speedy passage of digested food through the bowel. Waste that builds up in the body not only causes constipation but also brings the risk of cancer and bowel disease like diverticulosis. Fibre also helps to lower blood cholesterol levels and helps with weight control, and plays a role in steadying blood sugar, which is important for energy levels.

Fibre is particularly important as we get older as the digestive system functions less efficiently. Try to eat 20–35 g (about 1 oz) of fibre a day. Good sources include wholegrain cereal foods, vegetables, chickpeas, beans and lentils, seeds and fruit (especially dried fruit, prunes, figs, nectarines, dates and raspberries). Make sure you drink plenty of water to help this indigestible nutrient through your digestive system.

CHECK YOUR CHOLESTEROL

The body needs cholesterol to function, but too much of it in the bloodstream results in clogged and narrowed arteries, which can lead to heart disease (see pages 180–181). A few foods contain cholesterol (egg yolks, some shellfish and offal), but the main cause of high blood cholesterol levels is too great an intake of saturated fat (see page 72), which is converted into cholesterol in the body. Blood cholesterol levels also tend to rise with age and with stress. Lowering your blood cholesterol levels is paramount for good health – some foods are particularly good at doing this (see page 111).

See also ▶
Eat to stay young, pages 72–73
Vital vitamins and minerals for healthy ageing, pages 78–79
Healthy heart, Chapter 6

EATING TO BEAT AGEING

- Ensure that your diet is rich in nutrients, but lean in fat and calories for overall health and to reduce your risk of heart disease and cancer.

- Enhance your immune system with foods rich in antioxidants.

- Keep your digestive system healthy with plenty of fibre.

- Strengthen your bones by eating calcium-rich foods (see pages 144–147).

- Protect your eyesight by eating antioxidant foods.

EAT TO STAY YOUNG

Any dietary changes you can make – and it's never too late to start – to reduce the numbers of free radicals in your body will improve your chances of a healthier, longer life with fewer age-related illnesses. However, don't try so hard that you end up not being able to enjoy life – just try to follow at least some of the following 'rules'.

CHOOSING THE RIGHT FOODS

In a nutshell, you should be eating plenty of fruit and vegetables, whole grains and potatoes, and not too many fatty, sugary or salty foods. Save these for the odd occasion rather than everyday eating.

- **Cut calories** Research has shown that reducing your intake of calories can bring down the levels of free radicals in your bloodstream and extend your life span (see page 74).

- **Eat loads of fruit and vegetables** They are our best defence against free radicals, so eat them at every meal (fresh, frozen, canned, dried or as juice). Aim for at least five servings a day (potatoes do not count), but try for ten. Research published in the *American Journal of Clinical Nutrition* has shown that eating lots of fruit and vegetables (particularly fruit) can reduce the risk of stroke by 30 to 40 per cent.

- **Eat less fat** Limit your fat intake to no more than a third of your total daily calories, and ensure that less than 10 per cent comes from saturated fats (animal-sourced fats like cheese, milk, butter and meat; plus coconut oil and palm oil, see page 183).

- **Focus on whole grains** Eat three or four 75 g (3 oz) servings of wholegrain carbohydrates every day, one of which should be a high-fibre breakfast cereal fortified with folic acid, which helps to lower levels of homocysteine in the body (see page 70).

- **Go (mostly) vegetarian** Vegetarians age more slowly and live longer than meat-eaters. This is probably due to higher levels of plant antioxidants in their bloodstream and because a vegetarian diet necessarily means fewer calories and no animal fat. If you cannot give up meat entirely, at least cut your consumption of red meat and replace it with fish or vegetable proteins to improve your health. Women should eat at least 50 g (2 oz) of protein a day.

- **Eat less sugar** Sugar is a major cause of free radicals and linked to increased risk of late-onset diabetes, so aim to consume less than 40 g (1½ oz) per day.

- **Watch your salt intake** Current recommendations are for no more than 5–6 g (about 1 teaspoon) of salt per day.

- **Imbibe a little** Too much alcohol can seriously damage your health, but a small amount (one or two 125 ml/4 fl oz glasses of wine on five or six days of the week) can be beneficial, improving IQ and boosting mental agility. In addition, the phytonutrients in red grapes mean that red wine can help keep your heart healthy.

- **Drink tea** Tea (green, black or oolong) contains antioxidants called flavonoids, and tea drinking has been proven to protect against various cancers, help heart health and reduce blood cholesterol. It also fights the bacteria that cause gum disease and tooth decay.

- **Eat a little chocolate** Chocolate contains very high levels of cocoa flavonoids, antioxidants that help thin the blood and lower blood cholesterol and blood pressure. Since studies by the Harvard School of Public Health, USA, have shown that chocolate-eaters live longer than those who give up sweets completely, aim for two small squares daily of a chocolate that is high in cocoa solids.

FATS: GOOD VERSUS BAD

Too much fat, especially saturated fat, in our diet is linked with heart disease (see page 183), high blood cholesterol, obesity and even cancer. However, our bodies need some fat for healthy functioning, in particular the naturally occurring 'good' fats called essential fatty acids, which are found in oily fish, nuts, seeds and some vegetable oils.

'Good' fats
Oily fish (see page 183)
Fish oils
Nuts, seeds and their oils (such as pumpkin seeds, linseeds and linseed oil, sesame seeds and oil, walnut oil, peanut oil, sunflower oil)
Soya (see page 183)
Olive oil (especially cold-pressed)
Avocado and avocado oil
Corn oil

'Bad' fats
Partially hydrogenated fats
Deep-fried foods
Refined vegetable oils
Coconut oil
Palm oil
Full-fat dairy fats (such as milk, cheese, butter)
Processed foods (such as pies, cakes, biscuits)
Meat and processed meat products (for example, suet, salami, sausages)

WEIGHT CONTROL

Our body weight is the result of the balance between the amount of energy (that is, food) taken in, usually measured in calories, and the amount used up through physical activity. As we get older, we naturally lose some of the muscle mass and strength that requires calories for maintenance and our metabolism slows down, so we don't need as many calories as we did when younger. The reason why many of us put on weight as we get older is that we don't alter our eating habits to reflect this need for fewer calories.

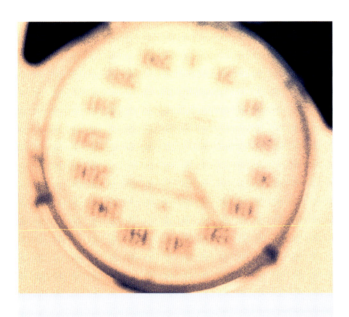

COUNT YOUR CARBS

More than half of your total daily calorie intake should come from unprocessed and unrefined carbohydrates. This means that fruit, vegetables and whole grains (like brown rice, porridge oats, wholemeal bread, wholewheat pasta and high-fibre breakfast cereal) should constitute the main part of every meal, providing you with a high-vitamin, low-calorie diet.

EXCESS TO REQUIREMENTS

If you regularly consume too many calories, the excess is stored as body fat. To prevent weight gain as you get older, you need to increase your activity levels, do muscle-toning exercises to maintain muscle mass (see pages 48–67) and eat fewer calories than previously.

KNOW YOUR CALORIE COUNT

To work out how many calories you can consume daily without gaining weight, do this calculation. Do bear in mind that it is only a rough guide, as many factors determine an individual's metabolic rate and the equation will be inaccurate if you are very muscular or very fat. (The following formulae apply only to women.)

- First, calculate your basal metabolic rate (see box, opposite).

- Next, multiply your BMR figure by an activity figure – 1.3 if your lifestyle is generally sedentary and you do little or no exercise; 1.5 if you are lightly active (exercise for 1 to 3 hours a week); 1.7 if you are active (exercise for more than 3 hours a week).

- The final figure you arrive at gives you the number of calories required to maintain your current weight.

To *lose* weight (and remove stored body fat), you need to consume 250–500 calories less than your calculated figure per day to create a calorie deficit. Alternatively, you can keep your calorie intake the same, but increase your activity levels. A combination of both these

approaches is the most effective way to achieve lasting weight loss.

Since 500 g (1 lb) of stored body fat is equivalent to 3,500 calories, you need to burn calories through physical activity and/or reduce the number of calories you eat for a total of 3,500 in order to lose just 500 g (1 lb) of fat.

APPLES AND PEARS

Where overweight people carry their excess weight is important for health reasons. Studies have shown that apple-shaped people (those with excess fat around their waist and abdomen) are at greater risk of heart disease, stroke and diabetes than those with a pear shape (who carry excess fat around their hips, bottom and thighs). This is because fat that is carried around the abdomen affects a range of risk factors, including raised blood pressure and blood-sugar levels. Therefore, if you are an 'apple' (rather than a 'pear'), you should make every effort possible to lose your excess weight.

Women whose waist measures more than 80 cm (32 in) have a slight health risk, while a waist of more than 88 cm (35 in) denotes a substantially increased health risk.

DELAY AGEING BY EATING LESS

Another reason to watch your food intake is that consuming fewer calories improves longevity. Evidence from a number of different animal studies in which a restricted calorific diet resulted in significantly increased life span suggests that we, too, would benefit. We are more likely to live to a healthy old age and avoid chronic illnesses and degenerative diseases like heart disease and cancer. This is because a limited calorie intake results in a strengthened immune system and fewer free radicals in the bloodstream (see page 70), as well as lower total body fat, better blood sugar control, lower blood pressure and lower blood cholesterol.

CALCULATING YOUR BASAL METABOLIC RATE

To calculate your basal, or resting, metabolic rate (BMR) – the number of calories your body requires to function at rest – you need to use the Harris Benedict formula:

$$655 + \left(9.6 \times \text{weight in kilos}\right) + \left(1.8 \times \text{height in cm}\right) - \left(4.7 \times \text{age in years}\right)$$

WHY WORRY ABOUT YOUR WEIGHT?

As you get older, maintaining a healthy weight is important because excess weight decreases your mobility, which is ageing in itself, and puts a strain on the body, increasing your risk of high blood pressure, heart attack, stroke, diabetes and arthritis.

WEIGHT-LOSS PLAN

This month-long diet focuses on both cutting calories and reducing the amount of fluid in the body resulting from stored unprocessed toxins. It does this by using foods that prevent fluid retention, cutting out the wheat- and dairy-based foods commonly linked to food intolerances, and by keeping the sodium content low. In addition, it uses detox foods (see page 82) and supplements to help neutralize any harmful toxins released into the body as the stored fat breaks down.

TIME SCALE

If necessary, continue with the diet when the month is up (and you have lost up to 6.5 kg/14 lb), now focusing on losing fat rather than fluid. Reintroduce wheat and dairy products – switch from soya to skimmed milk at breakfast; add cottage cheese or 50 g (2 oz) of reduced-fat hard cheese to your protein choices; and add wholegrain breads and wholewheat pastas to your evening carbohydrate choices (choose these new options once or twice a week).

Once you have reached your goal, maintain your new weight by sticking to your calorie maintenance level (see page 74) and keeping active.

07:00 **Early morning supplements** Multivitamin and mineral supplement + 1 g of vitamin C + 2,000 mg of conjugated linoleic acid (CLA, a healthy fat shown to help with fat loss) + 5 g of psyllium (a purified seed fibre supplement, which absorbs toxins and stimulates the bowel) + two glasses of water – drink at least eight more during the day.

07:30 **Breakfast** Half an hour after your supplements: ANTIOXIDANT COCKTAIL + one of the following high-fibre breakfasts:
- Bran cereal topped with soya milk and a handful of prunes.
- A cored apple filled with raisins and baked for 30 minutes at 220°C (425°F), Gas Mark 7, then topped with soya yogurt.
- Two slices of rye or pumpernickel bread, toasted and spread with honey + a boiled egg.
- Porridge made from oat flakes and water or soya milk, and mixed with a handful of chopped dried apricots.
- Two oatcakes topped with mashed banana and strawberries.

10:30 **Mid-morning snack** Two pieces of fruit + cup of dandelion tea (dandelion helps the body excrete excess fluid without destroying other vital nutrients).

13:00 **Pre-lunch supplement** Half an hour before lunch: 1,000 mg of CLA + 5 g of psyllium + at least two glasses of water.

13:30 **Lunch** CHELATING COCKTAIL + one of the following vegetable bases (using as much of each vegetable as you like, except for avocado), combined with a drizzle and a topping.

Bases:
- Spicy salad: alfalfa, tomato, red pepper, black olives, radish.
- Clarifying coleslaw: shredded white cabbage, grated carrot, sliced beetroot, sliced onion.
- Pure power: watercress, cucumber, tomato, artichoke hearts, ½ avocado.
- Stir-fry sensation: asparagus spears, bean sprouts, shredded green cabbage, mangetout and broccoli stir-fried in a tiny amount of oil with sliced ginger in it.
- Good-for-you grill: mushrooms, thinly sliced aubergine, red onions, yellow peppers and courgettes grilled until softened.

Drizzles:
- Balsamic vinegar; or 1 teaspoon of olive oil containing some chopped chilli (to boost the metabolism); or a spoonful of salsa, lemon juice or fat-free vinaigrette.

Toppings:
- 75 g (3 oz) of lean protein, such as chicken, turkey, salmon, tuna, mackerel, sardines, anchovies, lean ham, lean roast beef, a blend of kidney beans, green beans and chickpeas or grilled or marinated tofu.

16:00 **Afternoon snack** Two pieces of fruit.

19:00 **Evening meal** Another 1,000 mg of CLA + CHELATING COCKTAIL or SUPERCLEANSE SOUP + a vegetable base from lunch topped with 50 g (2 oz) of lean protein and 50 g (2 oz) of carbohydrates (for example a jacket potato, new potatoes, mashed potatoes, roast sweet potatoes, rye or pumpernickel bread, mashed swede, parsnips or pumpkin, sweetcorn or corn-on-the-cob, brown rice or wheat-free pasta).

21:30 **Evening snack** Slice of rye or pumpernickel bread topped with half a banana or 1 teaspoon of honey.

DETOX RECIPES

ANTIOXIDANT COCKTAIL
Blend 50 g (2 oz) each of prepared blueberries and strawberries, ½ mango and 250 ml (8 fl oz) orange juice in a blender until smooth.

CHELATING COCKTAIL
Juice together 2–3 peeled carrots, 1 beetroot and 1 apple, then serve.

SUPERCLEANSE SOUP
Cook 1 small onion in 2–3 tablespoons of 1.5 litres (2½ pints) chicken stock or water for 1 minute. Add 2 small, diced potatoes, salt and pepper and the rest of the stock/water. Bring to the boil and simmer until the potatoes are soft. Add 2 large handfuls of spinach and 1 large bunch of watercress (stems removed), and stir for 3 minutes. Remove from the heat and blend in a blender. (This recipe will make enough soup for a couple of days, so you can store it in the refrigerator until required.)

VITAL VITAMINS AND MINERALS FOR HEALTHY AGEING

NUTRIENT	FUNCTION	FOOD
Beta-carotene	A powerful antioxidant, which can help prevent cancer, heart disease and strokes (by preventing arteries from clogging up with fatty deposits), beta-carotene is converted by the body into vitamin A. Vitamin A boosts immunity, promotes strong teeth and bones, keeps skin healthy and is essential for good vision.	 Yellow, orange and dark green fruits and vegetables such as carrots, sweet potato, apricots, mango, pumpkin, spinach and kale.
Vitamin C	A powerful antioxidant, vitamin C also boosts immunity and fights infection; it is involved in collagen production and protects against skin damage; it helps prevent the development of age-related cataracts, and is thought to reduce the risk of stroke. Vitamin C also helps your body to absorb iron and folic acid effectively, and turn food into energy. A daily intake of the vitamin is vital.	 Fresh fruits and vegetables, especially blackcurrants, green pepper, broccoli, kiwifruit, mango, citrus fruit, strawberries, cabbage and spinach.
Vitamin E	Another powerful antioxidant, vitamin E has a key function as an anticoagulant and is therefore crucial for a healthy heart and blood supply. It also helps keep skin looking young and reduces the risk of dementia. Although fat soluble, it is stored in the body for only a short period of time and regular intake is essential. Absorption is reduced by high intakes of iron.	 Nuts and seeds, especially wheatgerm and wheatgerm oil, sunflower seeds and sunflower oil, olive oil, almonds, pine nuts, peanut butter, sweet potato, whole grains and blackberries.
Selenium	A key antioxidant, selenium is more powerful if taken with vitamin E, and vice versa; it helps protect the body from a wide range of diseases including cancer. Selenium stimulates the immune system; it is required for healthy muscles (including heart muscles), good eyesight and healthy skin. It also reduces the inflammation of arthritis.	 Brazil nuts, fish and shellfish, meat, sunflower seeds, wholemeal bread, walnuts, garlic.

NUTRIENT	FUNCTION	FOOD
Zinc	Zinc plays a crucial role in the protection and repair of DNA, and helps regulate hormone levels. A powerful antioxidant and immune system booster, it is also good for brain function and a healthy nervous system. It can help deal with arthritis.	Oysters, steak, wheatgerm, pumpkin seeds and brazil nuts.
Folic acid	A member of the B-complex family, folic acid works with other B vitamins, particularly vitamin B12. Folic acid is important for helping ward off anaemia, and reducing the risk of heart disease by lowering levels of the amino acid homocysteine (see page 70). It is found in many foods but is easily destroyed (up to two-thirds is lost in cooking, especially boiling).	Wheatgerm, offal, fortified breakfast cereals, black-eyed beans, green leafy vegetables (such as spinach, kale, broccoli), sprouted seeds, peanuts and eggs.
Flavonoids	These powerful antioxidants have anti-cancer properties. One type of flavonoids, anthocyanins, are thought to be 50 times more powerful than vitamin E.	Soya, tea, red wine, green vegetables, red, purple and blue fruits and oranges.
Co-enzyme Q10	This vitamin-like substance found in all cells is needed by the body to help convert food into energy. It improves immunity and works as an antioxidant, helping to protect the body from cell damage and the effects of ageing. Co-enzyme Q10 is thought to improve the strength of the heart muscles – since levels of it decrease as we get older, which is thought to play a significant role in age-related medical conditions, such as heart disease. Taking a supplement may be beneficial.	Meat, sardines, mackerel, peanuts, sesame seeds.
Manganese	Manganese acts as an antioxidant by activating an enzyme that breaks down potentially harmful free radicals. It is essential for brain function, improves brain strength and promotes wound healing.	Tea, wholemeal bread, avocados, hazelnuts, almonds and coconut.
Copper	An antioxidant that boosts the immune system, copper can also ease arthritis, regulates blood cholesterol levels and aids collagen production for healthy bones and skin.	Oysters, liver, shellfish, sardines, sunflower seeds and peanuts.

WHY DETOX?

Detox – short for detoxification – is possibly the biggest health topic of the 21st century. Studies have shown that we are feeling sicker and lower in energy than ever before. We know we have a problem and we know what we believe to be the reason: we are filling our bodies with toxins. These include the caffeine that we use to fuel our energy deficit, the fumes we breathe in, the junk food we eat and the alcohol we drink.

DETOXING

By using our detox plan you will:

- **Increase** production of the natural enzymes that your liver, skin and lungs use to neutralize harmful toxins, making it less likely that the body will suffer toxic overload.

- **Put in place** defence mechanisms to neutralize harmful compounds that toxins bring into the body, reducing the damage they can cause.

- **Boost** blood flow around the system, which ensures that toxins are removed faster and more effectively.

- **Strengthen** the power of the skin and lungs to detox more effectively.

- **Create** a healthy digestive system, also ensuring the fast and effective removal of toxins from the body.

WHEN TOXINS BUILD UP

You may not be aware that your body actually has a whole detox system of its own. It has to, otherwise it would become poisoned by natural toxins, including waste products from food, dead bacteria and debris from the millions of new body cells produced each day. When the body's natural detox system is working well, it can function at full power. However, if any one part of the system breaks down, toxins will not be eradicated and will start to build up in the body.

For example, the most simple (and probably most commonly experienced) sign of this is a hangover. If you exceed the amount of alcohol your body can process in one go, it starts to build up and effectively poisons the body, causing symptoms such as nausea, headache and an upset stomach. Once the body has had a chance to eliminate the alcohol, however, the symptoms begin to disperse. Now imagine this happening on a larger scale. If they are not removed effectively from the body, toxins can build up, stressing every system in our body and leading to problems like low energy, poor immunity, bad skin, cellulite, weight gain and even arthritis. This outcome is what detoxing tries to tackle. By reducing your exposure to toxins, you can help take pressure off the body's natural detox system and allow it to deal with those built-up toxins.

WORKING WITH YOUR BODY

What most people understand as 'detoxing', however, simply doesn't work. You can't atone for a year's worth of toxic overload by eating grapes or raw food for a weekend. The body just isn't designed that way. It is much better to work with your body to fight against toxic attack. You will still need to alter your diet to cleanse your system, but

you will work with foods and other elements to help reinforce your natural detox processes. This means that when you do expose your body to toxins, it will be able to deal with and process them more effectively. It will give you control over your body, as well as the strength, energy and the power to function at your best. You will have more energy, your skin and hair will look healthier, you will probably lose weight and you will sleep better.

TOXIC SIDE EFFECTS

All the unpleasant symptoms you normally get when you are on a traditional detox programme probably won't appear if you follow the advice in this book. Feelings of exhaustion, irritability, bad breath and so on happen not because your body is eliminating toxins but because you are starving it. Since you are not going to do that, these side effects are unlikely to occur.

CHANGING LONG-TERM HABITS

A good detox diet focuses your mind on eating healthily and helps you reassess your relationship with foods that can sometimes be bad for you. For example, by giving up coffee for a week, you become less dependent on it to wake you up and your natural energy becomes more balanced. By cutting out alcohol, you remember how good it felt not to have a hangover and you realize you can get through stressful situations without the aid of a glass of wine. By lowering your intake of sugar, you prevent the peaks and troughs in blood-sugar levels that can leave you 'down' and fatigued and needing more sweet stuff to boost your energy. You also re-educate your tastebuds, making you less dependent on the 'bad foods'.

COMMON TOXINS

- Alcohol
- Caffeine
- Nicotine
- Pesticides
- Pollutants
- Saturated fats
- Sugar
- Stress
- Allergy-related foods

'By reducing your exposure to toxins, you can help take pressure off the body's natural detox system and allow it to deal with those built-up toxins.'

See also ▶
Top 10 detox foods, pages 82–83
The three-day detox plan, pages 84–87
Juices for health, pages 88–93

THE TOP 10 DETOX FOODS

These top 10 detox foods have been shown to provide the best all-round nutrients that will work hard to rid your body of toxins. For information about free radicals and antioxidants, see pages 70–71 and 78–79.

1 APPLES

Contain vitamin C and quercetin, antioxidant nutrients that lower fat and cholesterol levels in the bloodstream, as well as pectin, a soluble fibre that binds heavy metals (such as lead and mercury) in the colon and encourages their excretion. Apples also help the body to excrete food additives.

2 AVOCADOS

Contain glutathione, an antioxidant that fights free radicals. This combines with fat-soluble toxins, particularly alcohol, to make them water-soluble. Levels of glutathione decrease as we age (one reason why hangovers worsen as we get older), making us more susceptible to arthritis.

3 ARTICHOKES

Increase production of bile, which carries toxins to the bowel where they can be excreted. Contains antioxidant nutrients. Damage to the liver caused by free radicals is dramatically lessened when artichoke extracts are present.

4 BEETROOTS

Contain methionine, a sulphur-containing essential amino acid that helps to purify natural waste products from the body, and betanin, which helps the rate at which the liver can break down fatty acids. These chemicals take the pressure off the liver, allowing it to fight more dangerous toxins.

5 CRUCIFEROUS VEGETABLES

Cabbage, kale, brussels sprouts, spinach and cauliflower are all cruciferous vegetables – members of the cabbage family – and are very powerful detoxers that neutralize particular toxins. These vegetables also contain glucosinolates, which prompt the liver to produce enzymes vital for body function.

6 GARLIC

Allicin is created when garlic is crushed, and it converts into a sulphur-based compound when it enters the body. Toxins such as mercury, certain food additives and chemical versions of the hormone oestrogen bind with sulphur, enabling the body to excrete the whole package. Sulphur also helps keep the body alkaline, which can help fight cravings caused by nicotine addiction.

7 KIWIFRUITS

Contain vitamin C, a powerful antioxidant, which also helps the body manufacture the vital detoxer glutathione (see Avocados, opposite).

8 PRUNES

These are the ultimate antioxidant food and provide twice as many antioxidants as blueberries, their nearest competitor. They are also important detoxifiers for other reasons. They contain tartaric acid, a natural laxative, and dihydrophenylisatin, which triggers the intestine to contract. Together, these reduce the time that faeces stay in the system, thereby reducing the risk of toxic reabsorption.

9 SEAWEED

Seaweed binds in the body with radioactive waste, which can reach us via food that has been grown where water or soil has been contaminated. It contains minerals in high doses, such as iron, calcium and magnesium, and also iodine and alginates. If your body doesn't get minerals from your diet, it will try to extract them from any heavy metals it takes in. Fortunately, alginates in seaweed have been shown to bind with them, which helps to prepare them for excretion from the body.

10 WATERCRESS

Increase detox enzymes in the body and may act directly on particular toxins. Contains chlorophyll, which helps build healthy red blood cells, thereby boosting your body's circulation.

OTHER USEFUL DETOX FOODS

Alfalfa High in a fibre called plantix, alfalfa has the ability to bind to toxins, including some drugs and food additives. It is also rich in minerals, amino acids and fatty acids.

Asparagus High in vitamin C, asparagus is also packed with fibre and the antioxidant rutin, and is a rich source of glutathione.

Bananas Exceptionally high in minerals, bananas can reduce the uptake of heavy metals. Bananas also provide potassium, which helps to regulate fluid in the body and reduce fluid retention.

Brazil nuts These contain the antioxidant nutrient selenium, which neutralizes free radicals created in the body, particularly those caused by smoking.

Carrots Vital sources of the antioxidants alpha- and beta-carotene, carrots also seem to have the ability to bind to heavy metals in the body. They also help to reduce cholesterol levels in the blood.

Eggs These contain high levels of lecithin, which helps improve fat digestion in the body and improves liver function. Eggs also include a detoxifier called cysteine, which is particularly potent against alcohol.

THE THREE-DAY DETOX PLAN

Using the format of the normal activities of three days (a weekend and a work day), this plan points out where you are commonly exposed to toxins, and reveals how to reduce them. In some cases, it actually just takes one thing, done over this one long weekend, to make a difference to other elements of your life. This three-day plan will show you how easy it is to make changes that you can carry out from now on.

SATURDAY

07:00 **Open your windows** The USA-based Environmental Protection Agency says that the air in the average home is 2–5 times more polluted than the average road. A build-up of the fumes from chemical cleaners and beauty products, like hairspray, and the gas given off by mouldy walls or by synthetic material used in furniture and fabrics, is to blame, and it can cause problems like fatigue, headaches, skin rashes and allergies. Opening your windows as often as possible helps all these disperse (and is vital if you have a new carpet or furniture). It is best to do this early in the morning as pollution fumes build up outside as the day progresses.

10:00 **Exercise safely** There is nothing better than exercising outside to boost your mood and energy – but it can also boost your exposure to airborne pollutants. After all, the average person exercising inhales 10 times more air when they exercise than at rest and breathes it into the lungs more deeply. You are also more likely to breathe through your mouth, which means that air is not passed through the tiny hairs in the nose that act as a partial filter against some pollutants. You can help reduce risk by working out away from the rush-hour (when carbon monoxide levels peak). On sunny days it may also be better to do your workout earlier in the day; sunlight increases the amount of a pollutant called ozone in the air, and this can trigger breathing problems.

11:00 **Take your shoes off when you come back in** When researchers at the Southwest Research Institute in San Antonio in Texas, USA, analysed the carpets of homes, they found residue from pesticides sprayed up to five years earlier. These had been brought in on people's shoes and lodged within

the carpet, and no amount of vacuum-cleaning could remove them. Studies have also shown that in homes where people do not routinely remove their shoes carpets contain high levels of lead. Removing your shoes before you enter the home is normal in Asian cultures, so make it a new policy in yours.

14:00 **Buy organic** Research carried out by the University of Ghent, Belgium, estimated that in the average daily diet a person was exposed to 54 different pesticides. You will cut this dramatically if the weekly shop contains as much organic produce as possible. The foods that will make the most difference if you swap to organic are bread, milk, soft fruits, salad crops (especially lettuce), peppers, spinach, cherries, apples and peaches.

19:00 **Avoid smoky atmospheres** Passive smoking is a pollutant many of us are exposed to, yet we don't realize how much it can harm us. A public health campaign in New Zealand estimated that one person a day died from the effects of passive smoking; their population is only three million people, so imagine the effects in somewhere like the UK or the USA. When you are out, try to sit in non-smoking or well-ventilated areas. Breathe through your nose, which gives some small level of filtration, rather than your mouth. If someone is blowing smoke right at you, ask them (nicely) if they can blow it the other way. If you are eating out, order something containing tomatoes: the antioxidant lycopene that tomatoes contain seems to have a protective effect on the lungs, even when they are exposed to smoke.

SUNDAY

07:00 **Get those windows open again**

10:00 **Rearrange the furniture** Some researchers believe that the electromagnetic fields (EMFs) created by electrical appliances like televisions and radios affect the body adversely. As yet, this has not been scientifically proven, but why be sorry when being safe is so easy? EMFs don't reach more than 2–2.5 m (7–8 ft), so move as many electrical appliances as possible this distance away from beds, chairs or any areas of the floor where you spend a significant amount of your time. EMF levels are highest at the rear of such electrical equipment, so at the very least make sure you are not facing the back of any appliance.

14:00 **Green clean your home.** Many modern cleaners use large amounts of chemicals to do the job, and these can be toxic; in fact, in close proximity to each other, chlorine bleach and ammonia products can create gases that may even be fatal. Cutting down on the amount of cleaning products you use, and using them in a well-ventilated room, is vital. It is even better to make your own green cleaners. Here are a few ideas.

- **Air freshener** Bicarbonate of soda is very good at absorbing odours. Sprinkle it on to the carpet and vacuum-clean or place in pretty bowls around the home.

- **Furniture cleaner** One cup of lemon juice mixed with one cup of vegetable oil makes a good basic polish. Put it on the cloth rather than the furniture itself and test on a small area first.

- **Window cleaner** Half-fill a spray bottle with water, then fill to the top with vinegar. Add a little washing-up liquid. Spray on the windows and wipe off.

- **Floor cleaner** Add half a cup of vinegar per 4.5 litres (1 gallon) of hot water and mop as usual.

- **Toilet cleaner** Vinegar kills germs and deodorizes smells. Pour one cup into your toilet bowl, leave for 10 minutes, then flush.

MONDAY

07:00 **Open the windows**

08:00 **Simplify your beauty programme** It is estimated that the average woman exposes her body to 150 chemicals a day during her beauty regime, and these have been blamed for the rise in sensitive skins. Recent research has also been published that links dark hair dyes to bladder cancer. Simplify your skincare regime by using only products you really need (see pages 16–17). You should also try to use ranges with minimal ingredients; hypoallergenic ranges are good for this. Switch to vegetable dyes for your hair, and skip nail polishes that contain formaldehyde or toluene, both of which have been linked to serious health problems. Don't believe the hype about antiperspirants causing breast cancer, though; it is not true.

08:30   **Make your trip to work more healthy** Even though we have cleaned up our cars, traffic fumes are still our main problem when it comes to air pollution, with the rush-hour offering you maximum exposure. If you drive to work, travel with your windows open and the air-conditioning off. Internal ventilation systems draw air from under the car, right by the exhaust of the car in front. It is better to drive with your windows open. This is even more important if you have a new car. Research from the Australian science researchers, CSIRO, has found that toxic gases in new cars can cause problems like headaches, skin rashes or fatigue for as long as six months after purchase when ventilation levels in the car are low. If you walk to work, stay as far away as possible from the kerb, where carbon monoxide levels are highest and try to breathe through your nose rather than your mouth.

10:00   **Rearrange your desk** EMFs are given off by computers and other office equipment as well as home electrical appliances, so try to avoid sitting close to anything but your computer, or next to the back of any equipment (see page 85). Then add some plants to the area. Printers and photocopiers give off gases called volatile organic compounds (VOCs), which can lead to symptoms like headache, fatigue and problems with concentration. However, studies by space agency NASA have shown that spider plants, Chinese evergreens and aloe vera all filter air and can reduce the effects of these VOCs. If your office has a no-plants rule, then use an air filter with a charcoal filter instead as it will help to absorb fumes.

17:00   **Change your outfit** If you work in an environment where toxic chemicals are used, it is advisable to get into the habit of changing out of your work clothes before you leave for home. Studies have produced evidence to show that people working with toxic dusts or radioactivity can actually carry minuscule particles home on their clothes.

HINT FOR HEALTH

Keep referring back to the list of common toxins (see box on page 81) and the top 10 detox foods (see pages 82–83) so that you can reduce the amount of toxins in your diet and increase the number of detox foods.

JUICES FOR HEALTH

Juicing fruit and vegetables removes the indigestible fibre, so that nutrients such as vitamins A, B, C and E, antioxidants, calcium, folic acid, potassium and zinc are available in much larger quantities and are utilized far more quickly by the body.

WHAT YOU NEED

It is possible to juice by hand, but this tends to be messy and time-consuming, so it is worth investing in a juicer. There is a wide range available, so it is best to look at all the options so you can make sure you buy the best machine for your needs.

PREPARING INGREDIENTS

As most enzymes, vitamins and minerals lie just below the fruit and vegetable skins, keep the skins on and wash all fruit and vegetables thoroughly. But if the vegetables are not organic, then remove the stems, skins or roots before juicing. However, don't include the skins from oranges, lemons, bananas, pineapples, mangoes and papayas. Remove the stones from apricots, peaches, mangoes and plums.

Cut the fruit or vegetable into manageable pieces for the juicer, then follow the manufacturer's directions. To get the maximum nutritional benefit, drink your juices as soon as you have made them.

Each recipe makes one serving, but quantities may vary depending on the type of juice.

COOL DOWN

This helps to relieve the symptoms of the menopause, such as irritability, hot flushes, mood swings, headaches, night sweats, vaginal dryness, loss of libido and anxiety. Beetroot is a rich source of folate, which can help to protect the heart and, together with carrots, helps to regulate hormones. Yam provides the hormone progesterone.

175 g (6 oz) carrot
100 g (3½ oz) beetroot
175 g (6 oz) yam or sweet potato
125 g (4 oz) fennel

Juice all the ingredients. Mix well and serve in a glass with ice cubes. Decorate with fennel fronds, if liked.

Nutritional values per serving • vitamin A 49,430 iu vitamin C 69.95 mg • iron 3.9 mg • folic acid 254 mcg folate 196 mcg • 296 kcal

POWER PACK

This revitalizing juice is a real tonic. If you are feeling lethargic or constantly tired, try to avoid processed foods and cut out salt and refined sugars. Carrots, beetroots and oranges are high in vitamins A and C, antioxidants and phytonutrients such as alpha- and beta-carotene.

250 g (8 oz) carrot

125 g (4 oz) beetroot

1 orange

125 g (4 oz) strawberries

Juice the carrot, beetroot and orange. Put the juice into a blender with a couple of ice cubes and the strawberries. Whizz for 20 seconds and serve in a tall glass. Decorate with strips of orange rind, if liked.

vitamin A 70,652 iu • vitamin C 166 mg
potassium 1,646 mg • magnesium 91.5 mg •
selenium 5.1 mcg • 259 kcal

EVERGREEN

An ideal stressbuster. High levels of stress deplete your body of essential nutrients and can cause symptoms such as headaches, indigestion, irritability and joint pain. This juice combines celery and fennel, which help the body to utilize magnesium, and calcium to calm the nerves. The lettuce also has a sedative effect.

50 g (2 oz) celery

50 g (2 oz) fennel

125 g (4 oz) cos lettuce

175 g (6 oz) pineapple

1 teaspoon chopped tarragon

Juice all the ingredients and whizz in a blender with two ice cubes. Serve in a tall glass and decorate with tarragon sprigs, if liked.

vitamin A 3437 iu • vitamin C 68 mg
magnesium 47 mg • calcium 95 mg • 128 kcal

KALE AND HEARTY

This juice is a great energy booster with nutritional benefits that far outweigh its flavour. Spirulina is one of the best sources of vitamin B12, which is essential for the functioning of all cells. Wheatgrass is high in chlorophyll, which combats anaemia. Kale has as much usable calcium as milk.

25 g (1 oz) kale

100 g (3½ oz) wheatgrass

1 teaspoon spirulina

Juice the kale and the wheatgrass, then stir in the spirulina powder. Serve in a small glass decorated with wheatgrass blades.

vitamin A 7,740 iu • vitamin B12 8 mcg

vitamin C 91 mg • chlorophyll 643 mg

iron 52 mg • calcium 462 mg • 30 kcal

HEAD BANGER

Juices are an ideal remedy for headaches and migraine, as the nutritional benefits of the fruits and vegetables enter quickly into your system. Lettuce and fennel contain calcium and magnesium, which are antispasmodic and produce feelings of calm and may alleviate headaches.

175 g (6 oz) lettuce

125 g (4 oz) fennel

½ lemon

Juice the lettuce, fennel and lemon, and serve on ice. Decorate with lemon slivers and lettuce leaves, if liked.

vitamin A 4,726 iu • vitamin C 67 mg

potassium 1,070 mg • calcium 124 mg

magnesium 32 mg • 72 kcal

HEART BEET

Packed with vitamin C and vitamin E, this juice is effective at combating heart disease. The onion and garlic thin the blood and help to lower cholesterol. Watercress oxygenates the blood and beetroot builds up the red blood cells.

125 g (4 oz) beetroot

125 g (4 oz) watercress

125 g (4 oz) red onion

250 g (8 oz) carrot

1 garlic clove

Juice all the ingredients and serve in a tall glass. Decorate with beetroot leaves and watercress, if liked.

vitamin A 41,166 iu • vitamin C 85 mg

magnesium 85 mg • niacin 2 mg

vitamin B6 0.56 mg • vitamin E 2.36 mg • 167 kcal

STICKS AND STONES

This juice helps to prevent osteoporosis. Turnip leaves contain more calcium than milk and broccoli contains calcium and folic acid. Dandelion leaves are an excellent source of magnesium, which helps the body utilize the calcium for healthy bones and teeth.

125 g (4 oz) turnip, including the tops

125 g (4 oz) carrot

125 g (4 oz) broccoli

handful of dandelion leaves

175 g (6 oz) apple

Scrub the turnip and carrot. Juice all the ingredients and whizz in a blender with a couple of ice cubes. Serve in a tall glass decorated with extra dandelion leaves, if liked.

vitamin A 50,391 iu • vitamin C 223 mg

magnesium 108 mg • calcium 398 mg

folic acid 210 mcg • 196 kcal

HARD AS NAILS

High in potassium, this juice is good for hair and nails. While there is nothing you can actually do to improve the appearance and texture of your hair and nails, as these cells are already dead, you can enhance the underlying, unseen parts: their roots.

175 g (6 oz) parsnip
175 g (6 oz) green pepper
100 g (3½ oz) watercress
175 g (6 oz) cucumber

Juice the ingredients together and serve over ice with a sprinkling of chopped mint.

vitamin A 6,331 iu • vitamin C 242 mg
potassium 1,400 mg • 211 kcal

GINGER ZINGER

This juice boosts the immune system and increases energy levels. In order to fight potential illnesses in your system, you need to increase your intake of antioxidants, which can help to rebalance your immunity. This juice is rich in antioxidants and the lime encourages the elimination of toxins.

125 g (4 oz) carrot
250 g (8 oz) cantaloupe melon
1 lime
2.5 cm (1 in) cube fresh root ginger, roughly chopped

Juice all the ingredients and serve in a glass over ice. Decorate with lime wedges and seeds from a cardamom pod, if liked.

vitamin A 4,262 iu • vitamin C 137 mg
selenium 2.7 mcg • zinc 0.84 mg • 166 kcal

WHAT'S UP BROC?

This vegetable juice is really good for the immune system, your body's natural internal defence system. High in protective antioxidants, including the mineral selenium, this is an ideal juice for smokers, to help guard against the threat of lung cancer.

250 g (8 oz) broccoli
175 g (6 oz) carrot
50 g (2 oz) beetroot

Juice all the ingredients and serve in a tall glass. Decorate with a coriander sprig, if liked.

vitamin A 52,304 iu • vitamin C 43 mg
selenium 9.86 mcg • zinc 1.6 mg • 172 kcal

JUICY LUCY

This juice is so delicious, it is not a chore to drink a glass every day. Watermelon is packed with beta-carotene and vitamin C. Strawberries, give you a boost of vitamin C, as well as helping your body fight against bacteria in your system. It is high in zinc and potassium, two great eliminators.

200 g (7 oz) watermelon
200 g (7 oz) strawberries

Juice the fruit and whizz in a blender with a couple of ice cubes. Serve decorated with mint leaves and whole or sliced strawberries, if liked.

vitamin A 6562 iu • vitamin C 195 mg
potassium 950 mg • zinc 0.58 mg • 130 kcal

PART 2
MAXIMIZING
YOUR HEALTH

CHAPTER 4
MINIMIZING THE EFFECTS OF THE MENOPAUSE

The menopause can bring with it a number of emotional and physical side effects as well as the increasing risk of developing serious illnesses such as breast cancer, so it is important that you optimize your health and wellbeing through your lifestyle. This chapter explains how diet, exercise and your attitude to life can help to reduce the effects of the menopause, helping you to enjoy day-to-day living to the full.

WHAT IS THE MENOPAUSE?

The menopause is a natural part of a woman's life, and one that signals an end to her child-bearing years. While some women sail through the menopause with little difficulty, others experience a range of symptoms, which vary in severity from mildly annoying to completely disrupting.

WHEN DOES IT HAPPEN?

The menopause is defined by those in the medical profession as the final menstrual period, and as such highlights the end of a woman's fertility. The term is more commonly used, however, to describe the time leading up to the final menstrual period and the time beyond. For most women, the start of the menopause is characterized by a change in regularity of their periods; they become increasingly irregular until they eventually stop altogether. The menopause is considered to be over when no periods have occurred for a year.

The average age at which women go through this change is 51 years, but it can occur at any time between the ages of 45 and 55. It is considered premature if it occurs before the age of 40, something which is thought to affect one in 100 women. It may also be suddenly induced at any age as a result of illness or a medical procedure, such as a hysterectomy where the ovaries are also removed.

WHAT CAUSES IT?

The menopause occurs when your ovaries no longer have a supply of eggs to release each month, as they did during your fertile years. Before puberty, the ovaries are packed with eggs and during a woman's life around 450 of them mature and are then released to travel down the fallopian tubes and into the womb – this is ovulation. If the egg is not fertilized, it will pass out of the body along with the womb lining (menstruation). The menstrual cycle is under the control of hormones, and these cause an egg to be released each month and prepare the body for possible fertilization. One of the main hormones involved is oestrogen, which is produced by the ovaries themselves.

Around the age of 45, few eggs remain and the ovaries start to reduce their production of the hormone oestrogen, until it stops altogether during the menopausal years. During this time, the female

body has to adapt from a life that has been dominated by oestrogen and the menstrual cycle, to a life without this hormone. It is this decline in oestrogen that results in the symptoms many women suffer.

HOW DO WOMEN REACT?

There is no universal reaction to the menopause; women experience symptoms and upset to varying levels. How women experience the menopause depends on several factors, including their diet and nutrition, their general fitness and their physical health; they may even be influenced by their beliefs and attitudes towards the menopause.

   Menopausal symptoms can last for just a few months or linger over the course of several years. It is estimated that three-quarters of Western women experience one or more of the common symptoms associated with the menopause (see page 100), and that for one-third of those women the symptoms are severe.

LONG-TERM EFFECTS OF THE MENOPAUSE

In the long term, the changing oestrogen levels in the body have far-reaching effects on the bones, heart and blood vessels. Oestrogen has a protective effect over the heart, arteries and veins, and helps promote bone density. As oestrogen levels decline, the risk of developing osteoporosis or heart disease increases significantly. By the age of 50, one in three women is affected by osteoporosis (see Chapter 5), and almost one-third of premature deaths in women are due to heart disease (see Chapter 6).

'How women experience the menopause depends on several factors, including their diet and nutrition, their general fitness and their physical health.'

See also ▶

Symptoms of the menopause, page 100

Health issues, page 102

Living with the menopause, page 106

Strong bones, Chapter 5

Healthy heart, Chapter 6

Breast watch, Chapter 7

Enjoy life's changes, Chapter 8

SYMPTOMS OF THE MENOPAUSE

The declining levels of oestrogen in the female body, a process which starts during the menopause, means that all women will experience at least some of the physical and emotional symptoms below. Some women sail through this period in their lives; but for about one-third of women the symptoms are a serious inconvenience. Consult your doctor or a qualified complementary practitioner, such as a homeopath, for treatment of the worst symptoms.

EARLY PHYSICAL SYMPTOMS

- **Changes to your periods** This is one of the earliest indicators of the approaching menopause – your periods can become heavier, lighter, less or more frequent than usual.

- **Hot flushes** This refers to a feeling of heat that suddenly sweeps across the body as a result of changing hormone levels affecting the stability of the circulatory system. They vary in severity, ranging from an experience of gentle warmth to intense all-over heat or sweats. They can last from a few seconds to a few minutes and typically occur four or five times a day, being worse at night.

- **Night sweats** Quite simply, these are hot flushes that occur at night, which can drench your bedding and disturb your sleep.

- **Insomnia** Again, this can be caused by ebbing levels of oestrogen in your body. It can also be due to anxiety or depression and is made worse by sleep-disturbing night sweats.

- **Tiredness and fatigue** This commonly results from lack of sleep at night thanks to the night sweats and insomnia described above.

- **Aches and pains** An increase in general aches and pains is another result of low oestrogen levels. These range from joint and muscular pains to backaches. Headaches and migraines often start, or are exacerbated, during the menopause. Frequent triggers include the normal culprits of caffeine, alcohol, chocolate and cheese.

- **Dizziness** Some women experience dizziness during the menopause. This might be related to falling oestrogen levels and the ensuing changes to the nervous system and blood vessels.

EMOTIONAL SYMPTOMS

- **Mood swings, depression or low self-esteem**
  You may become tearful, moody and irritable, and
  may experience lowered self-esteem. You may even
  suffer clinical depression, especially if you have
  suffered from premenstrual syndrome in the past.
  Hormonal changes are certainly likely to be
  responsible, although such symptoms may also be a
  response to other changes in your life – for example
  adjusting to the end of your reproductive years, and
  perhaps feeling unattractive and facing the implied
  loss of youth that comes with ageing.

- **Anxiety or an inability to cope** Feeling anxious at
  this time is hardly surprising, and frequent feelings of
  anxiety can result in panic attack symptoms like
  shortness of breath, palpitations and dizziness.

- **Loss of concentration and short-term memory**
  Research has shown that oestrogen plays a role in
  learning, clear thinking and articulation, and
  maintaining verbal memory. Thus, the reduced level
  of oestrogen in the body is again the culprit, this
  time causing a deterioration in brain function.

LATER PHYSICAL SYMPTOMS

- **Dry or itchy skin and dry hair** Skin inevitably thins
  as we get older, and without oestrogen in the body it
  is harder for it to retain moisture.

- **Urinary problems** Reduced oestrogen levels also
  affect the urethra, resulting in pain or difficulty when
  passing urine, reduced bladder capacity requiring
  you to visit the toilet more often and increased
  susceptibility to urinary infections like cystitis.
  Another possible result is stress incontinence,
  whereby loss of elasticity in muscle leads to the
  inability to hold urine, and anything that increases
  abdominal pressure, like sneezing, coughing or
  laughing, causes leakage.

- **Vaginal dryness** This can be an early symptom of
  the menopause but it worsens after the menopause.
  Without oestrogen, the walls of the vagina become
  thinner and drier, which can lead to uncomfortable
  or painful sexual intercourse.

- **Loss of libido** There are numerous reasons why
  women may be less interested in sex at this time.
  They include the decrease in female hormones,
  vaginal dryness, tiredness, loss of self-esteem, self-
  perceived unattractiveness and depression. However,
  some women actually find sex far more enjoyable
  after the menopause – freedom from worries about
  unwanted pregnancy being a big factor.

HEALTH ISSUES

Changing oestrogen levels caused by the menopause can lead to a number of serious health problems, including heart disease, osteoporosis and breast cancer. However, there are ways to minimize your chances of suffering from these conditions, the most important of which are to ensure that you have a good and balanced diet, and that you exercise regularly so that you are fit.

RISK FACTORS

Other factors that increase your risk of heart disease include:

- Smoking
- High blood pressure
- Diabetes
- High blood cholesterol levels
- Inactivity
- Being overweight
- Alcohol intake
- Low intake of fruit and vegetables

THE MENOPAUSE AND OSTEOPOROSIS

Osteoporosis is a condition caused by loss of bone mineral, resulting in bones that are weak, fragile and therefore extremely vulnerable to fracture. For a full description of this condition, see pages 134–141). A range of factors are required to maintain good bone health, one of which is oestrogen. During the menopause, levels of oestrogen (which influences calcium absorption) decline in a woman's body. Consequently, there is an increase in the normal rate of mineral loss from bone, and as a result makes postmenopausal women much more vulnerable to developing osteoporosis.

Hormone replacement therapy (HRT) (see page 105) is known to be effective in preventing osteoporosis, but women consuming diets rich in oestrogen-like compounds called phytoestrogens (found in soya products, other beans, linseed and rye) also have a much reduced incidence of osteoporosis, suggesting a role for phytoestrogens in preserving bone health (see pages 110–115).

THE EVIDENCE

Studies seem to suggest that postmenopausal women who are given phytoestrogen-rich soya have better bone density. The amounts consumed have been in the range of 45–90 mg of phytoestrogens per day, and better effects usually result from higher intakes.

So far, most studies have lasted only six months, whereas any significant improvements in bone structure take around two years. The main benefits have been seen in the spine, which is not surprising as bone 'turnover' here is much quicker than in other parts of the body. It is assumed that, given enough time, beneficial effects would be seen in the hips as well. However, the long-term effects of phytoestrogens on bone health still remain to be explored.

THE MENOPAUSE AND HEART DISEASE

It is a common but mistaken belief that heart disease affects men more than women. Heart disease is in fact the most common cause of death among both women and men in Western societies. For example, during 2001, 126,000 women died of heart disease in the UK – that is 50,000 more than died of cancer – so this cannot be overlooked as a serious health concern.

Heart disease occurs as a result of two processes which develop gradually over many years. The first process – atherosclerosis – is a build-up of a fatty substance called atheroma in the walls of blood vessels (similar to limescale building up inside a pipe), which reduces blood flow through that vessel. If this build-up affects blood vessels of the heart itself, it can lead to pain (angina) when the heart tries to work harder during exertion or at times of increased emotion.

The second process – thrombosis – occurs if the fatty deposits rupture, allowing a blood clot to form. This clot can then break off and travel around the body until it blocks a blood vessel completely. If a blood clot blocks one of the vessels in the heart, blood flow to the affected part of the heart is cut off, resulting in a heart attack and often permanent damage to that area of heart muscle. For a full description of this condition, see Chapter 6.

Before the menopause, women are afforded a certain amount of protecting against heart disease by the hormone oestrogen. But as the menopause progresses and oestrogen levels continue to dwindle, the incidence of heart disease in women rapidly escalates and within a few years matches that of men.

THE MENOPAUSE AND BREAST CANCER

Breast cancer affects one in ten women worldwide, and as the majority of cancers develop in women over the age of 50. It is especially important, therefore, that you are aware of the risks and what you should look out for if you are over this age.

Not only are there are ways to reduce the chances of developing breast cancer by ensuring that you lead a healthy lifestyle, but there are also medical screening services available to women and easy ways to check your own breasts for abnormalities. If you are worried about any lumps make sure you visit your doctor straight away so you can have it checked out. Even though most lumps turn out not to be cancerous do not delay seeking medical advice.

ARE YOU AT RISK?

There are certain factors that are thought to make some women more likely to develop breast cancer than others:

- Never having been pregnant, starting periods early or the menopause late.

- Having an unhealthy lifestyle, for example, being overweight, drinking too much alcohol or eating a diet high in saturated fats.

- Having a close family member with breast cancer or having an abnormal inherited gene.

- Being over the age of 50.

- Taking HRT may very slightly increase your risk.

Remember that even if you fall into these categories it does not mean that you will develop breast cancer.

See also ▶
Strong bones, Chapter 5
Healthy heart, Chapter 6
Breast watch, Chapter 7

MANAGING YOUR WEIGHT

Around the time of the menopause, many women have problems maintaining their normal bodyweight. In fact, by the age of 55–64 years, three-quarters of women are overweight or obese. While there is no direct evidence that the menopause is a cause of weight gain in itself, the symptoms of the menopause may dampen your enthusiasm for exercise. It does not take much for weight to start creeping on.

FOOD AND ACTIVITY DIARY

We often don't realize how much or how often we eat each day, or how inactive we actually are. Keep a diary for a few days of your eating and activity habits – be as honest as you can, then take a critical look.

- Are you eating regular meals – do you include breakfast every day?

- Are you eating at least five portions of fruit and vegetables every day?

- How often do you eat and drink between meals?

- Are there any times when you could be more active?

See also ▶

Loosen up and shape up, Chapter 2
Healthy eating for a longer life, Chapter 3

WHY WORRY ABOUT YOUR WEIGHT?

It is uncomfortable to be large, but a more pressing concern is the impact on your health. Carrying extra body fat places a strain on the heart, stresses the immune system so you are more susceptible to infections, makes you more likely to have joint problems, and increases the risk of diseases such as diabetes, cancer, gallstones and heart disease. Important, too, is where you carry your weight. Weight around your middle is most damaging to health. If your waist is bigger than 80 cm (31½ in), then now is the time to take action.

While 'quick-fix' diets promising overnight weight loss are tempting, remember they are just that – a quick fix that is temporary. The most effective approach to long-term weight control is a combination of healthy eating and increased activity levels.

KEEPING ACTIVE

Inactivity is the main cause of gradual weight gain. Only one-quarter of women achieve the recommended activity levels of 30 minutes of moderate activity per day. Becoming more active should be a major focus for anyone trying to manage their weight. How many hours each day do you spend sitting down? Think about all the times through the day that you could be more active – whether it is finding time for a quick walk, washing the car by hand instead of driving to the car wash, going bowling rather than spending another evening in front of the television or using the stairs instead of the lift.

It is surprising how quickly lots of little bits of extra activity can help you get fitter and burn off calories. If you simply went for a 20-minute brisk walk every day for a year, you could burn off 5 kg (11 lb) of body fat. Not a huge amount of effort, but the potential for great results.

HORMONE REPLACEMENT THERAPY

Hormone replacement therapy (HRT) can help alleviate menopausal symptoms. HRT replaces the hormones that are no longer produced by the body – these include oestrogen and progesterone. There are many different combinations and strengths of HRT, and different modes of delivery, including tablets, patches, gels and implants. Some continue to give a period every month, others every three months and some no periods at all.

SHOULD I TAKE HRT?

If you find that symptoms of the menopause – whether physical or emotional (see pages 100–101) – are severely disrupting your life then you should consider taking HRT to alleviate these problems.

Furthermore, if you know that you are at risk of certain conditions such as osteoporosis or cardiovascular disease, for example, for genetic reasons, then there is some evidence that HRT can help protect against such conditions (see below).

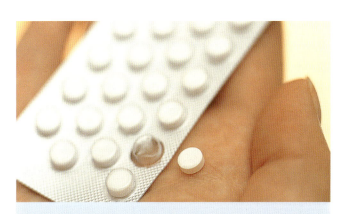

PROS AND CONS OF HRT

HRT helps to relieve symptoms such as hot flushes, night sweats and vaginal dryness. It may also offer some protection against heart disease, osteoporosis and Alzheimer's disease although, in order to gain most benefit, HRT needs to be taken for at least 5–10 years.

As with any drug treatment, however, HRT also holds some negative effects, which include an increased chance of breast cancer and deep vein thrombosis. As we have already seen, HRT is thought to protect women against heart disease, but recent evidence has suggested that specific types of HRT may actually increase the risk. Current advice by the British Heart Foundation (2003) is that women should not take HRT just to avoid heart problems.

HRT may also cause side effects including breast and nipple tenderness, headaches, an increase in appetite and leg cramps.

It is therefore important for all women to weigh up the benefits and drawbacks that come with HRT. Make your decision with the help of your doctor to ensure that you are making the best choice for your health, and also talk to your doctor about the alternatives offered by complementary medicines.

NATURAL ALTERNATIVES

If you do not want to take prescribed medication for the effects of the menopause then there are a number of alternative routes that may help, but check with your doctor first.

- Massage
- Reflexology
- Aromatherapy
- Yoga
- Meditation
- Acupuncture
- Homeopathy
- Traditional Chinese medicine
- Herbal medicines

LIVING WITH THE MENOPAUSE

Whether or not you decide to take HRT, there are a number of ways you can reduce the severity of menopausal symptoms – from simple lifestyle changes to complementary therapies that target specific symptoms.

BEATING MENOPAUSAL SYMPTOMS

- Avoid getting too warm by dressing in layers of clothing so you can easily add or remove a layer in response to different room temperatures.

- Sleep in a cool room.

- Keep cool by avoiding hot drinks and hot soups.

- Avoid triggers for hot flushes such as alcohol or spicy foods.

- Learn and develop effective ways of dealing with stress and also learn how to relax.

- When a hot flush starts to develop, take slow, deep breaths which may lessen the severity.

- Take regular moderate exercise.

- Maintain a healthy bodyweight.

- Have your blood pressure checked regularly.

- If you suffer from diabetes, ensure that your blood-sugar control is good.

A POSITIVE APPROACH

Many women go through the menopause with few or no serious symptoms or problems, although some may well have more than their fair share of troubles. No one can predict exactly what will happen, but your approach to this new stage of your life will have an important influence on how you deal with the changes that are taking place in your body. A positive outlook, an ability to adapt and making time to take a fresh look at your lifestyle will all help you to cope.

Some changes are likely to be beyond your control, such as children leaving home or changes in your role at work or your responsibilities towards ageing parents, and you may well wonder what you should do for the best. Taking steps to make sure you remain as healthy as possible and looking after your own emotional and psychological wellbeing will improve your chances of handling whatever should come along in this next phase of your life.

NON-TRADITIONAL THERAPIES

There are numerous alternative therapies that can help to alleviate some of the stress of the menopause, including acupuncture, aromatherapy (see right) and massage (see pages 274–281). Although no scientific evidence exists to suggest that these work, they will certainly not harm, and some women report great benefit from them. Some women also find relief in the form of herbal supplements such as Black Cohosh, Dong Quai and Ginseng. Always talk to your doctor before embarking on any of these therapies.

RELAXATION

Many women who practise relaxation on a daily basis find that these sessions help to ease hot flushes. Contrary to commonly held belief, there is much more to relaxation than simply sitting in a comfortable chair with a magazine or watching television; the techniques have to be learned and practised. Try joining a class or use videos or CDs at home. Yoga (see pages 264–273) and Pilates (see pages 46–67) exercises can also be very useful in relaxing both mind and body. Meditation (see pages 288–291) and visualization are effective ways of freeing your mind from distressing or worrying thoughts and, with practice, can help you achieve a very deep level of relaxation.

AROMATHERAPY OILS FOR THE MENOPAUSE

The following essential oils can be used to alleviate menopausal symptoms. Try a relaxing bath or even a full-body massage. See pages 282–287 for more information on aromatherapy.

Bergamot has a sedative yet uplifting character that is excellent for anxiety, depression and stress. It is also a cleansing tonic for the uterus.

Cypress is excellent for excessive sweating, oedema (fluid retention in body tissues), and heavy menstruation. It has a calming effect on the mind, soothing anger and frustration.

Fennel is an excellent body cleanser and is said to activate the glandular system by imitating the hormone oestrogen. This makes it useful for menopausal problems such as irregular periods, premenstrual tension and low sexual response.

See also ▶

Aromatherapy healing, pages 282–287

Yoga for body and soul, pages 264–273

Pilates to tone, shape and strengthen, pages 48–67

Massage techniques, pages 274–281

SEX AND THE MENOPAUSE

A woman's sexual drive and pleasure often actually increase as she gets older. However, many women erroneously believe that when they reach the menopause they no longer have the same right to sexual pleasure as they did when they were younger. This couldn't be more wrong, as lovemaking can be immensely beneficial for both your health and your happiness. Just because a woman is going through the menopause does not mean that her sex life should be put on hold. Sex makes people of every age feel beautiful, cherished, desirable and young – a perfect tonic for the older woman.

POSITIVE THINKING

The glow of wellbeing that comes with remembering all that is wonderful in your life is guaranteed to make you look and feel sexier. This could be your family, close friends, your partner, your life achievements so far, or your plans for the future. Many women celebrate the menopause itself, regarding it as a life-enhancing event that frees them from having periods and the risk of unwanted pregnancy. Their lives feel truly their own, and this sense of empowerment can be incredibly liberating sexually. After all, your brain is the most powerful sexual organ you possess.

SEX HAS NO AGE LIMIT

The wonderful thing about postmenopausal sex is that you are freed from many of the concerns you had when you were younger: you no longer worry about pregnancy or periods, and, if you have children, they are likely to be older, and more a source of delight than tiredness. You feel more sure of yourself and are less likely to worry about what other people think. These factors add up to a more carefree and confident state of mind that is not only enjoyable, but very attractive.

HORMONAL CHANGES

Certain physical changes that are linked to the menopause can have a direct bearing on the libido, and may interrupt an otherwise happy sex life if they are left untreated. The fall in the levels of the sex hormones oestrogen and progesterone has a number of effects on the body as a whole, but some can impact especially on your sex life.

- Skin becomes drier, affecting the whole body, including the face, breasts and the genital area.

- Facial and body hair growth increases.

- Sleep disturbances, headaches, hot flushes and fatigue can mean that women rarely feel 'in the mood'.

- Vaginal changes, especially dryness, can sometimes lead to pain during intercourse.

Luckily, most of these changes can be easily overcome or eased by making lifestyle changes, such as eating a healthy diet and improving physical fitness (see Chapters 2 and 3), as well as using products specifically produced to treat these problems. Your doctor will be able to advise you on the best ways to counteract some of these physical changes, while a good beauty therapist should probably become your new best friend. Remember that you are in the company of millions of women going through the same changes, and this guarantees that there will be both all sorts of solutions available and lots of animated discussion (on websites and in magazines) about which ones are the best available at any time.

Many women allow physical symptoms to affect their state of mind, saying that one or other physical changes makes them 'feel older' or 'less feminine'. While it is true that facial and body hair increases, for instance, it is also true that it can be quickly and easily removed; and it will have absolutely no bearing on how you feel about yourself as a woman – or how feminine you actually are – unless you choose to let it. Remember that some women have far more body hair than others all their lives, and feel no less feminine because of it. Don't allow a few physical symptoms to prevent you feeling good about yourself and your new-found freedom.

'Sex makes people of every age feel beautiful, cherished, desirable and young – a perfect tonic for the older woman.'

TAKING PRECAUTIONS

One word of caution – do remember to wait one full period-free year before abandoning contraception, as technically the menopause is only identifiable in retrospect. With your new-found confidence, it could be all too easy to get carried away in the heat of the moment.

The risk of catching a sexually transmitted infections (STIs) is also very real. Gonorrhea, non-gonococcal urethritis, genital warts, genital herpes, trichomoniasis, hepatitis B, syphilis and even HIV/AIDS are becoming more common among older people. Always practise safe sex by using a new condom for each act of sexual intercourse, and use only water-based lubricants. This is important as oil-based lubricants (such as massage oils, body lotions or cooking oil) can weaken latex.

See also ►
Enjoy life's changes, Chapter 8
The feel-good factor, Chapter 9

MIRACLE FOODS

Many symptoms of the menopause, such as hot flushes, mood swings, night sweats, osteoporosis and vaginal dryness, are a result of falling levels of oestrogen. One way to counteract this is to eat plenty of plant oestrogens, also known as phytoestrogens, as well as antioxidant fruit and vegetables (see also Chapter 3).

WHAT ARE PHYTOESTROGENS?

Phytoestrogens are chemicals found in certain plants, and they are very similar in structure to the human hormone oestrogen. Phytoestrogens appear to promote the effects of oestrogen in some parts of the body. One of the richest sources of phytoestrogens is soya, and foods made from this bean such as tofu, soya milk, soya yogurts and so on. They are also found in other beans, and in linseed (flax) and rye. How effective they are will depend on how often you eat them and how much you consume.

Compared with HRT, phytoestrogens provide much less oestrogen, but they can help to counteract the fall in levels around the time of the menopause. Phytoestrogens appear to reduce the effects of oestrogen in certain parts of the body, however. This is believed to be down to different types of body cell receptors for oestrogen.

PHYTOESTROGENS IN THE DIET

There are various different types of phytoestrogens and one type in particular – isoflavones – are found in the most commonly eaten foods (peas, beans, soya products, lentils and chickpeas). The average intake of phytoestrogens in a Western diet is estimated to be just 1–2 mg per day. This may be slightly higher among people eating vegetarian diets containing lots of beans and pulses. Women in Japan and other Eastern countries eat 50–100 mg per day, the amount shown by scientists to provide health benefits.

The great news is that foods that are rich in phytoestrogens are all extremely good for us anyway, containing protein, dietary fibre and a wide range of vitamins and minerals. So, even if we disregard the potential benefits from eating phytoestrogen-rich foods, we should try to include these foods in our diet on a regular basis.

PHYTOESTROGENS AND HOT FLUSHES

The menopause is much less of a problem in countries where a soya-based diet is eaten, such as Japan and China. In Europe, 80 per cent of menopausal women suffer from hot flushes, compared with 57 per cent in Malaysia and just 18 per cent in China. For one-third of women in Western countries, hot flushes are frequent and severe, and may be accompanied by other symptoms such as headaches, irritability and tiredness. In Japan, hot flushes are so rare that there are no words to describe this experience in the Japanese language.

However, Japanese women still have menopausal symptoms and report an increase in back and neck aches. It may be that a phytoestrogen-rich diet changes the symptoms of the menopause, or that Western women do in fact experience the same symptoms, but are more aware of the problems associated with hot flushes.

Most studies have shown that eating phytoestrogen-rich soya over two to three months can reduce the frequency and severity of hot flushes. In the main, trials have shown a significant impact when 40–80 mg of phytoestrogens are consumed per day. However, there have also been studies where no visible effects have been found. The greatest benefits will occur if at present you eat little soya, if your hot flushes are severe and if you start to eat at least 45 mg every day.

SOYA, CHOLESTEROL AND HEART DISEASE

The death rates from heart disease in Eastern countries, such as Japan and China, are six times lower than death rates in Western countries, such as the UK and the USA. The incidence of heart disease is also lower among vegetarians and vegans compared with those who eat meat. While many factors are likely to play a part, it is believed that a high intake of soya is one of the factors protecting the heart in those who eat Asian and vegetarian diets.

Soya protein, soya fibre and soya phytoestrogens are all known to have a positive influence over the heart, helping to lower the fat content of the diet, lower blood cholesterol levels, prevent cholesterol being deposited in the atheroma on blood vessel walls and lower blood pressure. If you include soya-based foods regularly in your diet, you will be gaining all these benefits at once.

ESSENTIAL NUTRIENTS

- **Vitamin B-complex** reduces anxiety and irritability.

- **Vitamin C** helps to maintain the skin's elasticity.

- **Vitamin D** controls calcium absorption.

- **Vitamin E** helps to reduce hot flushes.

- **Calcium** maintains bone density.

- **Iron** increases energy.

- **Magnesium** works with calcium to keep bones strong.

- **Phosphorus** slows loss of bone mass.

- **Selenium** reduces hot flushes.

- **Zinc** helps to regulate hormone levels.

- **Omega-3 fatty acids** help to maintain hormonal balance.

- **Omega-6 fatty acids** relieve symptoms.

- **Bioflavonoids** help relieve hot flushes.

- **Boron** increases oestrogen retention.

- **Co-enzyme Q10** improves energy levels.

'Foods that are rich in phytoestrogens are all extremely good for us anyway, containing protein, dietary fibre and a wide range of vitamins and minerals.'

HOW MUCH DO I NEED?

Scientific studies have shown that by eating 25 g (1 oz) of soya protein every day you can lower your cholesterol levels by up to 10 per cent. To get 25 g (1 oz) of soya protein, you need to eat around three servings of a soya-based food. This happens to be the same amount you need to provide 45 mg of phytoestrogens per day – exactly the quantity needed to relieve hot flushes. Each of your three servings must provide a minimum of 6.25 g (¼ oz) of soya protein.

WORDS OF CAUTION ABOUT PHYTOESTROGENS

It would be naïve to assume that consuming high doses of any substance is always beneficial, and phytoestrogens are no exception. Evidence suggests that the benefits from consuming both phytoestrogens and soya are far greater if they are derived from natural foods (as nature intended and where overdosing is less likely) rather than from concentrated supplements.

One group of women who should exercise caution are those who have breast cancer. Cancerous cells in the breast are generally stimulated by oestrogen, and it is unclear at present as to whether phytoestrogens stimulate or inhibit these cells. Research is under way to answer this question. Some experts believe that food-derived phytoestrogens do not present a risk to those with breast cancer, but do not recommend phytoestrogen supplements for these women. Other experts believe that any phytoestrogens can be damaging to any women with breast cancer. Until we have a definite answer it is prudent to be cautious and for those affected not to increase their intake of phytoestrogens, either by diet or by supplementation.

A second group who should be aware of the potential effects of a higher phytoestrogen intake are women taking thyroxine (a thyroid hormone that helps control metabolism). Phytoestrogens may affect thyroxine replacement therapy. If you increase your intake of phytoestrogens you should inform your doctor who will monitor your blood thyroxine levels more closely and adjust your therapy accordingly.

HOW TO EAT MORE PHYTOESTROGENS

The richest dietary sources include soya beans and foods made from these, lentils, chickpeas, sprouting beans, linseed, rye, most cereals, and fruit and vegetables (see the chart on pages 114–115). Reading

this list it may strike you that the richest sources are foods that you never eat, for example soya and linseed. Don't panic – you don't need to turn into a seed-nibbling vegetarian. There are many simple and easy ways to incorporate these into your daily diet. It is possible to achieve this without lots of home cooking, but the recipes in this chapter provide great ideas to add interest and variety to your diet.

The phytoestrogen content of foods will vary, and remember that processing may reduce a food's content. Many foods with phytoestrogen-rich ingredients, such as soya or linseed, do not provide information on the label with the actual phytoestrogen content. Rather than trying to count phytoestrogens, therefore, the best approach is to become familiar with the foods that contain them and to aim to include these in your diet several times each day.

HINT FOR HEALTH

Studies suggest that eating a diet rich in phytoestrogens, such as soya products, holds the potential to alleviate some menopausal symptoms, and may also help to prevent the development of breast cancer, osteoporosis and heart disease.

GETTING ENOUGH PHYTOESTROGENS

To get 45 mg of phytoestrogens, you need three servings of a phytoestrogen-rich food each day, for example:

- Two slices of a soya or linseed bread.

- One serving of a phytoestrogen-rich muesli.

- Soya milk in your tea or coffee, or make a fruit smoothie with soya milk.

SHOULD I TAKE A PHYTOESTROGEN SUPPLEMENT?

In short, the answer is no. Studies have found that naturally occurring phytoestrogens are far more effective than those presented in pill formulations. Reliability is also a problem. When phytoestrogen supplements have been analyzed, over two-thirds have been found to contain fewer phytoestrogens than the amount claimed by the manufacturer. As a result, experts advise women to boost their phytoestrogens as foods, not pills.

See also ▶

Healthy eating for a longer life, Chapter 3
Recipes for the menopause, pages 116–131
Strong bones, Chapter 5
Healthy heart, Chapter 6

PHYTOESTROGEN-RICH FOODS

FOOD		PHYTOESTROGENS PER 100 G (3½ OZ)	AVERAGE SERVING	PHYTOESTROGENS PER SERVING
Textured vegetable protein (TVP)		75 mg	75 g (3 oz)	56 mg
Tofu		13.5–67 mg	100 g (3½ oz)	40 mg
Linseed (flax)		60–370 mg	1 tablespoon	31 mg
Soya beans		37 mg	3 tablespoons	28 mg
Soya flour		131–198 mg	1 tablespoon	25 mg
Soya milk		5–10 mg	250 ml (8 fl oz)	12.5–25 mg
Tempeh		29–53 mg	25 g (1 oz)	10 mg
Soya cheese		6–31 mg	50 g (2 oz)	9 mg
Miso		45 mg	1 tablespoon	7 mg

FOOD		PHYTOESTROGENS PER 100 G (3½ OZ)	AVERAGE SERVING	PHYTOESTROGENS PER SERVING
Meat-free soya burgers		8–15 mg	50 g (2 oz)	6 mg
Blackberries		4 mg	100 g (3½ oz)	4 mg
Gooseberries		3 mg	100 g (3½ oz)	3 mg
China green tea/black tea		3 mg/1.1 mg	1 cup	3 mg/1.1 mg
Peas, lentils and split peas		3.28 mg	50 g (2 oz)	1.6 mg
Chianti/Cabernet Sauvignon wine		1.1 mg	125 ml (4 fl oz)	1.4 mg
Currants and raisins		2 mg	50 g (2 oz)	1 mg
Brown rice		0.3 mg	100 g (3½ oz)	0.3 mg
Miracle bread (see page 118)			2 slices	12 mg

RECIPES FOR THE MENOPAUSE

Because many of the symptoms of the menopause are caused by decreasing levels of oestrogen, it is important to try to increase your oestrogen levels through your diet. Here is a selection of tasty recipes to help you boost your intake of plant oestrogens (phytoestrogens), which may help to reduce the unpleasant side effects of the menopause, such as night sweats, mood swings and hot flushes, as well as prevent serious diseases, such as osteoporosis and heart disease.

STRAWBERRY MUESLI

Packed with seeds, nuts and fruit, muesli provides a delicious and extremely nutritious start to the day, while the soya milk is a great source of phytoestrogens. It will also slowly release energy throughout the morning, which should stop you being tempted by unhealthy snacks.

250 g (8 oz) strawberries, thinly sliced

250 g (8 oz) rolled oats

75 g (3 oz) flaked almonds

75 g (3 oz) pumpkin seeds

75 g (3 oz) sunflower seeds

25 g (1 oz) golden linseeds

75 g (3 oz) ready-to-eat dried cranberries, roughly chopped

soya milk, to serve

1 Blot away any juice from the strawberries with kitchen paper and lay them in a single layer on a baking tray lined with silicone paper. Place in a preheated oven at 110°C (225°F), Gas Mark ¼, for 1 hour, turn over and continue to cook for a further 1–1½ hours, or until crisp. Allow to cool.

2 Mix together the remaining ingredients, carefully stir in the strawberries and store the mixture in an airtight container. When ready to serve, pour into bowls and add soya milk.

Makes 12–14 servings

Preparation time 5 minutes

Cooking time 2–2½ hours

Nutritional values per serving • 200–229 kcal • 10–12 g fat • 0.7–1 g saturated fat • 2.5–3 g fibre

BANANA AND MANGO SMOOTHIE

1 small ripe banana, about 100 g
(3½ oz)

250 ml (8 fl oz) soya milk

1 small ripe mango, peeled,
stoned and diced

This fruit smoothie is packed with vitamins and minerals. Bananas are particularly rich in vitamin C, magnesium, calcium, phosphorus and potassium, while mangos are high in vitamin C, potassium and B vitamins. Mango is also good for controlling blood pressure and boosting the immune system.

1 Peel and slice the banana, then place in a freezerproof container and freeze for at least 2 hours or overnight.

2 Place all the ingredients in a blender or food processor and blend until thick and frothy. Pour into a glass and serve immediately.

Serves 1

Preparation time 2 minutes,
plus freezing

230 kcal • 3 g fat • 0.5 g saturated fat • 2 g fibre

MIRACLE BREAD

The seeds in this bread make it an excellent source of phytoestrogens, and the use of wholemeal and soya flour make this a much better breakfast alternative than white bread. If you prefer to make rolls instead of a loaf, then simply divide the mixture into 24 equal portions and reduce the cooking time to 15–20 minutes.

1 Mix the flours together in a large bowl. Stir in the remaining dry ingredients. Make a well in the centre and gradually add the warm water, oil and malt extract to form a soft dough.

Turn out on to a lightly floured work surface and knead the dough for about 10 minutes, or until smooth and elastic. To knead the dough, stretch it away from you with the heel of your hand, then gather it up towards you. It is ready when it will stretch without breaking. Return the dough to the bowl, cover with a clean, damp cloth and leave to rise in a warm place for at least 1½ hours, or until doubled in size.

2 Lightly oil two 1 kg (2 lb) loaf tins. Knead the dough again, knocking out the air, then divide in half. Shape the dough into two loaves and press into the prepared tins. Cover loosely and allow to rise for 30 minutes, or until the dough reaches the tops of the tins.

3 Brush each loaf with a little water and scatter over a few mixed seeds. Bake in a preheated oven at 220°C (425°F), Gas Mark 7, for 30–35 minutes, or until risen and golden brown. Leave in the tins for 10 minutes, then transfer to a wire rack to cool.

300 g (10 oz) strong plain white flour, plus extra for dusting

350 g (11½ oz) strong plain wholemeal flour

50 g (2 oz) soya flour

2 teaspoons salt

2 teaspoons fast-action dried yeast

1 teaspoon caster sugar

2 tablespoons sesame seeds

2 tablespoons poppy seeds

2 tablespoons golden linseeds

2 tablespoons sunflower seeds

2 tablespoons pumpkin seeds

450 ml (15 fl oz) warm water

1 tablespoon flaxseed oil

2 tablespoons malt extract

mixed seeds, for scattering

Makes 2 loaves

Preparation time 20 minutes, plus proving

Cooking time 30–35 minutes

110 kcal • 4 g fat • 0.2 g saturated fat • 2 g fibre

CAJUN POTATO, PRAWN AND AVOCADO SALAD

300 g (10 oz) baby new potatoes, halved

1 tablespoon olive oil

250 g (8 oz) cooked peeled king prawns

1 garlic clove, crushed

4 spring onions, finely sliced

2 teaspoons Cajun seasoning

1 ripe avocado, peeled, stoned and diced

handful of alfalfa sprouts

salt

This easy-to-prepare summer lunch is a great provider of antioxidants. Prawns are good sources of selenium, which helps to protect against ageing of many of the cells and tissues, while avocado, which is rich in Vitamins B and E and potassium, is also good for the skin. If you want to increase the fibre content of the salad then leave the skins on the potatoes, but make sure you wash them well.

1 Cook the potatoes for 10–15 minutes in a large saucepan of lightly salted boiling water, or until tender. Drain well.

2 Heat the oil in a wok or large, non-stick frying pan. Add the prawns, garlic, spring onions and Cajun seasoning, and stir-fry for 2–3 minutes, or until the prawns are hot. Stir in the potatoes and cook for a further minute. Transfer to a serving dish.

3 Stir in the avocado, top with the alfalfa sprouts and serve.

Serves 2

Preparation time 10 minutes

Cooking time 10–20 minutes

440 kcal • 23 g fat • 4.5 g saturated fat • 4.5 g fibre

FRAGRANT TOFU AND NOODLE SOUP

Tofu, which is a curd made from soya beans, is a very rich source of phytoestrogens, and as such can help to increase the body's oestrogen levels. It is also an excellent source of protein, having a similar protein content to beans and lentils.

1 Place the tofu on a plate covered with kitchen paper and allow to stand for 10 minutes to drain.

2 Heat the oil in a wok or frying pan until hot, add the tofu and cook for 2–3 minutes, stirring, or until the tofu is golden brown. Remove from the pan and drain on kitchen paper.

3 Meanwhile, soak the noodles in boiling water for 2 minutes, then drain.

4 Place the stock in a large saucepan. Add the ginger, garlic, lime leaves and lemon grass and bring to the boil. Reduce the heat, add the tofu, noodles, spinach or pak choi, bean sprouts and chillies and heat through for a couple of minutes. Stir in the coriander and the Thai fish sauce, then pour into warmed deep soup bowls to serve. Serve with lime wedges and chilli sauce.

125 g (4 oz) firm tofu, diced

1 tablespoon sesame oil

75 g (3 oz) thin rice noodles

600 ml (1 pint) vegetable stock

2.5 cm (1 in) piece of fresh root ginger, peeled and thickly sliced

1 large garlic clove, thickly sliced

3 kaffir lime leaves, torn in half

2 lemon grass stalks, halved

handful of spinach or pak choi leaves

50 g (2 oz) bean sprouts

1–2 fresh red chillies, deseeded and finely sliced

2 tablespoons fresh coriander

1 tablespoon Thai fish sauce

TO SERVE

lime wedges

chilli sauce

Serves 2

Preparation time 10 minutes, plus draining

Cooking time 10 minutes

250 kcal • 8 g fat • 1 g saturated fat • 0.5 g fibre

SMOKED CHICKEN SALAD

150 g (5 oz) asparagus, cut into
    5-cm (2-in) lengths

200 g (7 oz) smoked chicken
    breast, cut into bite-sized pieces

125 g (4 oz) cherry tomatoes,
    halved

300 g (10 oz) canned cannellini
    beans, drained and rinsed

handful of chives, chopped

DRESSING

2 tablespoons extra virgin olive oil

1 garlic clove, crushed

2 teaspoons clear honey

2 teaspoons balsamic vinegar

2 teaspoons wholegrain mustard

This is a filling salad that is rich in protein, minerals and vitamins. Chicken (with the skin removed) is a good low-fat meat option, while tomatoes can help to lower the risk of heart disease and various kinds of cancer as they contain the antioxidant lycopene.

1 Cook the asparagus in a large saucepan of lightly salted boiling water for about 4 minutes, or until just tender. Drain and plunge into cold water to prevent it cooking further. Pat dry with kitchen paper.

2 Place the chicken in a large bowl, add the tomatoes, beans, asparagus and chives and mix well.

3 To make the dressing, whisk all the ingredients together in a small bowl. Pour the dressing over the salad and toss well to coat.

Serves 2

Preparation time 10 minutes

Cooking time 5 minutes

350 kcal • 15 g fat • 3 g saturated fat • 8 g fibre • Source of phytoestrogens

LENTILS WITH BROAD BEANS, BACON AND POACHED EGGS

Lentils are a good source of minerals and are great phytoestrogen-rich foods. If you want a speedier dish, omit step 1 of the recipe and replace the dry lentils with 400 g (13 oz) of canned lentils, which should be drained and rinsed first.

1 Place the lentils, thyme, celery and garlic in a saucepan and pour over the water. Bring to the boil, then reduce the heat and simmer for 20 minutes until tender. Drain the lentils and discard the thyme, celery and garlic.

2 Fry the bacon in the oil for 2–3 minutes, then add the spring onions and broad beans and fry for a further 2–3 minutes. Add the lentils and continue to cook for 1 minute. Season to taste and stir in the vinegar.

3 Meanwhile, poach the eggs in simmering water for 3–5 minutes. Remove with a slotted spoon and drain on kitchen paper. Divide the lentil mixture between two plates and top each mound with a poached egg. Serve immediately.

75 g (3 oz) Puy lentils

1 thyme sprig

1 celery stick

1 garlic clove

1 litre (1¾ pints) water

1 tablespoon olive oil

3 rashers of smoked back bacon, roughly chopped

4 spring onions, finely sliced

200 g (7 oz) frozen broad beans, blanched and outer skins removed

1 tablespoon balsamic vinegar

2 eggs

salt and freshly ground black pepper

Serves 2

Preparation time 15 minutes

Cooking time 30 minutes

370 kcal • 16 g fat • 4 g saturated fat • 9 g fibre

CHILLI CON CARNE

1 tablespoon vegetable oil

1 red onion, finely chopped

1 garlic clove, finely chopped

250 g (8 oz) extra lean minced beef

1 small red pepper, cored, deseeded and diced

400 g (13 oz) canned chopped tomatoes

1 tablespoon tomato purée

1 teaspoon chilli powder

200 ml (7 fl oz) beef stock

400 g (13 oz) canned red kidney beans, drained and rinsed

salt and freshly ground black pepper

TO SERVE

brown rice

This milder version of the classic dish is full of antioxidants and phytoestrogens from the pepper, onion, tomatoes and kidney beans. Beef, like all red meat, is an excellent source of iron, but can be replaced with a soya meat substitute if you prefer.

1 Heat the oil in heavy-based, non-stick saucepan. Add the onion and garlic and cook for 5 minutes, or until beginning to soften. Add the mince and cook for a further 5–6 minutes, or until browned all over.

2 Stir in the red pepper, tomatoes, tomato purée, chilli powder and stock and bring to the boil. Reduce the heat and simmer gently for 30 minutes.

3 Add the beans and cook for a further 5 minutes. Season to taste and serve with brown rice, cooked according to the packet instructions.

Serves 2

Preparation time 15 minutes

Cooking time 45 minutes

480 kcal • 18 g fat • 6g saturated fat • 12 g fibre

GRIDDLED TUNA WITH BLACK-EYED BEAN AND AVOCADO SALSA

Tuna is an excellent source of B vitamins and selenium as well as omega-3 fatty acids, which reduce the levels of 'bad' cholesterol and boost the levels of 'good' cholesterol. It is good both for the skin and for the body's hormone systems, so can help to reduce some menopausal symptoms such as dry skin and mood swings.

1 To make the salsa, mix the avocado, tomatoes, onion and beans together in a large bowl. Stir in the coriander, lime rind and juice and seasoning to taste. Set aside.

2 Brush the tuna steaks with the oil. Place on a hot griddle pan and sear for 2–3 minutes on each side, or until cooked to your liking. Transfer the tuna to warmed serving plates and serve with the salsa.

1 large ripe avocado, peeled, stoned and diced

4 ripe plum tomatoes, quartered, deseeded and diced

1 small red onion, finely chopped

300 g (10 oz) canned black-eyed beans, drained and rinsed

2 tablespoons chopped fresh coriander

finely grated rind and juice of 1 lime

2 fresh tuna steaks, about 150 g (5 oz) each

1 tablespoon olive oil

salt and freshly ground black pepper

Serves 2

Preparation time 10 minutes

Cooking time 4–6 minutes

570 kcal • 28 g fat • 6 g saturated fat • 13 g fibre

MOROCCAN LAMB

1 teaspoon ground ginger

1 teaspoon ground cumin

1 teaspoon paprika

1 cinnamon stick

50 ml (2 fl oz) orange juice

250 g (8 oz) lean lamb, cut into
5 cm (2 in) cubes

125 g (4 oz) button onions or
shallots, unpeeled

1 tablespoon olive oil

1 garlic clove, crushed

2 teaspoons flour

2 teaspoons tomato purée

125 ml (4 fl oz) lamb stock

3 tablespoons sherry

50 g (2 oz) ready-to-eat dried
apricots

300 g (10 oz) canned chickpeas,
drained and rinsed

salt and freshly ground black
pepper

couscous, to serve

This hearty and exotic lamb dish is full of delicious flavours, as well as many of the vitamins and minerals your body needs. Ginger is known to have many benefits, including boosting circulation and preventing nausea, while apricots are a very potent antioxidant and chickpeas are a superb source of vegetable protein.

1 Place the spices in a large bowl and pour over the orange juice. Add the lamb and mix well, cover and leave in the refrigerator to marinate for at least 1 hour, or preferably overnight.

2 Place the onions or shallots in a saucepan of boiling water and cook for 2 minutes. Drain and refresh under cold water, then peel.

3 Heat the oil in a large, flameproof casserole. Remove the lamb from the marinade and brown over a high heat until golden all over. Using a slotted spoon, remove the lamb and set aside. Reduce the heat slightly and, adding a little more oil if necessary, cook the onions or shallots and garlic for 3 minutes, or until just beginning to brown. Return the meat to the pan and stir in the flour and tomato purée. Continue to cook for another minute.

4 Add the marinade to the pan with the stock, sherry and salt and pepper. Bring to the boil, then reduce the heat, cover and place in a preheated oven at 180°C (350°F), Gas Mark 4, for 1 hour. Add the apricots and chickpeas and return to the oven for a further 15 minutes. Serve with couscous cooked according to the packet instructions.

Serves 2

Preparation time 15 minutes,
plus marinating

Cooking time 1½ hours

490 kcal • 20 g fat • 6 g saturated fat • 8 g fibre

MONKFISH BROCHETTES WITH CANNELLINI BEANS AND PESTO

Fish should ideally be eaten two to three times a week, and monkfish is a good choice as it has a lovely flavour and is rich in omega-3 fatty acids. Peppers and tomatoes are rich in bioflavonoids, which help to prevent the harmful effects of free radicals, while cannellini beans are a good source of soluble fibre and can help to lower cholesterol levels.

250 g (8 oz) monkfish, cut into six pieces

6 slices of Parma ham

2 skewers

6 cherry tomatoes

1 yellow pepper, cored, deseeded and cut into six pieces

1 tablespoon olive oil

300 g (10 oz) canned cannellini beans, drained and rinsed

2 tablespoons ready-made fresh pesto

1 Wrap each piece of monkfish in a slice of Parma ham. Thread on to 2 skewers, alternating with tomatoes and yellow pepper pieces. Brush the kebabs with the oil and cook under a preheated hot grill for 3–4 minutes. Turn and cook for another 3 minutes till cooked through.

2 Place the beans in a non-stick saucepan and cook, stirring, over a low heat for 4–5 minutes, or until hot. Stir in the pesto. Spoon the beans on to 2 plates, top with the brochettes and serve immediately.

Serves 2

Preparation time 10 minutes

Cooking time 10–15 minutes

350 kcal • 11 g fat • 4 g saturated fat • 9 g fibre

TOFU WITH PAK CHOI AND SHIITAKE MUSHROOMS

4 teaspoons vegetable oil

200 g (7 oz) firm tofu, drained and cut into 2.5-cm (1-in) cubes

1 garlic clove, crushed

150 g (5 oz) shiitake mushrooms, roughly chopped

200 g (7 oz) pak choi, trimmed and roughly chopped

4 spring onions, finely sliced

2 tablespoons plum sauce

2 tablespoons light soy sauce

2 tablespoons water

125 g (4 oz) rice noodles

Research has shown that in Asian countries those people whose intake of soya-bean products, such as tofu, is high have a lower rate of heart disease. Tofu is a very versatile and rich source of phytoestrogens and protein, as well as being high in iron, potassium, calcium and magnesium, so it is a good staple to use in your cooking.

1 Heat half the vegetable oil in a wok or frying pan, add the tofu and cook for 2–3 minutes, stirring, or until it is golden brown. Remove with a slotted spoon and set aside.

2 Heat the remaining vegetable oil in the pan, add the garlic, mushrooms, pak choi and spring onions and cook for 2–3 minutes. Stir in the tofu, plum sauce, soy sauce and water, and cook for a further 2 minutes, or until the sauce is hot.

3 Meanwhile, cook the noodles according to the packet instructions. Divide them between the bowls, spoon over the tofu mixture and serve immediately.

Serves 2

Preparation time 15 minutes

Cooking time 10 minutes

310 kcal • 11 g fat • 2 g saturated fat • 1.5 g fibre

PENNE WITH BROAD BEANS AND FETA CHEESE

The Mediterranean diet, which uses olive oil rather than dairy products, is good for keeping cholesterol levels low. This delicious pasta dish has an oily sauce rather than a creamy one, which is better for your heart, while the feta cheese is a good source of calcium, and the broad beans are high in fibre.

1 Cook the penne according to the packet instructions. Refresh in cold water and drain well.

2 Meanwhile, cook the broad beans in a separate saucepan of lightly salted boiling water for 4–5 minutes, or until just tender. Drain and plunge into ice-cold water to cool. Peel away and discard the outer shells.

3 Whisk the dressing ingredients together in a small bowl and season to taste with salt and pepper.

4 Place the beans in a serving dish and stir in the pasta, tomatoes and herbs. Toss with the dressing. Season with freshly ground black pepper and sprinkle over the feta.

200 g (7 oz) penne or other pasta shapes

200 g (7 oz) fresh or frozen broad beans

50 g (2 oz) sun blush tomatoes in oil, drained and roughly chopped

handful of mixed herbs, such as parsley, tarragon, chervil and chives, roughly chopped

50 g (2 oz) feta cheese, crumbled or roughly chopped

salt and freshly ground pepper

DRESSING

2 tablespoons extra virgin olive oil

1 tablespoon sherry vinegar

½ teaspoon wholegrain mustard

Serves 2
Preparation time 15 minutes
Cooking time 10–12 minutes

523 kcal • 31 g fat • 5 g saturated fat • 7 g fibre

SPAGHETTI PUTTANESCA

1 tablespoon olive oil

1 garlic clove, crushed

pinch of chilli flakes

400 g (13 oz) canned chopped
tomatoes

50 g (2 oz) pitted black olives,
roughly chopped

1 tablespoon tomato purée

1 tablespoon capers

300 g (10 oz) canned flageolet
beans, drained and rinsed

125 g (4 oz) wholewheat spaghetti

handful of basil leaves

salt and freshly ground black
pepper

Parmesan shavings, to serve

This classic Italian dish is high in fibre and packed with bioflavonoids
and phytoestrogens from the tomatoes, olives, capers and beans.

1 Heat the oil in a non-stick frying pan.
Add the garlic and chilli flakes and
cook for 3–4 minutes. Add the
tomatoes, olives, tomato purée, capers
and beans. Reduce the heat and
simmer for 20 minutes, or until the
sauce is thick. Season to taste.

2 Meanwhile, cook the spaghetti
according to the packet instructions.

3 Drain the pasta and return to the pan.
Stir in the sauce and the basil and toss
well. Sprinkle over the Parmesan
shavings and serve.

Serves 2

Preparation time 10 minutes

Cooking time 25 minutes

441 kcal • 13 g fat • 1.5 g saturated fat • 14 g fibre

CHOCOLATE ICE CREAM

By using soya milk and cream you will be able to enjoy an ice cream that is richer in phytoestrogens and lower in saturated fat than ice cream made from cow's milk. This is very easy to make, particularly if you own an ice-cream machine.

500 ml (17 fl oz) vanilla-flavoured soya milk

250 ml (8 fl oz) soya cream

50 g (2 oz) caster sugar

3 large egg yolks

125 g (4 oz) plain chocolate, broken into pieces

1 Heat the soya milk and soya cream in a heavy-based saucepan until just below boiling point. Whisk the sugar and eggs yolks together in a large bowl until pale and thickened. Pour the hot liquid over the egg and sugar mixture, whisking all the time, then return the mixture to the pan. Place over a low heat and, stirring constantly, allow the mixture to thicken until it will just coat the back of a wooden spoon.

2 Remove from the heat and pour into a large, clean bowl, add the chocolate and stir well. Allow the mixture to cool, then pour it into an ice-cream machine and churn until the mixture becomes thick and frozen. If you don't have an ice-cream machine, transfer the mixture to a shallow, freezerproof container. Freeze for at least 1 hour, or until the mixture is just beginning to set around the edges. Remove the container from the freezer and beat the mixture until smooth, then return to the freezer. Freeze for a further 30 minutes, then beat again. Repeat the freezing and beating process several more times until completely frozen.

3 Allow the ice cream to soften in the refrigerator for 2 hours before serving. Any left over will keep for up to 4 weeks in the freezer.

Serves 4

Preparation time 10 minutes, plus freezing

Cooking time 15 minutes

380 kcal • 23 g fat • 7 g saturated fat • 0 g fibre

FROZEN STRAWBERRY YOGURT

250 g (8 oz) strawberries, roughly chopped, plus extra to serve

2 tablespoons purple grape juice

1 tablespoon crème de cassis

2 tablespoons icing sugar

300 ml (10 fl oz) soya yogurt

Strawberries are a fantastic source of vitamins, potassium, calcium, magnesium and phosphorus. They not only taste delicious but are also packed with antioxidants and can help to prevent cancer. Grape juice can also help to protect against the harmful effects of carcinogens, while soya yogurt is a good source of phytoestrogens.

1 Place the strawberries in a saucepan. Add the grape juice and warm gently, stirring occasionally, until the strawberries become soft and pulpy. Press the strawberries through a nylon sieve and collect their juice in a large bowl. Discard the seeds. Beat in the crème de cassis, icing sugar and soya yogurt.

2 Pour the mixture into an ice-cream machine and churn until the mixture becomes thick and frozen. If you don't have an ice-cream machine, transfer the mixture to a shallow, freezerproof container. Freeze for at least 1 hour, or until the mixture is just beginning to set around the edges. Remove the container from the freezer and beat the mixture until it's smooth, then return to the freezer. Freeze for a further 30 minutes, then beat again. Repeat the freezing–beating process several more times until completely frozen.

3 Store in the freezer for up to 2 weeks. Transfer from the freezer to the refrigerator 20 minutes before serving.

Serves 2–3

Preparation time 15 minutes, plus freezing

Cooking time 2 minutes

140–206 kcal • 4–6 g fat • 0.5–1 g saturated fat • 1–1.5 g fibre

CHAPTER 5
STRONG BONES

Osteoporosis, a debilitating condition caused by loss of bone mineral, makes the bones susceptible to fracture, especially at the hip, wrist and spine. It is most common in menopausal women as the decline in oestrogen levels leads to an increase in the normal rate of mineral loss from bone.

You can help prevent osteoporosis eating a varied diet rich in vitamins and minerals, by consuming less caffeine and alcohol, by exercising and by taking hormone replacement therapy (HRT). In this chapter you can find out if you are at risk of osteoporosis and what steps to take to lower your chances of developing it.

WHAT IS OSTEOPOROSIS?

The word 'osteoporosis' is derived from the Greek words *osteon* (bone) and *poros* (passageway, pore). Osteoporosis is defined as an absolute decrease in the total amount of bone-tissue mass, the remaining amount of bone being normal. The small structures that form the bone matrix gradually become smaller and thinner, and the spaces between them increase. As a result, bones become weaker, less dense and more porous. Small crush fractures occur from time to time, and gradually bone damage increases. The bones become progressively more fragile and more prone to breaking. This occurs because the natural bone breakdown activity in the body has begun to outweigh its bone-building equivalent. This process is accelerated when your intake of calcium is inadequate.

HINT FOR HEALTH

Eat a varied diet throughout your life as osteoporosis can start before the menopause. For strong bones, make sure your diet is especially rich in vitamins D and K, calcium and magnesium.

TYPE 1 OSTEOPOROSIS

Also known as postmenopausal osteoporosis, type 1 osteoporosis is thought to be brought about by the hormonal and other related changes that occur in women during the menopause (see Chapter 4). It is characterized by considerable bone loss in the spine.

Typically, oestrogen levels will have fallen, and this lack of oestrogen leads to reduced output of a hormone called calcitonin (see page 141). The lowered levels of calcitonin means that bone cells are allowed to break down too readily and leads to decreased production of the active form of vitamin D. Lack of vitamin D activity leads to reduced absorption of calcium from the digestive tract, and can lead to a loss of up to half your bone mass. At the same time, a lack of oestrogen leads to increased production of the important parathyroid hormone, which 'pulls' calcium from your bones into the bloodstream.

TYPE 2 OSTEOPOROSIS

The second type of osteoporosis, type 2, is a gradual and progressive osteoporosis, which is age-related and can start at any age. In addition to the loss of bone in the spine, there is also loss in the bones of the rest of the body. Weaknesses are most likely to show up in the long bones of the legs and arms. This type of osteoporosis results from the gradual changes that occur with age, such as a decline in the quality and mineral content of the diet and a decline in the body's ability to

synthesize vitamin D and to absorb calcium, magnesium and other necessary nutrients. These changes lead to increased activity of the parathyroid gland, and the increased amount of parathyroid hormone 'pulls' calcium from the bones throughout the body. The bones become weakened, and widespread osteoporosis develops.

SECONDARY OSTEOPOROSIS

Secondary osteoporosis is caused by, and is secondary to, some other health problem, including hormonal problems, partial stomach removal and multiple myeloma. It is less common than types 1 and 2.

MINIMIZING THE RISK OF OSTEOPOROSIS

Osteoporotic changes, particularly of the spine, can start several years before the menopause in many women. Indeed, it is believed that half the total bone loss may have already occurred before a woman's level of oestrogen has fallen, which means that the menopause cannot be the only cause of osteoporosis. In light of this, it is extremely important that your bones should remain strong throughout your life and particularly into old age. Remember that prevention is always better than cure, and simple urine tests can pick up early warning signs long before any bone weakness will show on an X-ray or DEXA scan (see page 137).

The rest of this chapter describes how you can maintain the strength and structure of your bones, but you should also undertake regular checks to make sure that you are not developing osteoporosis.

See also ▶
Health issues, pages 102–103
Symptoms of osteoporosis, pages 136–137

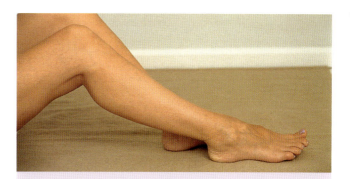

PROBLEM AREAS

Hip fractures are the most common type of break caused by osteoporosis, and are dramatic, life-changing events. The pain and disability of a hip fracture can be devastating and even, in very severe cases, fatal.

The spine or back is the second most frequent area affected by osteoporosis. Many people complain of having an aching back without being aware that the pain may be caused by disintegrating vertebrae.

The neck is also often affected, and the gradual osteoporotic weakening of the neck can lead to much pain and discomfort, which is worsened if there has been a previous injury. An old whiplash injury, for instance, may well come back to haunt you when, years later, the vertebrae of your neck are further weakened by the development of osteoporosis.

The wrist is also a vulnerable joint and is commonly affected by osteoporosis. It is easily injured or fractured during a fall.

SYMPTOMS OF OSTEOPOROSIS

Osteoporosis, generally, is a silent killer. For many years, while your bones are diminishing in density and strength, you may experience no symptoms whatsoever. For some people the first indication that they have osteoporosis may come as the result of an X-ray, possibly taken for some other reason. This is unfortunate, because it means there are no early warning signs until the osteoporotic process is fairly well advanced. Often, the first indication of the problem is when you suffer a fracture, and the consequences can be severe, life changing and even life threatening.

TYPE 1 OSTEOPOROSIS

Remember that type 1 osteoporosis, which is common among postmenopausal women, is most likely to involve the back. Over time, pain – which can often be low-level, mild back pain – may develop. Other symptoms may then appear.

ACUTE PAIN

There may be a growing number of incidences of acute pain. You may do something that puts slightly more pressure than usual on your back, such as picking up a heavy object. It may be something you used to be able to pick up easily and safely, but suddenly you find that this effort causes you an acute and stabbing or sharp pain as a crush fracture occurs. If you are lucky this will be felt as a dull ache for a few days and then clear up as the bone struggles to repair itself. If it happens several times or is severe, the pain is likely to get worse and to continue for longer; it is also likely to recur when you put a similar strain, even a very mild one, on the same place. Eventually, a persistent back problem may develop.

CURVATURE OF THE SPINE

If several vertebrae are involved, the spine will become misshapen and you could develop a 'dowager's hump', the instantly recognizable hump at the top of the back. The top of the spine becomes curved, and the typical bent-over posture leaves the sufferer staring at the ground, unable to look up or even, in extreme cases, to look straight ahead. It is often associated with pain and with loss of height. Even without this curvature and hump, you may lose a few centimetres in height.

TYPE 2 OSTEOPOROSIS

This type of osteoporosis develops gradually with age. The areas most likely to be affected include the hips, forearms and wrists as well as the back. There is commonly an overlap of both types in susceptible people – that is, women as they age and reach the menopause – and so the results can be detected in both the back and the limbs.

METHODS OF DIAGNOSIS

Many different methods of detection are available, although not all are ideal, and some are problematic. They indicate osteoporosis only once it has developed to a considerable extent.

Blood tests are useful only for detecting secondary osteoporosis. However, the information derived from blood tests, when combined with information from other diagnostic tools, can improve the overall assessment. X-rays can be helpful but only in detecting osteoporosis when it is relatively far advanced. They can show decreased vertebral bone density, but the structures become changed as the problem progresses, and their subjective assessment is open to error.

Other types of scans are available, including dual-energy X-ray absorptiometry (DEXA), which is non-invasive and rapid. It uses a low level of radiation and assesses bone density at specific at-risk areas, such as the lumbar spine, the top of the femur (thigh bone) and the lower arm. It can be used to document your current skeletal density and risk of fracture, and it helps to monitor the efficacy of therapy.

NEW PREDICTIVE TESTS

If osteoporotic change is detected at the start, something can be done to stop it developing further. There are two tests that may help to detect this, both of which involve measuring the amounts of collagen markers present in urine. These substances are lost from bones into the bloodstream and from there into urine during bone reabsorption or bone breakdown. The more of these compounds that show up in your urine the more likely you are to be developing osteoporosis. In other words, these tests show when a person has started to develop an osteoporotic pattern of bone metabolism. They distinguish between rapid losers and those who are slow losers of bone mass, and they also show this in appreciable time before there are visual osteoporotic changes in bone structure. If these tests show that bone reabsorption is starting to occur, it is time to start a serious prevention programme.

'Have regular medical check-ups to make sure that you are not developing osteoporosis.'

ARE YOU AT RISK?

Osteoporosis is more common in postmenopausal than premenopausal women, and in women who weigh less than 50 kg (110 lb; 7 st 12 oz). You may be unable to do anything about your genes and hereditary factors predisposing you to bone weaknesses, but you can do much to change your lifestyle to improve the strength and density of your bones.

HINT FOR HEALTH

Regular exercise can help to ensure your bones stay healthy and strong. With a little planning, weight-bearing exercises such as walking or running can quite easily be integrated into your daily routine (see also pages 152–161).

HEIGHT AND WEIGHT

Statistics show that tall women are more likely to develop osteoporosis. If you are tall, pay extra attention to the things you can do to minimize your risk of developing osteoporosis.

If you are too thin, you could run an increased risk of developing osteoporosis. An overactive thyroid gland could be causing your lack of bodyweight. In addition, if you don't have sufficient adipose tissue (fat) you will be less able to produce oestrogen from this source.

Carrying a slight amount of excess weight may actually help to push calcium into your bones. It is not helpful to be considerably overweight, however, as excess weight will put great pressure on your bones. If you do decide to lose weight, be careful. Research suggests that after the menopause it is better to stay the weight you are than to go on a sudden weight-loss programme and lose more than 10 per cent of your bodyweight, which can double your risk of getting osteoporosis.

EXERCISE

Lack of exercise is a significant risk factor in the development of osteoporosis. If you sit and do nothing, calcium tends to leave your bones; if you run, calcium tends to enter your bones. The critical factor is that the exercise should be weight-bearing, such as walking, running or push-ups. The more you use your bones and make demands on them, the stronger they become (see exercises on pages 152–161).

ALCOHOL

Heavy drinkers lose many nutrients in urine because of the diuretic effect of alcohol, including important minerals and vitamins needed by your bones. Alcohol also inhibits the absorption of calcium. It does

seem, however, that an average alcohol intake equivalent to one drink a day does not cause problems, and may actually be associated with greater bone density in postmenopausal woman.

CAFFEINE

Found in tea, coffee, chocolate, cola drinks and other soft drinks, caffeine is a diuretic. A high intake of caffeine is associated with an increased incidence of osteoporosis, probably because of loss of calcium and magnesium in urine. If you drink five or more cups of caffeine-containing drinks a day, your risk of getting osteoporosis is increased almost threefold. Although caffeine is addictive, it is relatively easy to give up. You may have withdrawal headaches for a few days, but after that there are rarely any symptoms.

CARBONATED DRINKS

Soft, fizzy drinks generally contain chemicals, including caffeine and phosphate compounds. A high intake of phosphates can lead to an increased loss of calcium in your urine. Equal amounts of calcium and phosphorus are needed to maintain the strength of your bones – there is little or no calcium in soft drinks, but a lot of phosphorus.

SMOKING

In postmenopausal women, smoking can reduce oestrogen levels by as much as 50 per cent. Smoking also depletes the body of ascorbic acid (vitamin C) and exposes it to toxins, such as cadmium and lead, which directly damage bone and interfere with calcium absorption.

'You can do much to change your lifestyle to improve both the strength and the density of your bones.'

SALT

A diet containing too much salt weakens bones by increasing the loss of calcium in urine – a good reason for cutting down or cutting it out.

MEDICINES

Many prescription drugs, such as some sleeping pills, have an adverse effect on bones. Steroid medications are particularly harmful: if you are taking, or have taken, them, you should try to build up your bones.

See also ▶
Exercises for strong bones, pages 152–161

THE OESTROGEN CONNECTION

Oestrogen, a female reproductive hormone, is closely associated with calcium metabolism as it increases the production of the hormone calcitonin and stimulates the synthesis of the active forms of vitamin D and the absorption of calcium from the intestine. Furthermore, oestrogen is understood to slow bone loss but to have only a limited effect on stimulating new bone growth.

POSSIBLE EFFECTS OF INSUFFICIENT OESTROGEN

- Inadequate intake and absorption of calcium.

- Increased levels of stress.

- Exhaustion of the adrenal glands, which produce oestrogen.

THE ROLE OF OESTROGEN

Oestrogen is not the most useful chemical in the body for stimulating bone growth; progesterone, ipriflavone and vitamin K are all more important. However, the publicity is focused on oestrogen. This has led to an assumption that the menopause (see Chapter 4), when a woman's oestrogen output falls, should be treated as a crisis, that doctors should be consulted and that replacement hormones should be taken. However, a consideration of a woman's life cycle suggests that this is not necessarily the case.

Before she reaches puberty, a girl cannot conceive, cannot carry a baby and does not need enhanced calcium absorption. She needs only to absorb sufficient calcium for herself and for her growing bones. At this time she produces a moderate amount of oestrogen.

At puberty, conception becomes possible and thus the possibility of the woman having to create a baby's skeleton arises. It is a useful metabolic development that the hormonal changes that lead to the body's being able to conceive and proceed with a pregnancy also encourage an increase in calcium absorption and availability.

After the menopause, conception is no longer possible; the female body will not have to make another set of bones, so enhanced calcium absorption is no longer necessary. The production of ovarian oestrogen is reduced at the menopause, but oestrogen continues to be produced from the adrenal glands provided they are not over-stressed.

Thus, it would seem that there is no need to worry. When the menopause occurs, the resulting drop in oestrogen output along with the lowered calcium absorption should leave a woman able to absorb all the calcium she needs for herself, now that child-bearing is no longer a possibility. If this does not hold true, we have to ask ourselves how women managed for thousands of years, before oestrogen supplements were available.

THE IMPORTANCE OF DIET

The above theory is based on the assumption that throughout her life the woman has eaten an adequate diet, rich in calcium, magnesium and other minerals, and that she continues to do so after the menopause. Unfortunately, today's diet contains insufficient calcium, and the enhanced oestrogen levels of a woman's fertile years are often needed simply to maintain the woman's own calcium level. Had she borne a child every year or two, as is biologically possible, it is likely that she would have become severely calcium-deficient. The diet of our ancient ancestors provided a much greater supply of calcium than today's average Western diet does.

It is in these circumstances that the reduced level of oestrogen production after the menopause increases the risk of osteoporosis. The problem is not so much the reduced oestrogen level but a prolonged inadequate intake of calcium. It would be better to have an adequate calcium intake throughout life than simply to rely on taking oestrogen supplements later on.

BENEFITS AND RISKS OF OESTROGEN THERAPY

Oestrogen therapy must be taken for several years, usually 10 or more, to get the full benefits. Considerable dangers result from taking oestrogen, including an increased risk of developing a number of types of cancer, such as uterine and breast cancers.

Remember that all hormones are powerful compounds. They have profound effects on your body, acting on and instructing a variety of target organs and tissues to change the ways they behave. In addition to producing the results you desire, they may well, and often do, produce undesirable and even dangerous effects.

'Unfortunately, today's diet contains insufficient calcium, and the enhanced oestrogen levels of a woman's fertile years are often needed simply to maintain the woman's own calcium level.'

CALCITONIN

The hormone calcitonin is produced by your thyroid gland in response to a rise in blood calcium level, and helps in the process of depositing calcium in the bones. It also helps to hold calcium in the bones. If your calcium intake is inadequate or if your blood calcium level never rises above normal, as it would after a high intake of calcium, calcitonin production will not be stimulated. A lack of calcitonin is worrying as it could mean that you fail to deposit calcium in your bones, even when it is present in the bloodstream in an adequate amount.

See also ▶

What your bones need, pages 142–143
Sources of calcium and magnesium, pages 144–147
Recipes for strong bones, pages 162–177

WHAT YOUR BONES NEED

Your bones require many of the vitamins and minerals found in fruits, vegetables and other foods. First, think about improving your diet (see also Chapter 3), and then consider what supplements you could take.

CALCIUM LOSS

Many factors increase the body's loss of calcium in urine. These include the following, which should be reduced or avoided:

- A high phosphorus intake
- A high protein intake
- Caffeine
- Salt
- Sugar
- A magnesium deficiency

Substances that reduce urinary loss of calcium are boron, oestrogen and vitamin K.

CALCIUM

This mineral is a major component of the structure of bones. You lose some calcium every day, mainly in your urine, and it is vital that this is replaced. A daily dose of 1,000 mg is recommended, with an increase to 1,500 mg close to and after the menopause. Make sure your diet supplies a large amount of calcium. If it doesn't, make some positive changes and consider taking a calcium supplement, if necessary.

PHOSPHORUS

Calcium's 'partner' in bones is phosphorus. The ideal diet would provide them in equal amounts, but the Western diet usually contains an excess of phosphorus. A high phosphorus intake can remove calcium from bones and can also lead to reduced vitamin D activity and hence reduced absorption of calcium from the digestive system.

Meat, grains and protein-rich foods in general are rich in phosphorus, so reduce your intake of these foods to the minimum that will provide adequate protein. Most fruits and vegetables have a good balance of calcium and phosphorus. Avoid carbonated soft drinks (see page 139).

MAGNESIUM

About 70 per cent of the body's magnesium is stored in the bones, where it replaces some of the calcium and has an important influence on bone structure. People with osteoporosis often have a deficiency of magnesium. Many medications prescribed for osteoporosis contain calcium and vitamin D but little or no magnesium, even though some people may needed it even more urgently than calcium.

OTHER ESSENTIAL MINERALS

In addition to those listed above, make sure that you are supplying your body with adequate levels of manganese, zinc, copper, silica and boron.

VITAMIN A

Also known as retinol, vitamin A stimulates the production of progesterone, thought to be more useful than oestrogen in the prevention of osteoporosis. It is found in eggs and meat, especially liver. Carotenes, the precursors of vitamin A, are available from orange, red or green plant foods, such as carrots, beetroot and leafy green vegetables.

VITAMINS B6 AND B12 AND FOLIC ACID

These B vitamins help to minimize levels of the harmful compound homocysteine. This effect can be enhanced by taking a supplement with as much as 5 mg folic acid. This is a safe dose, but it should always be taken in combination with vitamin B12.

VITAMIN C

Vitamin C is essential for healthy collagen and increases the production of progesterone. It is usually found in combination with bioflavonoids in foods such as oranges, strawberries, tomatoes and green vegetables. If choosing a supplement, look for one that contains vitamin C in calcium form (calcium ascorbate) in combination with bioflavonoids.

VITAMIN D

By promoting calcium absorption from the intestinal tract vitamin D helps to maintain normal levels of blood calcium. An adequate intake of vitamin D will, for most people, make a big difference to calcium levels.

VITAMIN K

This vitamin encourages calcium deposition in the bones. Many post-menopausal women stop losing calcium in urine when they take vitamin K. Leafy green vegetables are the richest sources. Because it is fat-soluble, vitamin K should be eaten or taken with some form of fat.

Another form, vitamin K2, is produced by bacteria and other micro-organisms in the digestive tract. For most healthy people, this is a major source of vitamin K. Vitamin K is not stored in the body, and so is less likely to be toxic in high doses. A recommended dose is 10 mg a day, but up to 50 mg a day has been used without adverse effects.

HINT FOR HEALTH

Most people do not eat enough fruit and vegetables, but it is easy to increase your intake by drinking more fruit juices, snacking on fresh or dried fruit instead of cakes or biscuits, and including an additional kind of vegetable in your evening meal.

See also ▶
Sources of calcium and magnesium, pages 144–147
Recipes for strong bones, pages 162–177

SOURCES OF CALCIUM AND MAGNESIUM

TABLE 1: CALCIUM PER 100 g (3½ oz)
This shows the amount of calcium in a fixed weight (100 g/3½ oz) of each food. However, note that the calorie content of each food varies widely (see Table 2).

TABLE 2: CALCIUM PER 100 kcal
This shows the amount of calcium in 100 calories of each food. The most nutrient dense food is the food with the most nutrient per calorie.

TABLE 1

FOOD	CALCIUM (mg)/100 g (3½ oz)
Cheese, Cheddar	721
Cheese, Camembert	388
Soya beans	277
Almonds	266
Parsley	260
Watercress	192
Hazelnuts	188
Brazil nuts	176
Milk, goats'	134
Broccoli	123
Yogurt, natural	121
Milk, cows'	119
Beet greens	119
Sunflower seeds	116
Buckwheat	114
Spinach	101
Walnuts	94
Cream	82
Okra	81
Macadamia nuts	70
Cheese, cottage	60
Peanuts	58
Swedes	58
Eggs, hens'	56
Leeks	56
Oats	55
Parsnip	54
Red lentils	51
Swiss chard	51
Kohlrabi	50
Turnips	49
Globe artichokes	48
Beans, green	48
Celery	48
Cabbage, white	47
Cabbage, Chinese	46

TABLE 2

FOOD	CALCIUM (mg)/100 kcal (418 kJ)
Watercress	914
Beet greens	496
Parsley	473
Spinach	404
Broccoli	351
Cabbage, Chinese	329
Celery	267
Marrows	250
Okra	238
Yogurt, natural	198
Milk, goats'	194
Lettuce	188
Cucumber	186
Cabbage, white	181
Cheese, Cheddar	179
Milk, cows'	178
Radish	176
Kohlrabi	172
Swiss chard	170
Turnips	169
Courgette	165
Swedes	161
Beans, green	150
Cabbage, red	135
Leeks	130
Cheese, camembert	129
Globe artichokes	120
Carrots	111
Asparagus	105
Onions	89
Oranges	85
Pumpkin	81
Cauliflower	81
Parsnip	77
Tomatoes	68
Soya beans	67

TABLE 3

FOOD	MAGNESIUM (mg)/100 g (3½ oz)
Broccoli	388
Sunflower seeds	354
Almonds	296
Hazelnuts	285
Soya beans	280
Buckwheat	229
Brazil nuts	225
Peanuts	180
Walnuts	169
Wheat	160
Oats	144
Macadamia nuts	116
Cabbage, white	113
Red lentils	107
Beet greens	106
Spinach	88
Okra	57
Kidney bean	45
Broad beans	38
Kohlrabi	37
Dates	35
Beans, green	32
Parsnip	32
Sweet potatoes	31
Watercress	30
Brussels sprouts	29
Brown rice	29
Bananas	29
Salmon	29
Cheese, Cheddar	28
Cod	28
Beetroot	25
Cream	25
Cauliflower	24
Leeks	23
Carrots	23

TABLE 4

FOOD	MAGNESIUM (mg)/100 kcal
Broccoli	1109
Beet greens	442
Cabbage, white	435
Spinach	352
Okra	168
Watercress	143
Kohlrabi	128
Celery	122
Beans, green	100
Cabbage, Chinese	100
Asparagus	95
Cauliflower	92
Radish	88
Swiss chard	81
Cucumber	79
Sweet peppers	69
Turnips	69
Buckwheat	68
Soya beans	67
Lettuce	65
Eggplant	64
Carrots	64
Tomatoes	64
Beetroot	63
Sunflower seeds	62
Brussels sprouts	59
Mushrooms	59
Leeks	53
Almonds	50
Wheat	48
Pumpkin	46
Parsnip	46
Hazelnuts	45
Swedes	42
Oats	37
Raspberries	37

TABLE 3: MAGNESIUM PER 100 g (3½ oz)

This shows the amount of magnesium in a fixed weight (100 g/3½ oz) of each food. However, note that the calorie content of each food varies widely (see Table 2).

Food	mg	Food	mg
Cabbage, red	42	Brussels sprouts	65
Oranges	40	Beetroot	65
Carrots	40	Cheese, cottage	58
Shallots	37	Shallots	51
Wheat	36	Aubergines	48
Figs	35	Figs	47
Dates	32	Strawberries	47
Sweet potatoes	32	Milk, breast	46
Milk, breast	32	Almonds	45
Brussels sprouts	32	Raspberries	45
Lettuce	32	Sweet peppers	38
Onions	31	Jerusalem artichokes	38
Radishes	30	Eggs, hens'	35
Kidney beans	28	Buckwheat	34
Courgette	28	Mushrooms	32
Jerusalem artichokes	26	Hazelnuts	30
Beetroot	26	Apricots	29
Cucumber	26	Sweet potatoes	28
Broad beans	22	Brazil nuts	27
Raspberries	22	Cream	23
Asparagus	22	Kidney beans	22
Pumpkin	21	Broad beans	21
Cauliflower	21	Sunflower seeds	21
Chicken	16	Grapes	20
Tomatoes	15	Red lentils	15
Marrow	15	Walnuts	15
Apricots	14	Oats	14
Strawberries	14	Cod	13
Bamboo shoots	13	Apples	12
Aubergines	12	Dates	12
Brown rice	11	Bamboo shoots	11
Grapes	11	Wheat	11
Cod	10	Peanuts	10
Sweet peppers	10	Macadamia nuts	10
Lamb	9	Potatoes	9
Pork chop	8	Brown rice	9
Salmon	8	Chicken	8
Beef	7	Bananas	7
Potato	7	Lamb	5
Apples	7	Salmon	4
Mushrooms	7	Pork chop	3
Bananas	6	Beef	2

TABLE 4: MAGNESIUM PER 100 kcal

This shows the amount of magnesium in 100 calories of each food. The most nutrient dense food is the food with the most nutrient per calorie.

Food	mg	Food	mg
Celery	22	Broad beans	36
Potato	22	Cod	36
Turnips	20	Kidney beans	35
Cheese, Camembert	20	Brazil nuts	34
Asparagus	20	Onions	34
Raspberries	18	Strawberries	33
Sweet peppers	18	Peanuts	32
Figs	17	Red lentils	32
Aubergines	16	Bananas	32
Beef	16	Potatoes	32
Radish	15	Sweet potatoes	29
Swedes	15	Walnuts	27
Pork chop	14	Parsley	26
Parsley	14	Brown rice	25
Cabbage, Chinese	14	Figs	24
Milk, goats'	13	Oranges	23
Tomatoes	13	Milk, goats'	21
Milk, cows'	13	Yogurt, natural	20
Mushrooms	12	Milk, cows'	20
Lamb	12	Apricots	19
Yogurt, natural	12	Macadamia nuts	17
Onions	12	Jerusalem artichokes	17
Pumpkin	11	Salmon	16
Eggs, hens'	11	Dates	13
Lettuce	10	Apples	13
Cucumber	8	Grapes	8
Jerusalem artichokes	8	Eggs, hens'	8
Oranges	8	Lamb	8
Strawberries	7	Cheese, Cheddar	7
Apricots	7	Cream	7
Grapes	7	Cheese, Camembert	7
Cheese, cottage	7	Pork chop	7
Apples	6	Cheese, cottage	6
Milk, breast	5	Beef	5
Bamboo shoots	5	Milk, breast	5
Marrows	5	Bamboo shoots	4
Swiss chard	4	Marrows	3
Courgettes	3	Courgettes	0
Cabbage, red	0	Cabbage, red	0
Globe artichokes	0	Globe artichokes	0
Shallots	0	Shallots	0
Chicken	0	Chicken	0

TABLE 5: KCAL PER 100 g (3½ oz)

This table presents the list of foods that are covered in all the tables and their calorie content per 100 g (3½ oz).

TABLE 6: MAGNESIUM:CALCIUM RATIO

This table has been calculated by dividing the amount of magnesium by the amount of calcium per 100 kcal. Broccoli, for example, has 3.15 mg of magnesium to every 1 mg of calcium. A ratio of between 0.5:1 and 3:1 is ideal.

TABLE 5

FOOD	KCAL (kJ)/ 100 g (3½ oz)
Almonds	589 (2,465)
Apples	59 (247)
Apricots	48 (201)
Asparagus	21 (88)
Aubergine	25 (105)
Bamboo shoots	113 (473)
Bananas	92 (385)
Beans, green	32 (134)
Beef	353 (1,477)
Beet greens	24 (100)
Beetroot	40 (167)
Brazil nuts	656 (2,745)
Broad beans	105 (439)
Broccoli	35 (146)
Brown rice	120 (502)
Brussels sprouts	49 (205)
Buckwheat	335 (1,402)
Cabbage, Chinese	14 (59)
Cabbage, red	31 (130)
Cabbage, white	26 (109)
Carrots	36 (151)
Cauliflower	26 (109)
Celery	18 (75)
Cheese, Camembert	300 (1,256)
Cheese, Cheddar	403 (1,687)
Cheese, cottage	103 (431)
Chicken	199 (833)
Cod	78 (326)
Courgettes	17 (71)
Cream	364 (1,523)
Cucumber	14 (59)
Dates	275 (1,151)
Eggs, hens'	158 (661)
Figs	74 (310)
Globe artichokes	40 (167)
Grapes	71 (297)

TABLE 6

FOOD	MAGNESIUM: CALCIUM
Bananas	4.83:1
Wheat	4.44:1
Salmon	3.63:1
Broccoli	3.15:1
Potatoes	3.14:1
Peanuts	3.10:1
Sunflower seeds	3.05:1
Cod	2.80:1
Brown rice	2.64:1
Oats	2.62:1
Cabbage, white	2.40:1
Beef	2.29:1
Red lentils	2.10:1
Buckwheat	2.01:1
Pork chop	1.88:1
Mushrooms	1.86:1
Sweet peppers	1.80:1
Walnuts	1.80:1
Broad beans	1.73:1
Macadamia nuts	1.66:1
Kidney beans	1.61:1
Hazelnuts	1.52:1
Lamb	1.44:1
Aubergines	1.33:1
Brazil nuts	1.28:1
Cauliflower	1.14:1
Almonds	1.11:1
Dates	1.09:1
Soya beans	1.01:1
Sweet potatoes	0.97:1
Beetroot	0.96:1
Tomatoes	0.93:1
Asparagus	0.91:1
Brussels sprouts	0.91:1
Beet greens	0.89:1
Spinach	0.87:1

TABLE 7

FOOD	CALCIUM: PHOSPHORUS
Watercress	3.69:1
Parsley	3.61:1
Beet greens	2.98:1
Oranges	2.86:1
Figs	2.50:1
Milk, breast	2.29:1
Raspberries	1.83:1
Spinach	1.74:1
Broccoli	1.60:1
Cabbage, white	1.57:1
Turnips	1.53:1
Swedes	1.49:1
Celery	1.41:1
Cheese, Cheddar	1.41:1
Cream	1.37:1
Okra	1.29:1
Milk cows'	1.28:1
Yogurt, natural	1.27:1
Marrows	1.25:1
Milk, goats'	1.21:1
Cabbage, red	1.20:1
Cabbage, Chinese	1.15:1
Lettuce	1.14:1
Cheese, Camembert	1.12:1
Carrots	1.11:1
Swiss chard	1.11:1
Cucumber	1.08:1
Leeks	1.06:1
Beans, green	1.04:1
Apples	1.00:1
Kohlrabi	0.98:1
Radish	0.97:1
Courgettes	0.97:1
Grapes	0.85:1
Dates	0.80:1
Onions	0.78:1

TABLE 8

FOOD	PHOSPHORUS: CALCIUM
Salmon	23.25:1
Cod	19.40:1
Pork chop	19.00:1
Beef	17.57:1
Chicken	16.75:1
Mushrooms	16.57:1
Lamb	14.44:1
Wheat	10.64:1
Red lentils	8.90:1
Brown rice	8.18:1
Potatoes	7.57:1
Oats	6.75:1
Peanuts	6.60:1
Sunflower seeds	6.08:1
Kidney beans	5.07:1
Broad beans	4.32:1
Bamboo shoots	3.85:1
Brazil nuts	3.41:1
Walnuts	3.37:1
Bananas	3.32:1
Eggs, hens'	3.21:1
Cauliflower	3.05:1
Sweet peppers	3.00:1
Jerusalem artichokes	3.00:1
Soya beans	2.54:1
Buckwheat	2.47:1
Brussels sprouts	2.47:1
Asparagus	2.36:1
Cheese, cottage	2.20:1
Aubergines	2.17:1
Tomatoes	2.13:1
Pumpkin	2.10:1
Almonds	1.95:1
Macadamia nuts	1.94:1
Globe artichokes	1.83:1
Hazelnuts	1.66:1

TABLE 7: CALCIUM:PHOSPHORUS RATIO

A diet with approximately equal amounts of calcium and phosphorus, a ratio of around 1:1, is desirable. Few foods contain much more calcium than phosphorus.

TABLE 8: PHOSPHORUS:CALCIUM RATIO

Too much phosphorus can reduce calcium absorption, but too little encourages calcification (where calcium is deposited outside the bone). Again, the ideal ratio is 1:1.

Sources of calcium and magnesium (continued)

Food	Content
Hazelnuts	632 (2,645)
Jerusalem artichokes	68 (285)
Kidney beans	127 (531)
Kohlrabi	29 (121)
Lamb	186 (778)
Leeks	43 (180)
Lettuce	17 (71)
Macadamia nuts	702 (2,938)
Marrows	6 (25)
Milk, goats'	69 (289)
Milk, breast	70 (293)
Milk, cows'	67 (280)
Mushrooms	22 (92)
Oats	388 (1,624)
Okra	34 (142)
Onions	35 (146)
Oranges	47 (197)
Parsley	55 (230)
Parsnip	70 (293)
Peanuts	567 (2,373)
Pork chop	234 (979)
Potatoes	76 (318)
Pumpkin	26 (109)
Radish	17 (71)
Raspberries	49 (205)
Red lentils	338 (1,415)
Salmon	217 (908)
Shallots	72 (301)
Soya beans	416 (1,741)
Spinach	25 (105)
Strawberries	30 (126)
Sunflower seeds	570 (2,385)
Swedes	36 (151)
Sweet peppers	26 (109)
Sweet potatoes	114 (477)
Swiss chard	30 (126)
Tomatoes	22 (92)
Turnips	29 (121)
Walnuts	642 (2,687)
Watercress	21 (88)
Wheat	330 (1,381)
Yogurt, natural	61 (255)

Table 7: Calcium:Phosphorus Ratio

Raspberries	0.82:1
Kohlrabi	0.74:1
Strawberries	0.71:1
Apples	0.71:1
Okra	0.70:1
Beans, green	0.67:1
Parsnip	0.59:1
Carrots	0.58:1
Pumpkin	0.57:1
Apricots	0.57:1
Grapes	0.55:1
Radish	0.50:1
Figs	0.49:1
Swiss chard	0.48:1
Celery	0.46:1
Cucumber	0.42:1
Jerusalem artichokes	0.42:1
Leeks	0.41:1
Turnips	0.41:1
Onions	0.39:1
Lettuce	0.34:1
Cream	0.30:1
Cabbage, Chinese	0.30:1
Swedes	0.26:1
Oranges	0.25:1
Bamboo shoots	0.23:1
Eggs, hens'	0.21:1
Watercress	0.16:1
Milk, cows'	0.11:1
Milk, goats'	0.10:1
Yogurt, natural	0.10:1
Milk, breast	0.09:1
Cheese, cottage	0.08:1
Parsley	0.05:1
Cheese, Camembert	0.05:1
Cheese, Cheddar	0.04:1
Courgettes	*
Cabbage, red	*
Globe artichokes	*
Shallots	*
Marrows	*
Chicken	*

Table 8: Phosphorus:Calcium Ratio

Food	Ratio	Food	Ratio
Shallots	1.62:1	Strawberries	0.74:1
Sweet potatoes	1.47:1	Apricots	0.74:1
Parsnip	1.46:1	Beetroot	0.68:1
Beetroot	1.46:1	Parsnip	0.68:1
Strawberries	1.36:1	Sweet potatoes	0.68:1
Apricots	1.36:1	Shallots	0.62:1
Onions	1.29:1	Hazelnuts	0.60:1
Dates	1.25:1	Globe artichokes	0.55:1
Grapes	1.18:1	Macadamia nuts	0.51:1
Courgettes	1.04:1	Almonds	0.51:1
Radish	1.03:1	Pumpkin	0.48:1
Kohlrabi	1.02:1	Tomatoes	0.47:1
Apples	1.00:1	Aubergines	0.46:1
Beans, green	0.96:1	Cheese, cottage	0.45:1
Leeks	0.95:1	Asparagus	0.42:1
Cucumber	0.92:1	Brussels sprouts	0.41:1
Swiss chard	0.90:1	Buckwheat	0.40:1
Carrots	0.90:1	Soya beans	0.39:1
Cheese, Camembert	0.89:1	Sweet peppers	0.33:1
Lettuce	0.88:1	Jerusalem artichokes	0.33:1
Cabbage, Chinese	0.87:1	Cauliflower	0.33:1
Cabbage, red	0.83:1	Eggs, hens'	0.31:1
Milk, goats'	0.83:1	Bananas	0.30:1
Marrows	0.80:1	Walnuts	0.30:1
Yogurt, natural	0.79:1	Brazil nuts	0.29:1
Milk, cows'	0.78:1	Bamboo shoots	0.26:1
Okra	0.78:1	Broad beans	0.23:1
Cream	0.73:1	Kidney beans	0.20:1
Cheese, Cheddar	0.71:1	Sunflower seeds	0.16:1
Celery	0.71:1	Peanuts	0.15:1
Swedes	0.67:1	Oats	0.15:1
Turnips	0.65:1	Potato	0.13:1
Cabbage, white	0.64:1	Brown rice	0.12:1
Broccoli	0.63:1	Red lentils	0.11:1
Spinach	0.57:1	Wheat	0.09:1
Raspberries	0.55:1	Lamb	0.07:1
Milk, breast	0.44:1	Mushrooms	0.06:1
Figs	0.40:1	Chicken	0.06:1
Oranges	0.35:1	Beef	0.06:1
Beet greens	0.34:1	Pork chop	0.05:1
Parsley	0.28:1	Cod	0.05:1
Watercress	0.27:1	Salmon	0.04:1

*no magnesium content

OSTEOPOROSIS PREVENTION PLAN

It is possible to prevent osteoporosis occurring in later life by making some simple improvements to your diet and lifestyle – and the earlier you start, the better. Being aware of the factors that cause osteoporosis and taking action to combat these is crucial in prevention.

MULTISTEP PLAN

- **Be aware** of all the known risk factors.

- **Make** necessary lifestyle changes.

- **Maximize** your intake of necessary nutrients and minimize harmful factors.

- **Eat** soya-based foods and seaweeds.

- **Ensure** an adequate intake of calcium supplements as appropriate.

- **Have** an adequate intake of all the other nutrients needed by the bones and taking supplements as necessary.

- **Exercise** regularly (see pages 152–161).

- **Take** oestrogen with progesterone if advised by your doctor.

- **Optimize** the function of the organs involved in bone metabolism: the liver, kidneys, parathyroid gland, thyroid gland, adrenal glands and digestive system.

NUTRITION AND THE MEDICAL PROFESSION

What you eat is crucially important to your health and general wellbeing. Yet it is amazing that medicine does not give diet the serious attention it deserves or take a more thorough and careful approach to assessing the effect it has on our health. No one would say that the type of fuel you put in your car is unimportant, yet a car is a simple machine compared with the complexities of the human body. There may be some rational explanation for how and why this happened in the past, but there is no excuse, given our knowledge of nutrition and human biochemistry, for continuing with this attitude in the present day.

Multinational drug companies make drugs and medications that are patented and make the companies wealthy. Vitamins, minerals and raw foods cannot be patented. The drug companies have the advertising power, the sales forces and the resources to produce multiple technical brochures, to run seminars and more. For the busy doctor, it can be all too easy to accept the latest information on the latest drug. Furthermore, because doctors do not generally study nutrition in medical school, learning about it when they are practising with a view to offering constructive and detailed dietary advice is generally not considered.

As a result, modern medicine has never fully embraced nutrition, even though the science, biochemistry and application of it are well researched and widely written up in the scientific literature. At best, if you are concerned about osteoporosis, your doctor will tell you to take more calcium and eat a well-balanced diet.

HOW TO IMPROVE YOUR DIET

The changes suggested (see box, opposite) may not produce a diet exactly like that of our 'cave-age' ancestors, consisting of two-thirds vegetables and fruits together with one-third low-fat, lean flesh foods with nuts, herbs and possibly some olive oil, but they are probably as far as you are willing to go. It is almost certainly a better diet than you are eating now and will be of great benefit to your bones.

You should also consider taking supplements to top up your intake as needed, making sure that the supplements provide the various nutrients discussed above and in the appropriate proportions.

These dietary suggestions may seem to be pretty radical. When you look at the list you may think you have so many changes to make that the process is impossible. If that is the case and if you are suffering from osteoporosis, you may have identified a major part of the cause. It could be your diet that has caused much of the problem.

PRESCRIPTION DRUGS

If you have osteoporosis you may be prescribed some of the drugs that have been suggested for treatment. They can generally be divided into two types: those aimed at preventing the breakdown of bones, and those aimed at promoting bone-building. The two processes are, however, closely linked, and if you alter one it is probable that you will also affect the other. This means that many of the drugs that help to prevent bone breakdown also reduce bone-building activity. This is particularly true when they are used on a long-term basis.

The first group of drugs described above includes oestrogen (hormone), calcium, bisphosphonates and calcitonin (hormone). The second group includes sodium fluoride, anabolic fragments of parathyroid hormone and insulin-like growth factor. Unfortunately, these drugs have other side effects. For example, sodium fluoride increases bone density, but it also changes the crystalline structure of the bones and actually makes them more fragile. Therefore, it is often better to adopt a naturopathic approach to treatment.

NATUROPATHY

In naturopathic treatment, there are generally several clearly defined steps to take, although the precise details may vary from one practitioner to another.

- **Make appropriate changes** to your lifestyle, such as exercising and relaxing.

- **Correct your diet** to make sure that it contains the maximum amounts possible of all the necessary nutrients and to eliminate all kinds of harmful foods, substances and practices.

- **Add special foods** and nutritional herbs, which can generally be added to your diet and included in the various dishes you prepare.

- **Add supplements** of specific nutrients as appropriate.

- **Take specific remedies**, herbal or homeopathic medicines.

See also ▶

What your bones need, pages 142–143

Sources of calcium and magnesium, pages 144–147

Exercises for strong bones, pages 152–161

Recipes for strong bones, pages 162–177

EXERCISES FOR STRONG BONES

The following exercises are aimed at strengthening your bones without taking a large amount of time, without needing special equipment or another person to work with, and without necessitating a change of clothing. They are exercises that can be done within the normal course of your day and at any odd moment when you have time to spare.

CHAIR TWIST

While holding the telephone, use the time to do this simple exercise. Put your phone on remote, or hold it in your left hand and twist to the right – then do the reverse.

Care Sit up straight as you turn.

Repetitions Once each side

1 Sit upright in your chair, keep your buttocks firmly in place and your spine straight. Twist round to the right using your right hand to pull you round, then back.

2 Change the phone to your right hand, if necessary, and swing round to the left, grasping the back of your chair with your left hand.

Care Keep your spine straight as you bend.

Repetitions Once each side

CHAIR PICK-UP

The next time you need to pick something up off the floor, do the following exercises to increase flexibility and boost circulation.

1 Start by sitting up straight, with your arms hanging by your side.

2 Instead of gently leaning forwards and down, keep your spine straight and bend down sideways to pick the item up. You will feel the extra load on the near leg.

3 If you have time, extend this exercise by bringing your other hand down to join the first. If you are in a restaurant, this may be all you do; if you are at home, and perhaps waiting for someone else to finish their meal, you can take the time to repeat the exercise on the other side.

4 You can extend this exercise further by swinging the other arm above your head.

WALL LEAN

Walls are always available. As you go about your business of the day, at home, at work or in the office, take a few minutes to lean against a wall and practise this exercise.

Care Keep your spine straight as you lean into the wall.

Repetitions Once only

1 Stand a short pace away from the wall and place your palms flat against it with your elbows bent.

2 Gradually walk your feet backwards, making sure you keep your spine straight.

3 Bend your arms further and let them take more of your bodyweight.

WALL PUSH

Many people have trouble doing push-ups. However, they need not be done lying down. Use a wall and do this vertical version, which is simpler.

Care Keep your back straight as you lean towards the wall.

Repetitions 10 for each variation

1 Stand a short pace away from the wall and place your palms flat against it with your elbows bent slightly.

2 Keeping your back and legs in a straight line, and your elbows by your side, lean towards the wall, controlling the movement with your hands. Then push yourself back up to the start position.

3 By changing the position of your hands in this variation, different pressure is applied to the forearms. Change the position of your hands so that the fingers point towards each other, and your elbows point out.

4 Keeping your back and legs in a straight line, fall towards the wall, then push yourself away from it back to the start position.

BELT PULL

Strengthen your shoulders with this belt pull. You can use a belt, a tea towel or any handy object that can be made long and thin and pulled.

Care Don't thrust your head forwards as you pull the belt.

Repetitions Once only

1 Grasp one end of the object in either hand and pull.

2 Lift your arms above your head while still pulling.

3 Lower your arms so the object is across the back of your neck and keep pulling.

4 Lower your arms again and reverse the exercise with the object behind your back.

Care Keep your shoulders relaxed and down.

Repetitions Once only

TELEVISION PULL

Next time you are watching television, use the time to improve the strength of your bones in the lower arms.

1 Hold your hands in front of you, palm to palm, as in prayer. Keep your lower arms horizontal and your elbows out to the side. Take this opportunity to pump more calcium into your bones and press your hands firmly together.

2 Then twist your arms, link your fingers together and pull firmly, as if trying to part your hands.

3 Slide your hands over your wrist and grab each one with the opposite hand and pull.

4 Swap positions by releasing your hold and twisting the hand that was facing your body so it faces away from you. Twist the other hand in the opposite direction. Re-grasp your wrists and pull again.

LEG SWING

This exercise will improve flexibility and boost your circulation. If your joints are uncomfortable when leant on, use a cushion for protection.

Care Make sure you don't let your back dip downwards as you swing your leg behind you.

Repetitions Once each side

1 Kneel on all fours. You can do this exercise with or without small hand weights. If you choose to use them, place one in the bend of your right knee. Lift your lower leg slightly to keep the weight in place.

2 Lift the bent knee until it is level with your (flat) spine and your right foot is pointing up to the ceiling.

3 Swing your bent leg down and through until your knee is under your chest. Return it to the start position and lower to the ground. Repeat the exercise using the other leg.

Care To avoid putting undue pressure on your lower spine, make sure that your spine is kept straight by not letting your head hang.

Repetitions 4

KNEELING HAND WALK

This simple exercise places much-needed pressure on your hand and arm joints and bones. At the end of the exercises, roll up to a standing position gradually – do not be tempted to pull yourself up by a piece of furniture.

1 Kneel down on all fours, keeping your back straight.

2 Keeping your knees and feet still, slowly walk your hands forward until your arms are carrying much of your weight. Be sure to keep your spine straight while you are doing this.

3 Now walk your hands out to the side. This will greatly increase the strength of the bones in your arms. Then walk your hands back in the reverse pattern until you are kneeling comfortably, balanced on all fours again. Repeat four times.

4 To stand up, lift your knees off the ground and then walk your legs forward until they are underneath your body, and roll up from there. As you slowly straighten your knees, try to keep touching your toes for as long as possible as this is another useful stretch for the back of your legs.

HIP STRETCH

This is perfect for doing when watching television or while playing with the children on the floor. Ensure that you provide sufficient support for your head with your hand.

Care Keep your hips in line with each other as you move your legs.

Repetitions 15 on each side

1 Lie on your left side, resting on your left elbow and using your hand to support your head. Steady yourself by putting your right hand on the floor in front of you. Your left leg should be slightly bent with your right knee pulled towards the body.

2 Extend the right leg in front of you, with the toe slightly raised from the floor. Hold this position for 5 seconds.

3 Lift your right leg to hip height and hold for 2 seconds, then lower to the floor. Repeat the sequence on the other side.

Care Move forwards into the resting position slowly and gradually.

Repetitions Once only

WIND DOWN

Relaxation is an important part of exercise – just as it is vital that you exercise the bones you should also allow them to rest and recover.

1 Assume a kneeling position on the floor. Place a cushion behind your knees and go to sit down. Your leg joints will be supported by the cushion. This is a comfortable position to relax in. You could also use this technique when gardening or doing any work on the floor to ensure that your joints are protected at all times.

2 Keep the cushion behind your knees. Place another cushion in front of you on the floor, and lower yourself on to all fours, resting on your elbows. Your forehead and lower arms should be resting on the cushion. Hold for as long as is comfortable.

RECIPES FOR STRONG BONES

The following recipes are excellent for building up and maintaining your bones' structure and strength. By ensuring that, throughout your life, your bones receive all the vitamins and minerals they need – such as calcium, magnesium, phosphorus and vitamins A, B, C, D and K – you can help to prevent osteoporosis in later life. These delicious recipes will provide you with inspiration to cook food in new and different ways, drawing on Eastern and Mediterranean influences as well as updating classic dishes such as colcannon and fruit crumble.

GRANOLA

Dried fruits are rich in potassium, which is involved in the function of all the cells in the body, while sesame, sunflower and linseeds are rich sources of essential fatty acids.

1 Place the butter, honey and vanilla essence in a small saucepan. Cook over a medium heat, stirring occasionally, for 5 minutes, or until the honey and butter are combined.

2 Place all the remaining ingredients, except the fruit, in a large bowl and mix well. Carefully stir in the butter mixture. Spread the mixture over the base of a large, non-stick roasting tin and place in a preheated oven at 160°C (325°F), Gas Mark 3, for 20 minutes, or until the grains are crisp and browned. Stir occasionally to prevent the mixture from sticking.

3 Remove from the oven and allow to cool. Stir in the dried fruit and serve with natural yogurt.

75 g (3 oz) butter

5 tablespoons clear honey

1 teaspoon vanilla essence

300 g (10 oz) rolled oats

50 g (2 oz) dried shredded coconut

50 g (2 oz) flaked almonds

3 tablespoons sunflower seeds

3 tablespoons pumpkin seeds

1 tablespoon sesame seeds

1 tablespoon linseeds

75 g (3 oz) rye flakes

75 g (3 oz) ready-to-eat dried mixed fruit salad, roughly chopped

TO SERVE

natural yogurt

Serves 4

Preparation time 3 minutes

Cooking time 15 minutes

Nutritional values per serving • 940 kcal • 52 g fat • 20 g saturated fat • 140 mg calcium

EGGS FLORENTINE

500 g (1 lb) spinach leaves, without stems

2 tablespoons thin cream or Greek yogurt

4 eggs

4 slices Swiss cheese

salt and freshly ground black pepper to taste

Spinach is a good source of iron, carotenes, B vitamins, vitamin C and the associated antioxidant chemicals (bioflavonoids and pycnogenols) and vitamin K. Eggs are a beneficial low-calorie source of protein, providing more nutrients per calorie than almost any other food. They are also rich in methionine, an important amino acid that benefits your liver. Although cream may have more appeal, a thick Greek-style yogurt would provide better nutrition.

1 Wash the spinach leaves, shake lightly and place in a dry saucepan. Put the lid on and cook over a gentle heat. When cooked, squeeze, drain off the excess liquid and chop the leaves finely. Add the cream or yogurt, season and place in an ovenproof dish.

2 Poach the eggs in gently simmering water. When cooked, place them on the bed of spinach. Cover each one with a slice of Swiss cheese and place the dish in a hot oven or under a warm grill until the cheese has melted.

Serves 4

Preparation time 3 minutes

Cooking time 15 minutes

195 kcal • 13 g fat • 6 g saturated fat • 423 mg calcium

BROCCOLI AND CHEESE SOUP

The minerals in the broccoli combine well with the calcium in the cheese and yogurt. Broccoli is a good source of vitamin K, carotenes and other antioxidant nutrients such as vitamin C, the bioflavonoids and pycnogenols. It is a good source of fibre if you include generous amounts of the stems, and the yogurt will help your digestive system.

1 Remove all the very tough stems and leaves from the broccoli. Cut off the stalks, peel them and cut, crossways, into thin slices. Break the florets into small pieces and set them aside.

2 Melt the butter or olive oil in a large saucepan. Add the onion and broccoli stalks and cook, covered, for 5 minutes over a moderate heat. Stir frequently.

3 Add the broccoli florets, potato and vegetable stock to the pan. Bring the mixture to the boil and cook, partially covered, for 5 minutes. Use a slotted spoon to remove 6 or more florets for a garnish and set aside. Season the mixture and continue to cook over a moderate heat for a few minutes until all the vegetables are just soft.

4 Use a blender or food processor and purée the mixture in batches until smooth, then transfer each batch to a saucepan. Add the lemon juice, Worcestershire sauce and a few drops of Tabasco sauce to the pan. Simmer for 3–5 minutes. Stir in the yogurt.

5 Just before serving, stir in the grated cheese and garnish each portion with the reserved florets and sprigs of watercress.

1 kg (2 lb) broccoli

50 g (2 oz) butter or olive oil

1 onion, chopped

1 large potato, peeled and quartered

1.5 litres (2½ pints) vegetable stock

1 tablespoon lemon juice

1 teaspoon Worcestershire sauce

few drops Tabasco sauce, or to taste

125 ml (4 fl oz) natural yogurt

125 g (4 oz) mature Cheddar cheese, grated

salt and freshly ground black pepper

TO GARNISH

sprigs of watercress

Serves 6

Preparation time 10 minutes

Cooking time 20 minutes

249 kcal • 16 g fat • 10 g saturated fat • 294 mg calcium

VEGETABLE BITES WITH DIPPING SAUCE

about 500 g (1 lb) vegetables of your choice

DIPPING SAUCE

125 g (4 oz) yellow bean sauce

½ onion, chopped

1 tablespoon tamarind (see right)

200 ml (7 fl oz) coconut milk

200 ml (7 fl oz) water

2 eggs

2 tablespoons honey

1 tablespoon soy sauce

TO GARNISH

1 large fresh red chilli, sliced lengthways

This dish allows you to use a variety of vitamin- and mineral-rich vegetables such as carrots, cucumber and courgette sticks, French beans, Chinese leaves, cauliflower florets and strips of red, orange and yellow peppers. Tamarind is a sour-tasting fruit, usually sold in blocks and soaked in hot water to extract the flavour. It can also be bought in paste form and mixed with water to give a runny consistency. Lemon juice can be used instead in this recipe, although it has less flavour.

1 Choose a mixture of raw vegetables and chop them into lengths.

2 To make the dipping sauce: blend the yellow bean sauce and the onion in a blender or food processor and then pour into a saucepan. Add the rest of the sauce ingredients and bring gradually to the boil, stirring. Remove from the heat and pour into a bowl.

3 Garnish the prepared sauce with slices of chilli and serve warm, with the vegetables.

Serves 4

Preparation time 15 minutes

Cooking time 5–6 minutes

160 kcal • 5 g fat • 1 g saturated fat • 95 mg calcium

CARROT, DAIKON AND RED PEPPER SALAD

Carrots are a good source of carotene and are high in fibre. Peppers, particularly the red ones, are an excellent source of vitamin C and contain nearly twice as much magnesium as calcium. Sesame seeds contain calcium and several of the B group of vitamins.

1 Cut the carrots, daikon and red pepper into julienne strips. Alternatively, you can peel them lengthways with a potato peeler. Lightly combine the vegetables and sesame seeds. Divide the mixture into four and arrange on four individual serving plates.

2 Warm the sesame oil, rice wine vinegar and coriander powder to blend the flavours. Allow to cool and pour the dressing over and around the salad. Garnish with spring onions and fresh coriander leaves.

3 carrots

1 small daikon (white radish)

1 large, firm red pepper

1 tablespoon toasted sesame seeds

DRESSING

1 teaspoon sesame oil

1 tablespoon rice wine vinegar

¼ teaspoon coriander powder

TO GARNISH

4 spring onions, finely shredded

coriander leaves

Serves 4

Preparation time 5–10 minutes

Cooking time 2–3 minutes

83 kcal • 4 g fat • 1 g saturated fat • 64 mg calcium

SWEET POTATO, ROCKET AND HALOUMI SALAD

500 g (1 lb) sweet potatoes, sliced

3 tablespoons olive oil

250 g (8 oz) haloumi cheese, patted dry on kitchen paper

100 g (3½ oz) rocket

DRESSING

5 tablespoons olive oil

3 tablespoons clear honey

2 tablespoons lemon or lime juice

1½ teaspoons black onion seeds

1 red chilli, deseeded and finely sliced

2 teaspoons chopped lemon thyme

freshly ground black pepper

This filling salad can be served as a light meal or with other leafy salad dishes. The calcium in the haloumi combines with the calcium and other minerals in the vegetables to make a nutritious meal. Sweet potatoes are an excellent choice for people with arthritis or other joint problems that might be aggravated by potatoes of the nightshade family. The rocket leaves provide a range of vitamins and minerals including vitamin K.

1 Mix together all the ingredients for the dressing in a small bowl. Do not be tempted to add salt because there is plenty in the haloumi cheese.

2 Cook the sweet potatoes in boiling water for 2 minutes and drain well. Heat the oil in a large frying pan, add the sweet potatoes and fry for about 10 minutes, turning once, until golden.

3 Meanwhile, thinly slice the cheese and place on a lightly oiled, foil-lined grill rack. Cook under a preheated moderate grill for about 3 minutes until golden, turning once.

4 Pile the sweet potatoes, cheese and rocket on to serving plates and spoon the dressing over them.

Serves 4

Preparation time 10 minutes

Cooking time 15 minutes

548 kcal • 37 g fat • 12 g saturated fat • 312 mg calcium

VEGETABLE RICE PANCAKES

Who says vegetables are dull? These paper-thin rice pancakes make interesting wraps for a variety of tempting fillings such as this light combination of vegetables. Served with a highly flavoured sauce, they make an intriguing starter to any meal. Allow two rice pancakes for each person or one each if there is a heavy meal to follow.

1 Place all the ingredients for the sauce, except the sesame seeds, in a food processor or blender and process to a thin paste. Alternatively, crush the garlic, grate the ginger and whisk in with the remaining ingredients. Stir in the sesame seeds and transfer to a serving bowl.

2 Soften the rice pancakes by following the instructions on the packet. Combine the carrots, bean sprouts or sprouting beans, mint, celery, spring onions and soy sauce.

3 Divide the vegetable mixture among the pancakes, spooning it into the middle of each. Fold in the bottom edge of each pancake to the middle, then roll up from one side to the other to form a pocket.

4 Steam the pancakes in a vegetable steamer or bamboo steamer for about 5 minutes until they are heated through. Alternatively, place the pancakes on a wire rack set over a roasting tin of boiling water and cover with foil. Serve immediately with the sauce, garnished with sesame seeds.

SAUCE

1 **garlic clove, roughly chopped**

5 **cm (2 in) piece fresh root ginger, peeled and roughly chopped**

3 **tablespoons light muscovado sugar or honey**

4 **teaspoons soy sauce**

5 **teaspoons wine or rice vinegar**

2 **tablespoons tomato purée**

2 **tablespoons sesame seeds, plus extra to garnish**

8 **rice pancakes**

PANCAKE FILLING

2 **medium carrots, cut into fine shreds**

100 **g (3½ oz) bean sprouts or mixed sprouting beans**

small handful of mint, roughly chopped

1 **celery stick, thinly sliced**

4 **spring onions, thinly sliced diagonally**

1 **tablespoon soy sauce**

Serves 4
Preparation time 15 minutes
Cooking time 5 minutes

183 kcal • 6 g fat • 1 g saturated fat • 97 mg calcium

CELERIAC AND POTATO REMOULADE

500 g (1 lb) celeriac, peeled

375 g (12 oz) potatoes, peeled

1 tablespoon extra virgin olive oil, plus extra for drizzling (optional)

500 g (1 lb) asparagus, trimmed

SAUCE

150 ml (5 fl oz) mayonnaise

150 ml (5 fl oz) Greek yogurt

1 teaspoon Dijon mustard

6 cocktail gherkins, finely chopped

2 tablespoons capers, chopped

2 tablespoons chopped tarragon

salt and freshly ground black pepper

Make this into a complete meal for a light lunch or supper by lightly poaching some eggs and arranging them over the asparagus. Celeriac, the root vegetable with a flavour similar to celery, is a good source of minerals and fibre and the yogurt adds calcium and protein to the dish.

1 Cut the celeriac and potatoes into matchstick-sized pieces. Cook the celeriac in lightly salted boiling water for 2 minutes or until softened. Add the potatoes and cook for a further 2 minutes or until just tender. Drain the vegetables then refresh them under cold running water.

2 Mix together the ingredients for the sauce and set aside.

3 Heat the oil in a frying pan or griddle pan. Add the asparagus and fry for 2–3 minutes until just beginning to colour. Mix the celeriac and potato with the sauce and spoon on to 4 serving plates. Arrange the asparagus spears on top and serve immediately, drizzled with a little extra olive oil if wished.

Serves 4

Preparation time 10 minutes

Cooking time 10 minutes

456 kcal • 36 g fat • 7 g saturated fat • 156 mg calcium

SPICY ROAST VEGETABLES

These lightly spiced roast vegetables are delicious as a starter, a side dish or a finger snack. Although called roast vegetables, they are actually better cooked in a large, heavy-based grill pan. Since the vegetables in this dish are mainly 'fruits', it is not surprising to find it is an excellent source of vitamin C and the antioxidant bioflavonoids and pycnogenols.

1 Heat the grill pan for 2 minutes. Pour in the olive oil, then add the cumin seeds. Lower the heat to medium.

2 Arrange all the vegetables in the pan with a pair of tongs, then add the green chillies, garlic, ginger and red chillies. Sprinkle with salt. Increase the heat and cook the vegetables for 7–10 minutes, turning them with tongs.

3 Serve hot garnished with the lemon wedges and fresh coriander. Some thick Greek-style yogurt served as an accompaniment adds an interesting contrast, provides both protein and calcium and benefits your digestion.

2 tablespoons extra virgin olive oil

½ teaspoon white cumin seeds

1 green pepper, cored, deseeded and thickly sliced

1 red pepper, cored, deseeded and thickly sliced

1 orange pepper, cored, deseeded and thickly sliced

2 courgettes, diagonally sliced

2 tomatoes, halved

2 red onions, quartered

1 aubergine, thickly sliced

2 thick fresh green chillies, sliced

4 garlic cloves

2.5 cm (1 in) piece fresh root ginger, peeled and shredded

1 teaspoon dried, crushed red chillies

½ teaspoon salt

TO GARNISH

1 tablespoon chopped fresh coriander

lemon wedges

TO SERVE

thick Greek-style yogurt (optional)

Serves 6

Preparation time 10 minutes

Cooking time 15 minutes

85 kcal • 4 g fat • 1 g saturated fat • 34 mg calcium

LEMON GRASS AND TOFU NUGGETS WITH CHILLI SAUCE

1 bunch of spring onions

5 cm (2 in) piece of fresh root ginger, peeled and chopped

2 lemon grass stalks, roughly chopped

small handful of coriander

3 garlic cloves, roughly chopped

1 teaspoon honey

1 tablespoon light soy sauce

300 g (10 oz) tofu, drained

75 g (3 oz) wholemeal breadcrumbs

1 egg

oil, for shallow-frying

salt and freshly ground black pepper

DIPPING SAUCE

1 tablespoon clear honey

2 tablespoons soy sauce

1 red chilli, deseeded and sliced

2 tablespoons orange juice

Including generous amounts of soya beans and soya products in your diet will have special benefits for the health of your bones. You can buy soya mince, fine or coarse, and use it in a range of dishes just as you would use beef mince. Simply add it instead of the meat and use extra liquid (stock or water) to allow for the fact that it is a dried product and will soak up a lot of the liquid from the recipe.

1 Thinly slice a spring onion and set aside. Roughly chop the remaining ones and place in a food processor with the ginger, lemon grass, coriander and garlic. Process lightly until mixed together and chopped but still chunky. Add the honey, soy sauce, tofu, breadcrumbs, egg, salt and pepper, and process until just combined.

2 Take dessertspoonfuls of the mixture and pat into flat cakes using lightly floured hands.

3 Make the dipping sauce. Mix together all the ingredients, adding the reserved sliced spring onion, and place in a small serving bowl.

4 Heat the oil in a large non-stick frying pan. Add half the tofu cakes and fry gently for 1–2 minutes on each side until golden. Drain on kitchen paper and keep warm while frying the remainder. Serve on a platter with the dipping sauce.

Serves 4

Preparation time 10 minutes

Cooking time 10 minutes

205 kcal • 11 g fat • 2 g saturated fat • 422 mg calcium

ROOT VEGETABLE BAKE

These root vegetables are a source of many nutrients as well as fibre. Watercress, a rich source of minerals and vitamins, and alkalizing alfalfa sprouts, would be an alternative garnish. For a creamier texture serve the vegetable bake with a dish of natural yogurt.

1 Cook the potatoes in a pan of boiling water until just tender. Lift out and cut into 5 mm (¼ in) slices and set aside. Return the water to the boil, add the remaining vegetables and simmer until just tender. Drain the vegetables and place in layers in a deep ovenproof dish, alternating with the potatoes and finishing with a border of overlapping potato slices. Pour over the stock, sprinkle with the cheese and season with salt and pepper.

2 Preheat the oven to 180°C (350°F), Gas Mark 4, and bake for 15–20 minutes or until the cheese has melted and the vegetables are heated through. Brown under a moderately hot grill to finish, if wished.

3 Garnish with tomato slices and chopped parsley.

500 g (1 lb) new potatoes, washed

250 g (8 oz) swede, peeled and cubed

300 g (10 oz) parsnips, peeled and sliced

250 g (8 oz) carrots, peeled and cut into sticks

65 ml (2½ fl oz) vegetable stock

50 g (2 oz) reduced-fat cheese, preferably Edam or Cheddar, grated

salt and freshly ground black pepper

TO GARNISH

tomato slices

1 tablespoon chopped fresh parsley

Serves 4

Preparation time 20 minutes

Cooking time 40–50 minutes

208 kcal • 4 g fat • 2 g saturated fat • 198 mg calcium

KALE AND POTATO COLCANNON

500 g (1 lb) kale or green leaf cabbage, stalks removed and finely shredded

500 g (1 lb) potatoes, unpeeled

6 spring onions or chives, finely chopped

150 ml (5 fl oz) milk or natural yogurt

125 g (4 oz) butter

salt and freshly ground black pepper

Cabbage is a rich source of vitamins A, B and C, and a good source of iron, potassium and calcium, so this dish provides an excellent mix of nutrients and vitamins for the bones.

1 Place the kale or cabbage and the potatoes separately in large saucepans of boiling water and cook until tender – about 10–20 minutes for the kale or cabbage, longer for the potatoes.

2 Meanwhile, place the spring onions or chives and milk or yogurt in a small saucepan and simmer over a low heat for about 5 minutes.

3 Drain the kale or cabbage. Mash with a fork so that it is ready to be added to the potato when it has been drained and mashed.

4 Drain the potatoes. Holding them in a tea towel, peel them carefully while warm and mash well with a potato masher or fork. Add the hot milk or yogurt mixture, beating well to give a soft, fluffy texture.

5 Beat in the mashed kale or cabbage, season with salt and pepper, to taste, and add half the butter. The colcannon should be a speckled green colour.

6 Heat through thoroughly, and then serve in warmed individual dishes or bowls. Make a well in the centre of each serving and put a knob or the remaining butter in each one. Serve immediately.

Serves 4–6

Preparation time 20 minutes

Cooking time 20 minutes

386 kcal • 29 g fat • 18 g saturated fat • 224 mg calcium

STIR-FRIED CHICKEN WITH CRUNCHY VEGETABLES

In the interests of preventing osteoporosis, the main emphasis in this recipe section has been on vegetables, soya dishes and dairy products. Here are a couple of meat dishes in which mineral-rich vegetables play a part. These vegetables provide minerals, vitamins and fibre, thus benefiting your bones and your digestion, but you could also try other vegetables such as green beans or broccoli.

1   Prepare the sauce. Mix the cornflour to a thin paste with the water, then stir in the soy sauce. Set aside.

2   Heat a wok until hot. Add the oil and heat over a moderate heat. Add the chicken strips, increase the heat and stir-fry for 3–4 minutes until lightly coloured on all sides. Remove from the heat and transfer the chicken to a plate with a slotted spoon.

3   Return the wok to a moderate heat until hot. Add all the vegetables and garlic and stir-fry for 2–3 minutes or until the green pepper is just beginning to soften.

4   Stir the sauce to mix it, then pour into the wok. Increase the heat to high and toss the ingredients until the sauce thickens and coats the vegetables. Add the chicken with its juices and toss for 1–2 minutes or until all the ingredients are combined. Add pepper to taste and serve at once.

1 teaspoon vegetable oil

500 g (1 lb) chicken breasts, skinned, boned and cut into thin strips across the grain

125 g (4 oz) white cabbage, finely shredded

125 g (4 oz) bean sprouts

1 large green pepper, cored, deseeded and cut lengthways into thin strips

2 medium carrots, cut lengthways into thin strips

2 garlic cloves, crushed

freshly ground black pepper

SAUCE

2 teaspoons cornflour

4 tablespoons water

3 tablespoons soy sauce

Serves 4

Preparation time 15 minutes

Cooking time 6–10 minutes

205 kcal • 5 g fat • 1 g saturated fat • 49 mg calcium

SWEET AND SOUR CHINESE TURKEY

500 g (1 lb) turkey breast

2 tablespoons lemon juice

5 tablespoons orange juice

4–5 celery sticks

2 sharon fruits or firm tomatoes

8–10 radishes

½ Chinese cabbage

1 large green pepper, cored and deseeded

1 tablespoon oil

150 ml (5 fl oz) chicken stock

1½ teaspoons cornflour

1 tablespoon soy sauce

1 tablespoon clear honey

brown rice, to serve

vegetable salad, to serve

This is an excellent example of how to create dishes that combine meat with nutrient-rich vegetables to the benefit of your total health. Sharon fruit is a type of persimmon, which can be eaten like an apple. The skin is edible or, if you prefer, the fruit can be peeled.

1   Cut the turkey breast into thin strips. Marinate in the lemon and orange juices for 30 minutes.

2   Cut the celery, sharon fruits or tomatoes, radishes, Chinese cabbage and green pepper into small, neat pieces and set aside.

3   Heat the oil in a large non-stick frying pan or wok. Drain the turkey and reserve the marinade. Fry the turkey in the oil until nearly tender. Add the prepared vegetables and heat for just 2–3 minutes.

4   Blend the chicken stock with the marinade and the cornflour. Add the soy sauce and honey. Pour this mixture over the ingredients in the pan and stir until thickened and cooked through. Serve immediately, with brown rice and a large fresh vegetable salad.

Serves 4

Preparation time 15 minutes, plus marinating

Cooking time 15–20 minutes

209 kcal • 5 g fat • 1 g saturated fat • 60 mg calcium

SUMMER FRUIT COMPOTE

Berries are delicious and excellent sources of nutrients as they are high in the antioxidant vitamins C, E and betacarotene as well as sodium and sulphur. Oranges are also high in vitamins C and magnesium, while yogurt is a good source of calcium and vitamins A, B, D and E.

1   Place the fruit, orange rind and juice and redcurrant jelly in a large saucepan. Cover and cook gently for 5 minutes, or until the juices flow and the fruit is softened. Remove from the heat and set aside. Chill and serve with soya yogurt.

250 g (8 oz) mixed summer fruit, such as raspberries, blueberries and strawberries, thawed if frozen

finely grated rind and juice of 1 large orange

1 tablespoon redcurrant jelly

250 g (8 oz) plain soya yogurt, to serve

Serves 2
Preparation time 5 minutes
Cooking time 5 minutes

169 kcal • 6 g fat • 1 g saturated fat • 32 mg calcium

FRUIT AND NUT CRUMBLE

175 g (6 oz) dried apricots

125 g (4 oz) dried pitted prunes

125 g (4 oz) dried figs

50 g (2 oz) dried apples

600 ml (1 pint) apple juice

100 g (3½ oz) wholewheat flour

50 g (2 oz) margarine

50 g (2 oz) muscovado or soft
  brown sugar, sifted

50 g (2 oz) hazelnuts, chopped

TO SERVE

low-fat yogurt

TO GARNISH

rosemary sprigs

Dried fruit such as apricots and prunes add to the iron content of the diet. Absorption of iron is aided by vitamin C, but inhibited by a number of other factors, including drinking tea.

1   Place the dried fruits in a bowl with the apple juice and leave overnight to soak. Transfer to a saucepan and simmer for 10–15 minutes, until softened. Turn into an ovenproof dish.

2   Sift the flour into a bowl and rub in the margarine until the mixture resembles breadcrumbs. Stir in the sugar, reserving a little to serve, and the hazelnuts, then sprinkle the crumble over the fruit.

3   Bake in a preheated oven at 200°C (400°F), Gas Mark 6 for 25–30 minutes. Serve with low-fat yogurt, if liked, sprinkled with the reserved sugar and garnished with rosemary.

Serves 6

Preparation time 15 minutes,
  plus soaking

Cooking time 35–50 minutes

394 kcal • 13 g fat • less than 1 g saturated fat • 118 mg calcium

CHAPTER 6
HEALTHY HEART

Heart disease is caused by two processes. First, atherosclerosis can result from a build-up of a fatty substance called atheroma on the inner lining of blood vessels, which reduces blood flow to an area of the body and can result in pain. Second, thrombosis occurs when these fatty deposits rupture, allowing a blood clot to form, and then travel until it blocks a vessel, which may result in a heart attack or stroke.

Although premenopausal women are afforded some protection from heart disease by the hormone oestrogen, after the menopause their incidence of heart disease soon matches that of men. Following a balanced diet low in saturated fat is a great way to reduce your chances of developing heart disease. This chapter shows you the good food choices you can make and provides recipes to inspire you to healthier eating.

CHOLESTEROL

This white waxy substance is vital for the human body – it forms cell membranes, various hormones, bile salts and vitamin D. Excess blood cholesterol, however, can increase your risk of heart disease. Most cholesterol is made in the liver, but some is absorbed directly from food by the digestive system. Foods high in saturated fat, such as fatty meats and meat products, eggs, butter, cheese, whole milk, cream, pastries, cakes and confectionery, increase blood cholesterol levels.

TOTAL CHOLESTEROL

Depending on your case, your doctor may first want to find out what your total cholesterol level is. If it's higher than 5 mmol/L (200 mg/dL) then he or she may send another blood test for a breakdown of the different lipids in your blood.

'GOOD' AND 'BAD' CHOLESTEROL

Cholesterol travels to your body's cells through the bloodstream in tiny packages called lipoproteins. Scientists distinguish the types of cholesterol packages by their density, and the most important types are low-density lipoprotein (LDL) cholesterol and high-density lipoprotein cholesterol (HDL) cholesterol. Most blood cholesterol is carried as LDL cholesterol from the liver to other parts of the body.

Having a high level of LDL cholesterol increases your risk of heart disease because when oxidized it can slowly build up in the walls of coronary arteries and, ultimately, cause a heart attack. Doctors regard LDL cholesterol as 'bad' cholesterol, and so the lower your LDL cholesterol level the better. Your target level of LDL cholesterol should be below 3 mmol/L (195 mg/dL).

HDL cholesterol, on the other hand, is 'good' cholesterol. It acts as an arterial scavenger, carrying cholesterol away from body tissues, including artery walls, and back to the liver. The higher your HDL cholesterol level the lower your risk of heart disease. The target level of HDL for women is above 1.2 mmol/L (45 mg/dL). Experts believe that HDL removes excess cholesterol from atherosclerotic plaques on blood vessel walls, thereby slowing their build-up.

TRIGLYCERIDES

Calories that are not used immediately are converted into triglycerides and stored in fat cells. If you have a high triglyceride level (above 2.0 mmol/L (77 mg/dL)) you run an increased risk of heart disease.

HINT FOR HEALTH

There is a simple test that your doctor can do to check your blood cholesterol levels, which will enable you to make an informed decision about whether you need to change your current diet and reduce your intake of saturated fat.

See also ▶

Health issues, pages 102–103

What are your risk factors?, pages 182–183

Healthy eating for a healthy heart, pages 188–189

WHAT ARE YOUR RISK FACTORS?

A number of factors influence the incidence of heart disease. Ones you cannot change include your age and your family history; you are at increased risk if there is heart disease in your family. Factors that can be reduced or eliminated include high blood cholesterol levels, high blood pressure, smoking, diabetes, and being overweight and physically inactive.

FOUR STEPS TO A HEALTHY HEART

1 **Eat healthily** Avoid eating too much saturated fat and instead eat plenty of fish, poultry, fruit and vegetables, and maintain a healthy bodyweight.

2 **Be more active** Half an hour every day is enough to make a difference and it is easy to build into your daily routine. Start off gently and gradually build up.

3 **Be smoke-free** From the moment you stop smoking, your risk of heart attack starts to fall and is halved within one year of giving up.

4 **Reduce your alcohol intake** Binge drinking increases your risk of having a heart attack.

COMMON RISK FACTORS

Several factors influence the incidence of heart disease, but they can be reduced or even eliminated by changes in diet and lifestyle.

CHOLESTEROL

The lower your cholesterol level the more you reduce your risk of heart disease (see page 181). If you already have heart disease or are at a high risk of developing it, your doctor may have prescribed medication to modify your cholesterol levels. The benefits of these drugs are significant and their effect is enhanced by a healthy diet.

TRIGLYCERIDES

These lipids or fats are absorbed from food or made in the body, and people with high triglyceride levels have an increased risk of heart disease (see page 181). Diets high in carbohydrates and alcohol, as well as other factors, can raise triglyceride levels.

HIGH BLOOD PRESSURE

If you have high blood pressure, this adds to the workload of your heart, causing it to enlarge. As you age, your arteries harden and become less elastic, and high blood pressure speeds up this process.

DIABETES

People with diabetes are at high risk of heart disease, stroke and peripheral vascular disease. If you have diabetes, you should follow a healthy lifestyle and use appropriate drug therapy.

SMOKING

Smoking increases the risk of heart attack and stroke. Even passive smoking significantly increases the risk of heart disease.

NEGATIVE FACTORS

Low intake of fruit and vegetables If we all ate five portions a day, the incidence of heart disease, stroke and cancers would fall by 20 per cent.

Saturated fats These are mainly found in animal foods such as butter, cream, lard, fatty meats, burgers, sausages, pies and pasties, but also in some vegetable sources, particularly palm oil and coconut.

Adding extra fats Try to limit the amount of fat you add to foods – spread margarine or butter thinly, opt for tomato-based rather than cream-based sauces, and choose your cooking method carefully. Keep fried foods for a treat, roast without adding fat, stir-fry, boil or casserole.

Raised cholesterol levels Often caused by a diet high in saturated fats. If your cholesterol level is high, choose a cholesterol-lowering spread in place of butter or margarine.

Low-fibre diet This leaves you feeling hungry, constipated and sluggish. Increasing fibre intake reduces fatigue and boosts energy levels by 10 per cent.

Weight gain Bad for both your self-esteem and your general health. The most common cause is inactivity.

POSITIVE FACTORS

Antioxidants These hugely beneficial chemicals are found in fruit, vegetables, red wine and grape juice. Try to eat at least five portions of fruit and vegetables each day.

Polyunsaturated and monounsaturated fats These help to moderate cholesterol levels if eaten in moderation. They include olive, sunflower, soya, rapeseed (canola) and corn oils, and spreads or margarines made from these.

Soya and phytoestrogens Phytoestrogen-rich soya foods are proven to lower cholesterol levels and protect the heart. Try to include three servings of a soya food in your diet daily.

Oily fish Try to eat herring, mackerel, trout, salmon, pilchards or sardines once or twice every week.

High-fibre cereal foods These provide a long-lasting source of energy, keep you feeling full and offer a great source of dietary fibre, which helps to control cholesterol and blood-sugar levels. Choose wholegrain breads, cereals and pasta as often as you can.

Increased activity This helps the heart and muscles get fitter, boosts the metabolism, helping with weight control, and is a fantastic mood-enhancer.

'The lower your cholesterol level the lower your risk of heart disease.'

See also ▶
Healthy eating for a longer life, Chapter 3
Healthy eating for a healthy heart, pages 188–189
Top 10 tips to protect your heart, pages 190–191
A healthy heart diet, pages 192–193

KEEPING YOUR BODY AND HEART ACTIVE

Exercise is absolutely essential for a healthy heart. Your heart is a muscle, and like any other muscle it can be trained to become strong so that it can pump more blood with each heartbeat, giving you more stamina. Being active is also a great way to help you relax and to control stress levels, another risk factor for heart disease.

'Your heart is a muscle, and like any other muscle it can be trained to become strong.'

TAKING DAILY EXERCISE

There is no need to join an expensive gym or take part in organized sport unless you want to and will therefore keep it up. Simple activities like walking, gardening, cycling and generally incorporating more activity into your daily life can be just as effective as a more structured exercise programme. The exercise you choose should be both enjoyable and safe, especially if you have already been diagnosed with atherosclerosis or if you have had a heart attack.

CHOOSING THE BEST EXERCISE FOR YOU

There are three main types of exercise to help you become fitter and healthier: aerobic exercise, strength and muscular endurance exercises, and flexibility exercises. These are commonly summed up as stamina, strength and suppleness. Although aerobic exercise often receives the most attention, especially in relation to heart disease, it is important not to overlook the other types of exercise for overall fitness.

STAMINA

Aerobic exercise, also known as endurance or cardiovascular exercise, is designed to increase the strength of your heart muscle and thus your stamina. Over a period of time, regular aerobic exercise improves your body's ability to extract oxygen from the blood and transport it to the rest of the body, including your lungs. It also improves the ability of your body to use oxygen efficiently and to burn (or metabolize) fats and carbohydrates for energy, which is vital if you are trying to control your weight. As time goes on, your heart is able to pump more blood with each stroke and so is able to do more for less effort.

In practice, aerobic exercise means any exercise that makes you feel hot and sweaty and slightly breathless. This includes activities like

walking, running, cycling, tennis, swimming or using any of the cardiovascular machines you may find in a gym, such as the stairwalker, treadmill or rowing machine.

STRENGTH

The second type of exercise helps to make your muscles stronger; it is also known as anaerobic exercise because it does not involve the muscles using oxygen as with aerobic exercise. It may involve the use of free weights and machines or any kind of exercise in which you use your own bodyweight to load the muscles – for example, press-ups, lunges and squats or some of the exercises involved in Pilates and yoga (see Chapter 2 and pages 152–161). Using this type of exercise, makes muscle more active metabolically than fat, so even at rest, you'll burn more calories. It is therefore excellent as an adjunct to aerobic exercise if you want to control your weight.

SUPPLENESS

Suppleness exercises include any kind of exercise which involves stretching your muscles. Stretching helps to relax and lengthen muscles, encouraging improved blood flow to the muscles, which in turn aids muscle healing. Yoga and Pilates are gentle forms of exercise which can be especially beneficial to people with heart problems as they help to calm the mind and body and reduce stress.

HOW MUCH EXERCISE SHOULD YOU DO?

Experts now recommend that you should aim to do some kind of moderate aerobic exercise, such as walking, swimming or cycling for 30 minutes, on most days. If you find it hard to do this amount of exercise in one session, you can split it up into shorter periods.

HOW INTENSELY SHOULD YOU EXERCISE?

For aerobic fitness, you need to work at somewhere between 60 and 75 per cent of your heart's maximum capacity. By and large, this means that while you are exercising you should aim to be slightly out of breath, but not so breathless that you are unable to carry on a conversation, and feel hot and slightly sweaty, but not so exhausted that you feel you cannot go on. As a rule of thumb, you should feel that the effort you are applying is moderately hard.

WHEN TO AVOID EXERCISE

Do not exercise if you are suffering from any of the following:

- Chest pain – consult a doctor immediately.
- Uncontrolled high blood pressure.
- Injured bones or joints.
- Severe sunburn.
- Severe hangover.
- Nausea or dizziness.
- Swelling or sudden weight gain.
- Dehydration.
- Asthma or other lung problems – especially if it is very hot, humid or cold.
- Chronic medical condition.

HOW MUCH IS ENOUGH?

If you experience any or all of the following, you may be exercising too intensively:

- Dizziness, light-headedness or confusion.
- Cramp-like pains in the legs.
- Pale or bluish skin tone.
- Breathlessness lasting for more than 10 minutes.
- Palpitations (rapid or irregular heartbeat).
- Continued fatigue (lasting for 24 hours or more).
- Insomnia.
- Fluid retention.

If you have been sedentary, you must check with your doctor before embarking on any form of exercise programme; this is especially important if you are also overweight, have heart disease, or any heart-disease risk factors such as high blood pressure, a family history of heart disease or other chronic conditions such as arthritis, diabetes or a bad back. If you do decide to join a gym or exercise class, the instructors should be made aware if you have high blood pressure and/or any symptoms of heart disease so that a programme can be devised that is both safe and healthy. If you have not exercised for some time, it is important to start gradually and build up slowly.

MOVING ON

As you get fitter, you may get bored or find that your exercise becomes easy. You can then increase the complexity of what you do – for example, by including some hills in your walk or programming in some hills on the treadmill at the gym. You may also want to start to include more complex activities such as dance, tennis or windsurfing, which involve working at a different pace for varying lengths of time.

ACTIVITY AFTER A HEART ATTACK

If you are recovering from a heart attack or heart surgery, exercise can aid recovery and help you feel better more quickly. It can also help to prevent further damage to your heart and blood vessels. Some hospitals, physiotherapists and/or doctors run rehabilitation programmes designed to improve your overall fitness, which may include advice on diet, exercise and stress management training.

KEEPING AT IT

There are a few pointers to take on board to make your goals for becoming more active and more healthy a more permanent feature of yourlife, rather than a short-lived phenomenon.

- **Pick an activity you enjoy** If you join a gym when you hate gyms, you are unlikely to keep up your exercise programme. The secret is to choose a sport you always enjoyed at school, or something unusual like a flamenco class.

HINT FOR HEALTH

Before you start any new kind of exercise routine, always check with your doctor first, especially if you already have a medical condition, are unfit or are overweight.

- **Take it slowly** Too much too soon and you risk developing injuries or giving up because of pain or exhaustion. Always warm up for a few minutes (see pages 42–45) before you start.

- **Plan for setbacks** It can be difficult to find time for exercise, especially if you have a busy job or a young family to look after. Have a look at your daily timetable and find ways in which you might be able to fit in exercise. For example, get up an hour earlier, have a walk in the lunch hour or get a friend to babysit while you go to the gym or an exercise class.

- **Stay motivated** One of the best ways to keep up your enthusiasm is to join a class (where the teacher supplies the motivation) or to exercise with a friend. You are more likely to stick to your exercise plan if you enlist support.

- **Pay attention to comfort** Wear loose, comfortable clothing that allows you to move easily and that absorbs sweat. You should choose a good pair of 'cross training' shoes that support your heels and your arches.

- **Drink water** It is important to stay hydrated when you exercise in order to replace fluids that are lost in sweating. Take a bottle of water with you and take regular gulps, topping up as necessary. See also page 19.

- **Listen to your body** Exercise can be uncomfortable, especially if you are not used to it, when you first start. But it should not be painful or completely exhausting. Your body is the best judge of how much exercise you are capable of doing. Learn to listen to it and heed any warning signs.

'Yoga and Pilates can be especially beneficial to people with heart problems as they help to calm the mind and body and reduce stress.'

EVERYDAY EXERCISE

Keeping fit doesn't have to mean going to the gym everyday. The following activities can count as aerobic exercise. Try to do at least 30 minutes of exercise a day, and if you don't have 30 minutes at a time to spare, try to do 15 minutes twice, or ten minutes three times, a day.

- **Getting off the bus** a stop earlier than your usual one and walking the rest of the way to work.

- **Walking or cycling** short journeys instead of taking the car.

- **Pedalling on an exercise bike** while reading or watching television.

- **Energetic housework**, such as cleaning floors or windows.

- **Vigorous gardening**, such as weeding or clearing leaves.

See also ▶
Loosen up and shape up, Chapter 2
The feel-good factor, Chapter 9

HEALTHY EATING FOR A HEALTHY HEART

There is a wealth of information that links diet and the risk of heart disease. The emerging picture is that we should adopt a pattern of healthy eating (see Chapter 3) that can protect against heart disease. But there is no single individual dietary intervention that will guard you against heart disease, and you must look to make several changes to maximize the cardioprotective potential of what you eat.

LOW GI FOODS

There is now evidence that men and women who keep to foods with a low glycaemic index (GI) are less likely to develop insulin resistance, diabetes and heart disease. Glycaemic index is a measurement of the effects of carbohydrate-rich foods on blood glucose levels. Starchy foods that take a long time to be digested and absorbed into the body have a low GI, and these foods have a favourable effect on blood glucose and insulin. This improves the balance of blood lipids, increasing the protective HDL cholesterol and lowering triglyceride levels.

SATURATED FAT

In the 1960s, a study now known as the Seven Countries Study led by Ancel Keys showed a link between saturated fat intake and the rate of heart disease in seven countries. Keys showed that in Japan and the rural Mediterranean countries of Southern Europe, such as Greece and Italy, where the intake of saturated fat from meat and dairy products was low, there were significantly lower rates of heart disease than in the UK and the USA, where intakes of saturated fat were higher.

THE MEDITERRANEAN DIET

The characteristic Mediterranean diet is high in fruit, vegetables, bread and other forms of cereals, potatoes, beans, nuts and seeds. It features olive oil as an important fat source, while dairy products, fish, poultry and eggs are consumed in low to moderate amounts. Little red meat is eaten, but a glass or two of wine compensates! A Mediterranean-style diet certainly has a favourable effect on blood cholesterol concentrations. So what are the possible heart-protective mechanisms behind the Mediterranean-style diet?

FRUIT AND VEGETABLES

The Mediterranean-style diet is high in fruit and vegetables, which are rich in vitamins and minerals, essential fatty acids and antioxidants. There are about 600 antioxidants and these include the ACE vitamins, (beta-carotene, which is converted to vitamin A in the body, vitamin C and vitamin E), minerals (selenium and zinc) and various other compounds that give fruit and vegetables their fabulous colours (flavonoids and phenols). Red wine and tea are also known to be good sources of antioxidants.

The antioxidants do exactly what their name implies – they protect LDL cholesterol from becoming oxidized. Oxidized LDL cholesterol is much more toxic than LDL cholesterol and more likely to accumulate in the artery walls. Fruit and vegetables also supply other protective nutrients. For example, folic acid is found in dark green vegetables, fruit and whole grains, and helps to maintain lower levels of homocysteine in the blood. High levels of homocysteine are linked to an increased risk of heart disease.

OLIVE OIL

Containing mainly monounsaturated fats, olive oil replaces saturated fat in the Mediterranean diet and lowers total and 'bad' LDL cholesterol without decreasing the 'good' HDL cholesterol (see page 181). However, substituting saturated fat with high levels of polyunsaturated fat or 'good' carbohydrates can decrease HDL cholesterol.

THE BENEFITS OF SOYA BEANS

In Asian countries, with high intakes of soya-bean products, there is also a lower incidence of cardiovascular disease. Soya beans contain phytoestrogens (see pages 110–115), naturally occurring compounds that bear a structural similarity to oestrogen. Phytoestrogens have a beneficial effect on the lipid pattern, especially in postmenopausal women. Isoflavones in soya products also exert a favourable effect on the lining of blood vessels and improve vascular tone.

THE BENEFITS OF OMEGA-3 FATTY ACIDS

One of the most remarkable dietary discoveries in recent years has been the role fish can play in preventing heart disease. People who eat fish and shellfish regularly, such as the Japanese and Greenland Inuits, have fewer heart attacks than non-fish-eaters. Oily fish is the richest source of the polyunsaturated fatty acids – eicosapentanoic acid (EPA) and docosahexanoic acid (DHA), or omega-3 fatty acids.

Omega-3 fatty acids are also found in plants. An example is alpha-linolenic acid, found in seed oils, soya, nuts and green vegetables, which can actually make EPA and DHA in the body. Omega-3 fatty acids can play an important part in blood-clotting mechanisms, making the blood less sticky and reducing the risk of thrombosis. They also reduce irregular and potentially fatal heart arrhythmias.

APPLE- OR PEAR-SHAPED?

The shape you are has a link with heart disease. If you are apple-shaped, where fat is deposited around your stomach, you are at greater risk of heart disease than if you are pear-shaped, with fat distributed over your hips and thighs. This is because fat cells over the stomach make the body more resistant to the hormone insulin. To compensate, more insulin is produced, which in turn increases blood pressure, cholesterol and triglycerides, lowers HDL cholesterol and increases the tendency for the blood to form clots; and of course your risk of becoming diabetic is increased. This clustering of risk factors is known as the insulin resistance syndrome.

See also ▶

Healthy eating for a longer life, Chapter 3
What are your risk factors?, pages 182–183
Top 10 tips to protect your heart, pages 190–191
A healthy heart diet, pages 192–193
Recipes for a healthy heart, pages 194–209

TOP 10 TIPS TO PROTECT YOUR HEART

1 ENJOY A WIDE VARIETY OF NUTRITIOUS FOODS

Eat a combination of different foods, which will help to give you all the essential nutrients in balanced proportions. Try to adopt the Mediterranean diet most of the time (see pages 188–189), making simple changes one at a time. Above all, enjoy your food.

2 BE A HEALTHY WEIGHT FOR YOUR HEIGHT

Make sure you maintain a healthy weight for your height, or lose weight sensibly if you know you're overweight. You should aim to keep your waist circumference under 80 cm (31½ in). If it is more than this, you should try to lose some weight.

3 EAT PLENTY OF FRUIT, VEGETABLES AND SALAD

Eat at least five portions of fruit or vegetables a day – one portion is about the size of a clenched fist and five portions should add up to 500 g (1 lb) in weight.

4 EAT FISH TWO OR THREE TIMES A WEEK

Eat more fish, particularly oily fish such as mackerel, pilchards, trout and salmon, especially if you have had a heart attack. Oily fish are the richest source of omega-3 fatty acids (see page 189). White fish and shellfish also contain some omega-3 fatty acids.

5 BASE MEALS AND SNACKS AROUND WHOLEGRAIN FOODS

Wholegrain foods include bread, cereals, rice, pasta and starchy food, such as potatoes. They are filling yet not fattening and are great sources of fibre, both soluble and insoluble. Soluble fibre lowers cholesterol and is found in oats, beans, apples, strawberries and citrus fruits. Insoluble fibre prevents bowel problems and is found in wholegrain bread and cereals, brown rice, wholemeal pasta, fruit and vegetables.

6 EAT A DIET LOW IN FAT, ESPECIALLY SATURATED FAT

All fatty foods are made up from a mixture of three main types, but are classified according to the type of fat present in the largest amount. **Saturated fats**, which raise cholesterol, are found in fatty meats, full-cream dairy products such as milk, cream and cheese, coconut and palm oil used in convenience foods, cakes, pastries, biscuits, sweets, prepacked foods and take-away meals. **Polyunsaturated fats**, which lower cholesterol and have other beneficial effects, are found in vegetable oils such as

sunflower, corn, safflower, soya, grapeseed and nut oils and many margarines and spreads contain omega-6 polyunsaturated fatty acids. **Monounsaturated fats**, which also lower cholesterol, are found in olive and rapeseed (canola) oil, peanut oil and spreads, avocados and nuts.

You should avoid saturated fat and choose fats that are unsaturated, particularly olive oil and rapeseed (canola) oil. New spreads, which contain plant sterols, are available for people with raised cholesterol.

7 CHOOSE LEAN MEAT, POULTRY, EGGS, BEANS, NUTS, SOYA AND LOW-FAT DAIRY FOODS

Eat a variety of protein foods. Pulses – peas, beans (including baked, kidney, soya, borlotti and butter beans), lentils and chickpeas – are great sources of soluble fibre, which can help lower cholesterol. Soya protein has a similar benefit. Nuts protect you from heart disease, so eat a few unsalted nuts every day. You can safely eat up to four eggs a week.

8 AVOID TOO MUCH SALT

Three-quarters of our salt intake now comes from salt added to processed food, so choose fresh foods rather than processed wherever possible. Avoid obviously salty foods – salted nuts, crisps, canned fish, ham, bacon, sausages, corned beef, canned foods, packet soups, commercial pies, cheeses and salad dressings. Don't add salt to food, either while cooking (commercial stock cubes are very high in salt) or at the table. Replace the taste with fresh and dried herbs as well as other flavourings such as lemon juice, garlic, ginger and vinegars. Some foods that do not appear to be salty, such as bread and some cereals, do contain large quantities of salt.

9 ENJOY ALCOHOL WITH YOUR FOOD BUT BE SENSIBLE

If you like alcohol, enjoy a unit or two each day with your meal. It is the pattern of drinking and the amount you consume that are the important factors rather than the type of drink. Avoid binge drinking and keep to safe levels of alcohol, with some alcohol-free days.

10 TRY TO WALK FOR HALF AN HOUR MOST DAYS

Eating for a healthy heart is part of a whole healthy lifestyle, which involves not smoking and being physically active. Brisk walking, cycling or climbing the stairs will benefit your heart.

See also ▶

Healthy eating for a longer life, Chapter 3

What are your risk factors?, pages 182–183

Healthy eating for a healthy heart, pages 188–189

A healthy heart diet, pages 192–193

Recipes for a healthy heart, pages 194–209

A HEALTHY HEART DIET

FOODS	BEST CHOICE	IN MODERATION	BEST AVOIDED
Cereals and starchy foods	Bread, chapattis, breakfast cereals, oats, porridge, rice, pasta, popcorn (without butter), all other cereals	Naan bread	Poppadoms (fried), waffles, croissants, Danish pastries, fried rice, noodles in cartons
Potatoes	Boiled, mashed, jacket, instant mashed (without fat)	Oven chips, roast potatoes cooked in best-choice oil, fat-free crisps	Chips, potato croquettes, all other crisps
Vegetables and fruit	A wide variety of vegetables, fruit, salads, pulses – raw, baked, boiled, steamed, and all fresh, frozen, dried, canned	Stir-fried vegetables in best-choice oils, coleslaw in homemade dressing, canned fruit in syrup	Ready-made coleslaw; vegetables in batter
Fish	White fish: cod, haddock, plaice, lemon sole, whiting; oily fish: mackerel, herring, salmon, tuna and trout; canned fish in water or tomato sauce: tuna, pilchards, sardines; shellfish: oysters, mussels, clams, whelks, winkles, scallops; squid	Canned fish in oil (drain or rinse off excess oil); fish in breadcrumbs; shellfish: shrimps, prawns, lobster, crab	Fried fish in batter: scampi, whitebait; roe, fish pâté, taramasalata
Meat	Well-trimmed grilled steak, chicken and turkey (with skin removed), venison, rabbit	Lean lamb, beef, pork; lean minced beef; grilled lean burgers; lean ham, gammon and lean bacon; liver and kidney; low-fat sausage	Fatty meats, crackling and skin; duck, sausages, sausagemeat, luncheon meat, corned beef, pâté, Scotch eggs, meat pies and pasties

FOODS	BEST CHOICE	IN MODERATION	BEST AVOIDED
Vegetarian choices	Mycoprotein (Quorn), tofu, soya protein, pulses, chestnuts	All fresh nuts	Check fat content of vegetarian ready-made dishes
Eggs and dairy	Egg white, skimmed milk, low-fat yogurt, very low-fat cheese: cottage, fat-free fromage frais	Semi-skimmed, soya, goats', sheep's milk and their products; Greek yogurt, fromage frais, crème fraîche, evaporated milk; cheese: reduced-fat hard cheese, Edam, brie, camembert, feta, ricotta, mozzarella, cheese spread	Whole eggs (no more than four a week); whole milk, condensed milk, cream; cheese: Cheddar, Gouda, Gruyère, Roquefort, Stilton, cream cheese
Oils	Olive oil, rapeseed (canola) oil	Sunflower, corn, safflower, groundnut and sesame seed oils	Lard, suet, ghee and some vegetable oils, particularly palm and coconut oil
Spreads	Plant sterol or stanol spreads, low-fat spreads	Olive, rapeseed (canola), sunflower and soya oil spreads	Butter, hard margarines
Flavourings, sauces, jams and sweets	Pepper, herbs, spices, lemon juice, vinegar, garlic, tomato purée, mustard; homemade salad dressings and sauces made with best-choice ingredients; jam, marmalade, honey	Tomato ketchup, brown sauce, Worcestershire sauce, pickles, Bovril, Marmite, stock cubes, gravy granules, reduced-calorie mayonnaise and salad cream; hummus, peanut butter; mints and boiled sweets	Salt, salad cream, mayonnaise, cream sauces, ready-made cook-in sauces, chocolate spread, chocolates, toffees, fudge

RECIPES FOR A HEALTHY HEART

By eating vitamin- and mineral-rich foods and by reducing your intake of saturated fats, you can reduce the likelihood of developing heart disease and make a real difference to your health. You don't even need to give up all your favourite foods, just modify your recipes to use low-fat equivalents such as skimmed milk, yogurt or fromage frais instead of full-fat milk or cream. The sodium content is also given for each recipe to help you monitor your intake of salt. The Guideline Daily Amount (GDA) of sodium is 2.5 g which is equivalent to 6 g of salt.

WALNUT AND BANANA SUNRISE SMOOTHIE

Smoothies are a great way to increase your intake of soya protein. Make the recipe with soya milk and soya yogurt to give you 10 g of soya protein. There is 5 g in each 150 ml (¼ pint) soya milk and each 150 g (5 oz) soya yogurt.

1 orange, segmented

1 banana, peeled

150 ml (5 fl oz) soya or skimmed milk

150 g (5 oz) soya or natural yogurt

25 g (1 oz) walnuts

3 teaspoons honey

1 Place all the ingredients in a food processor or blender and blend until smooth and frothy. Pour into two glasses.

Serves 2

Preparation time 10 minutes

Nutritional values per serving • 300 kcal • 10 g fat • less than 1 g saturated fat • 110 mg sodium

LIGHT 'N' LOW PANCAKES

125 g (4 oz) brown or wholemeal plain flour

1 egg

300 ml (10 fl oz) skimmed milk (if using wholemeal flour you will need a little more)

1 teaspoon vegetable oil, plus a little extra for cooking, or use an oil-water spray

TOPPING IDEAS

chopped fresh fruit

chopped apple, raisins and ground cinnamon

cottage cheese

low-fat cream cheese

fruit spread or preserve

Pancakes offer another way in which you can base meals and snacks around starchy carbohydrates. They provide a good balance of many essential nutrients and can be low in fat if cooked with care.

1 Sift the flour into a bowl. If using wholemeal flour, also add the bran in the sieve to the flour in the bowl.

2 Beat the egg, milk and oil together, then slowly add to the flour. Stir the mixture until a smooth batter forms.

3 Leave to stand for about 20 minutes, then stir again.

4 Heat a little oil in a non-stick frying pan, or spray with an oil-water spray. When the oil is hot, add 2 tablespoons of the pancake mixture and shake the pan so that it spreads.

5 Cook the pancake for 2 minutes until the underside is lightly browned, then flip or turn over and cook the other side for a minute or so.

6 Keep the pancake warm in the oven while you cook the rest – you can stack one on top of the other as they are cooked. The mixture should make eight pancakes in all. Serve with your chosen topping.

Serves 4

Preparation time 10 minutes, plus standing

Cooking time 20 minutes

150 kcal • 3 g fat • less than 1 g saturated fat • 60 mg sodium

PUMPKIN SEED AND APRICOT MUESLI

Nuts may help to lower your risk of heart disease as they are high in cardioprotective nutrients such as vitamin E, folate, magnesium, copper and arginine. Almonds are the richest nut source of vitamin E, one of the antioxidants believed to help reduce the risk of heart disease by preventing the oxidation of LDL cholesterol. Like all nuts, they have a high fat content but most of it is monounsaturated fat, so go easy if you are watching your weight.

50 g (2 oz) rolled jumbo oats

1 tablespoon sultanas or raisins

1 tablespoon pumpkin or sunflower seeds

1 tablespoon chopped almonds

25 g (1 oz) ready-to-eat dried apricots, chopped

2 tablespoons fruit juice, such as apple or orange juice, or water

2 small eating apples, peeled and grated

3 tablespoons skimmed milk, soya milk, natural yogurt or soya yogurt

1 Place the oats, sultanas or raisins, seeds, almonds and apricots in a bowl with the fruit juice or water.

2 Add the grated apple and stir to mix.

3 Top with skimmed milk, soya milk, natural yogurt or soya yogurt.

Serves 2

Preparation time 10 minutes

340 kcal • 12 g fat • less than 1 g saturated fat • 65 mg sodium

FENNEL AND WHITE BEAN SOUP

900 ml (1½ pints) vegetable stock

2 fennel bulbs, trimmed and chopped

1 onion, chopped

1 courgette, chopped

1 carrot, chopped

2 garlic cloves, finely sliced

6 tomatoes, finely chopped, or 400 g (13 oz) can tomatoes

2 x 400 g (13 oz) cans butter beans, rinsed and drained

2 tablespoons chopped sage

freshly ground black pepper

When choosing canned vegetables, go for the 'no added salt' varieties. If these aren't available, rinse and drain vegetables such as beans and sweetcorn. This removes some but not all of the salt.

1 Place 300 ml (10 fl oz) of the stock in a large saucepan. Add the fennel, onion, courgette, carrot and garlic. Cover and bring to the boil. Continue boiling for 5 minutes, then remove the lid, reduce the heat and simmer gently for about 20 minutes until the vegetables are tender.

2 Stir in the tomatoes, beans and sage. Season with pepper and pour in the remaining stock. Simmer for 5 minutes, then let the soup cool slightly.

3 Transfer 300 ml (10 fl oz) of the soup to a food processor or blender and process until smooth. Stir back into the pan and heat through gently.

Serves 4

Preparation time 15 minutes

Cooking time 30 minutes

155 kcal • 1 g fat • less than 1 g saturated fat • 550 mg sodium

ORANGE AND ALMOND COUSCOUS SALAD

Almonds (see also page 196) contain the amino acid arginine (among other vital nutrients), which is thought to improve the health of artery linings and reduce the risk of heart disease.

1   Place the apple juice in a saucepan and bring to the boil. Slowly stir in the couscous. Remove the pan from the heat. Cover and leave to stand for 10 minutes. Fluff up with a fork.

2   Add the pepper, herbs and currants to the couscous and toss to combine. Transfer to a serving bowl. Scatter with the orange segments and onion.

3   For the dressing, place the ingredients in a small saucepan and heat gently to dissolve the honey – do not allow to boil. Drizzle over the salad. Scatter with the almonds.

250 ml (8 fl oz) apple juice

175 g (6 oz) couscous

½ red pepper, cored, deseeded and diced

4 tablespoons chopped parsley

3 tablespoons chopped mint

25 g (1 oz) currants

2 oranges, segmented

1 red onion, sliced

25 g (1 oz) flaked almonds

DRESSING

juice of 1 orange

juice of 1 lemon or lime

2 teaspoons olive or hazelnut oil

1 teaspoon honey

Serves 6

Preparation time 15 minutes, plus standing

Cooking time 5 minutes

160 kcal • 4 g fat • less than 0.3 g saturated fat • 6 mg sodium

SWEET POTATO AND CANNELLINI FALAFEL

6 pitta breads, warmed

1 tablespoon low-fat hummus

100 g (3½ oz) shredded lettuce

175 g (6 oz) tabbouleh

1 red onion, thinly sliced

lemon juice, to serve

FALAFEL

400 g (13 oz) orange sweet
potato, cut into chunks

2 teaspoons olive oil

1 clove garlic, crushed

2 teaspoons ground cumin

1 teaspoon ground coriander

1 tablespoon tomato purée

400 g (13 oz) can cannellini beans,
rinsed and drained

2 tablespoons chopped fresh
coriander

1 tablespoon tahini (sesame seed
paste)

1 tablespoon lemon juice

75 g (3 oz) dry breadcrumbs

flour, for coating

Serves 6

Preparation time 20 minutes

Cooking time 10 minutes

Sweet potatoes are full of antioxidants, particularly the ACE vitamins and beta-carotene. Like yams and new potatoes, they are digested more slowly than all other potatoes and help to lower the overall glycaemic index (GI) of your diet.

1 Boil or microwave the sweet potato until tender, then drain. Place in a bowl and mash. Set aside.

2 Heat the oil in a non-stick frying pan, add the garlic, cumin and ground coriander. Cook, stirring, for 1–2 minutes until fragrant. Stir in the tomato purée. Cook for 3–4 minutes until the mixture becomes deep red and develops a rich aroma. Stir in the cannellini beans.

3 Place the fresh coriander, tahini and lemon juice in a food processor or blender and process until they form a coarse paste.

4 Mix the bean mixture and breadcrumbs with the sweet potato. Shape the mixture into 2.5 cm (1 in) round patties. If the mixture feels too wet to shape into patties you may need to add some extra breadcrumbs. Roll in flour to coat. Place on a plate lined with clingfilm. Cover and refrigerate until ready to cook – the patties can be made up to a day in advance.

5 Grill the falafel under a preheated hot grill for 3–4 minutes each side until golden and crispy.

6 Spread the bread with hummus. Top with lettuce, tabbouleh and onion. Place 3 falafel in each pitta and flatten slightly. Sprinkle with lemon juice to taste and serve immediately.

215 kcal • 8 g fat • 1 g saturated fat • 245 mg sodium

THAI-STYLE MONKFISH AND MUSHROOM KEBABS

Fish is a good low-fat option: monkfish, sole, cod, halibut, haddock, hake, red snapper, mullet, plaice, pollock, trout, turbot and whiting all have fewer than 5 g of fat per 100 g. When you eat out, try to choose any of these fish from the menu.

1 Combine the ingredients for the marinade in a large bowl. Cut the fish into large cubes and add to the marinade with the onion, mushrooms and courgette. Cover and refrigerate for 1 hour for the flavours to blend.

2 Brush the rack of a grill pan lightly with oil to prevent the kebabs from sticking. Thread 4 skewers with the chunks of fish, mushrooms, courgette and onion alternately. Brush with a little oil and grill under a preheated hot grill for about 10 minutes, turning at intervals. Garnish with watercress or flatleaf parsley.

500–750 g (1–1½ lb) monkfish tails, skinned

1 onion, quartered and layers separated

8 mushrooms

1 courgette, cut into 8 pieces

vegetable oil, for brushing

watercress or flatleaf parsley, to garnish

MARINADE

grated rind and juice of 2 limes

1 garlic clove, finely chopped

2 tablespoons finely sliced fresh root ginger

2 fresh chillies, red or green, or 1 of each, deseeded and finely chopped

2 lemon grass stalks, finely chopped

handful of chopped fresh coriander

1 glass of red wine

2 tablespoons sesame oil

freshly ground black pepper

Serves 4

Preparation time 15 minutes, plus marinating

Cooking time 10 minutes

192 kcal • 5 g fat • less than 1 g saturated fat • 34 mg sodium

PUY LENTILS WITH FLAKED SALMON AND DILL

500 g (1 lb) salmon tail fillet

2 tablespoons dry white wine

4 red peppers, halved, cored and deseeded

175 g (6 oz) Puy lentils, well rinsed

large handful of dill, chopped

1 bunch of spring onions, finely sliced

lemon juice, for squeezing

freshly ground black pepper

DRESSING

2 garlic cloves

large handful of flatleaf parsley, chopped

large handful of dill, chopped

1 teaspoon Dijon mustard

2 green chillies, deseeded and chopped

juice of 2 large lemons

1 tablespoon extra virgin olive oil

Serves 4

Preparation time 30 minutes

Cooking time 45 minutes

As well as creating a delicious and unusual flavour combination, lentils and salmon make an excellent cardioprotective duo. Lentils are high in protein, low in fat and high in soluble fibre, which will help reduce cholesterol levels. Salmon is an oily fish, providing a rich source of omega-3 fatty acids, which will have a beneficial effect on reducing blood clotting and an irregular heartbeat.

1 Place the salmon in the centre of a sheet of foil and spoon over the wine. Gather up the foil and fold over at the top to seal. Place on a baking sheet and bake in a preheated oven, 200°C (400°F), Gas Mark 6, for 15–20 minutes until cooked. Allow to cool, then flake, cover and chill.

2 Flatten the pepper halves slightly. Grill skin side up under a preheated hot grill until charred. Enclose in a plastic bag for a few minutes. Remove from the bag, peel away the skin and cut the flesh into 2.5 cm (1 in) cubes, reserving any juices.

3 Place all the dressing ingredients, except the oil, in a food processor or blender and process until smooth. While processing, drizzle in the oil until the mixture is thick.

4 Place the lentils in a large saucepan with plenty of water, bring to the boil, then simmer gently for about 15–20 minutes until cooked but still firm to the bite.

Drain and place in a bowl with the red pepper, dill, most of the spring onions and pepper to taste.

5 Stir the dressing into the hot lentils and allow to infuse. To serve, top the lentils with the salmon and gently mix through the lentils and dressing, squeeze over a little lemon juice and scatter with the remaining spring onions.

450 kcal • 18 g fat • 3 g saturated fat • 70 mg sodium

GRIDDLED HONEY-GLAZED TUNA WITH PARSNIP PURÉE

Griddling is a healthy way to cook, since it requires little or no added fat, and any fat from the food can drain away. Using a griddle therefore allows you to easily reduce the amount of fat in your diet, as well as giving food a delicious flavour.

1 Place the ingredients for the glaze in a small saucepan. Bring to the boil, then reduce the heat and simmer until the mixture reduces and is of a glaze consistency. Keep hot.

2 For the parsnip purée, steam the parsnips and potatoes until tender. Drain if necessary and place in a food processor or blender with the yogurt, horseradish (if using) and pepper to taste. Process until blended. Keep warm or reheat prior to serving.

3 Brush the tuna with oil. Cook on a preheated, very hot griddle or barbecue, or in a frying pan or under a grill, for 1–2 minutes. Turn and spoon the glaze over the tuna. Cook for a further 1–2 minutes – it is best if moist and still slightly pink in the centre.

4 To serve, top a mound of the purée with a tuna steak and spoon over the remaining glaze. Accompany with steamed green vegetables, if liked.

4 tuna steaks, about 125 g (4 oz) each

2 teaspoons olive oil

GLAZE

1 tablespoon honey

2 tablespoons wholegrain mustard

1 teaspoon tomato purée

2 tablespoons orange juice

1 tablespoon red wine vinegar or balsamic vinegar

freshly ground black pepper

PARSNIP PURÉE

2 parsnips, cut into chunks

2 potatoes, cut into chunks

50 g (2 oz) natural yogurt

2 teaspoons horseradish sauce (optional)

Serves 4

Preparation time 15 minutes

Cooking time 15 minutes

310 kcal • 10 g fat • 2 g saturated fat • 300 mg sodium

SEA BASS WITH MUSHROOM AND MIXED HERB STUFFING

1 tablespoon olive oil

125 g (4 oz) mixed mushrooms, preferably wild, sliced

grated rind and juice of 1 lemon

handful of mixed herbs (such as flatleaf parsley, thyme, green or purple basil), roughly chopped

14 tiny new potatoes

1 garlic clove, crushed

2 sea bass fillets, about 125 g (4 oz) each

freshly ground black pepper

chopped herbs, to garnish

Experts recommend that we eat fish a couple of times a week, and this recipe has a lovely fresh taste, perfect for a summer evening. Sea bass contains a moderate amount of omega-3 fatty acids at 0.4 g per serving (100 g/3½ oz). Our average intake of EPA and DHA (see page 189) is estimated at only 0.2 g per day, far short of the ideal 1 g per day.

1 Heat 1 teaspoon of the oil in a non-stick frying pan and gently cook the mushrooms for about 5 minutes until tender. Season to taste. Remove the pan from the heat and add the lemon rind and juice and herbs.

2 Meanwhile, cook the potatoes in boiling water or a steamer for about 10 minutes until just tender. Drain and allow to cool. Place the potatoes and garlic in a roasting tin, brush with most of the remaining oil and roast in a preheated oven, 200°C (400°F), Gas Mark 6, for about 20 minutes, until golden brown.

3 Make a crisscross incision on the skin side of the fish (to prevent the fish from curling). Make a cut lengthways down the side of each fillet into the centre and fold open creating a pocket for the stuffing. Brush with the remaining oil and stuff with the mushroom and herb mixture. Close up the fish to its original shape.

4 Season the fish with pepper to taste and arrange on top of the potatoes. Return to the oven and bake for 5–6 minutes (depending on size) until cooked through.

5 Serve the fish on top of the potatoes and garnish with chopped herbs.

Serves 2

Preparation time 15 minutes

Cooking time 40 minutes

TAGLIATELLE WITH BACON, MUSHROOMS AND PINE NUTS

It is easy to make your favourite recipes healthier by using skimmed-milk products, natural yogurt or fromage frais instead of soured cream, crème fraîche and double, whipping or single cream. At less than 1 g fat per 100 g (3½ oz), yogurt and fromage frais are both very low in fat. To prevent yogurt and fromage frais from separating during cooking mix a teaspoon of smooth mustard into them before you start to cook.

1 Cook the tagliatelle according to the packet instructions.

2 Meanwhile, heat the oil in a non-stick frying pan, add the pepper and cook for 2–3 minutes. Stir in the garlic, mushrooms, bacon, parsley and pepper to taste.

3 Reduce the heat and stir in the fromage frais or yogurt. Heat through very gently.

4 Drain the pasta and toss with the sauce. Sprinkle with the pine nuts before serving. Serve with salad.

375 g (12 oz) green and white tagliatelle

1 tablespoon olive oil

1 yellow pepper, cored, deseeded and chopped

2 teaspoons garlic purée, or crushed garlic

125 g (4 oz) button mushrooms, sliced

125 g (4 oz) rindless lean back bacon, grilled and cut into thin strips

1 tablespoon chopped parsley

500 g (1 lb) natural fromage frais or yogurt

25 g (1 oz) pine nuts, toasted

freshly ground black pepper

Serves 4

Preparation time 10 minutes

Cooking time 10 minutes

535 kcal • 14 g fat • 2 g saturated fat • 740 mg sodium

LEAN LASAGNE

200 g (7 oz) precooked sheets of lasagne

freshly ground black pepper

MEAT SAUCE

2 aubergines, peeled and diced

2 red onions, chopped

2 garlic cloves, crushed

300 ml (10 fl oz) vegetable stock

4 tablespoons red wine

500 g (1 lb) extra-lean mince

2 x 400 g (13 oz) cans chopped tomatoes

CHEESE SAUCE

3 egg whites

250 g (8 oz) ricotta cheese

175 ml (6 fl oz) skimmed milk

6 tablespoons freshly grated Parmesan cheese

Serves 8

Preparation time 30 minutes

Cooking time about 1 hour

Despite its Mediterranean origins, lasagne can be even higher in fat and calories than fried foods and chips. But this reduced-fat version, which uses ricotta cheese for the white sauce tastes deliciously sweet and heavenly creamy – you'd never know it was low in fat.

1 For the meat sauce, place the aubergines, onions, garlic, stock and wine in a large non-stick saucepan. Cover with a lid and simmer briskly for 5 minutes.

2 Remove the lid and cook the sauce gently for about 5 minutes until the aubergine is tender and the liquid is absorbed, adding a little more stock if necessary. Remove from the heat, allow to cool slightly, then purée in a food processor or blender.

3 Meanwhile, brown the mince in a non-stick frying pan. Drain off any fat. Add the aubergine mixture, tomatoes and pepper to taste. Simmer briskly, uncovered, for about 10 minutes until the sauce is thickened.

4 For the cheese sauce, beat the egg whites with the ricotta. Beat in the milk and four tablespoons of Parmesan. Season to taste with pepper.

5 To assemble the lasagne, alternate layers of meat sauce, sheets of lasagne and cheese sauce. Start with meat sauce and finish with cheese sauce. Sprinkle with the remaining Parmesan. Bake in a preheated oven, 180°C (350°F), Gas Mark 4, for 30–40 minutes until browned.

340 kcal • 11 g fat • 5 g saturated fat • 180 mg sodium

CHICKEN ENCHILADAS WITH MANGO SALSA

Mexican food has a number of high-fat traps, but it also offers many healthy and delicious dishes. If chosen carefully, and with some minor adjustments, you can enjoy this rich and flavourful cuisine. Enchiladas can be one of the traps because of the high cheese content. In this version, a small amount of reduced-fat cheese is used and the corn tortillas are packed with plenty of high-fibre beans instead.

1 Put all the ingredients for the mango salsa in a bowl and mix together. Cover and refrigerate for 30 minutes or more to allow the flavours to infuse.

2 Heat the oil in a saucepan, add the onion and cook for about 5 minutes until softened. Stir in the beans, chicken, chillies, oregano and fresh tomato. Heat through, then remove from the heat.

3 Place the chilli powder, cumin and blended tomatoes or passata in a saucepan and simmer for 2 minutes. Remove from the heat.

4 Dip each tortilla into the tomato mixture and set aside on a plate. Fill each tortilla with 3 tablespoons of the chicken mixture. Roll up and place seam-side down in an ovenproof dish. Pour two-thirds of the mango salsa over the enchiladas. Sprinkle with the grated cheese and serve with the remaining salsa.

5 Bake in a preheated oven, 180°C (350°F), Gas Mark 4, for about 20 minutes. Place two enchilladas on each plate and serve.

2 teaspoons vegetable oil

1 large onion, chopped

250 g (8 oz) canned pinto beans, rinsed and drained

300 g (10 oz) cooked chicken breast, skinned and cubed

4 green chillies, deseeded and chopped

1 teaspoon dried oregano

1 large tomato, chopped

¼ teaspoon chilli powder

¼ teaspoon ground cumin

400 g (13 oz) can tomatoes, blended or passata

12 corn tortillas

75 g (3 oz) grated low-fat mozzarella cheese

MANGO SALSA

1 mango, peeled and diced

200 g (7 oz) ripe tomatoes, skinned, deseeded and chopped

1 green chilli, deseeded and finely chopped

1 tablespoon chopped mint

1 tablespoon chopped fresh coriander

juice of 1 lime

1 tablespoon olive oil

freshly ground black pepper

Serves 6

Preparation time 20 minutes, plus chilling

Cooking time 25 minutes

240 kcal • 3 g fat • less than 1 g saturated fat • 190 mg sodium

THAI SESAME AND TOFU STIR-FRY

1 teaspoon sesame oil

2 tablespoons teriyaki sauce

400 g (13 oz) firm tofu, cut into 4 thick slices

2 tablespoons sesame seeds

1 tablespoon rice wine vinegar or sherry

2 teaspoons reduced-salt soy sauce

1 tablespoon groundnut oil

16 mangetouts

1 carrot, cut into thin strips

125 g (4 oz) bean sprouts

2 spring onions, white parts cut into 5 cm (2 in) batons, green tops shredded for garnish

250 g (8 oz) rice noodles, prepared according to the packet instructions

50 g (2 oz) watercress, broken into sprigs

Serves 4

Preparation time 15 minutes

Cooking time 10 minutes

Tofu (soya bean curd) is rich in protein and B vitamins, low in saturated fat and sodium and an important non-dairy source of calcium. Soya protein has been shown to decrease total and LDL cholesterol (see page 181). Firm tofu can be cubed and served in soups, casseroles, stir-fried and threaded on kebabs. Silken tofu is a creamy custard-like food for use in cheesecakes, creamy sauces and salad dressings.

1 In a small bowl, combine the sesame oil and 1 tablespoon teriyaki sauce. Brush over both sides of the tofu. Sprinkle 1 side of each piece of tofu with half the sesame seeds. Mix together the remaining teriyaki sauce, vinegar or sherry and soy sauce. Set aside.

2 Heat a large wok or frying pan. Brush with a little of the groundnut oil. Add the tofu, seed side down, and cook for 2 minutes. Sprinkle the remaining sesame seeds over the tofu. Turn over and cook for 2 minutes more until crisp. Remove the tofu from the pan and keep warm.

3 Brush the pan with a little more groundnut oil, then add the mangetouts, carrot, bean sprouts and spring onion batons. Stir-fry for 2–3 minutes until tender yet still crisp. Add the reserved teriyaki sauce mixture. Stir-fry for another minute.

4 Divide the hot noodles between warmed serving bowls. Add the watercress, spoon over the vegetables and top with the tofu. Garnish with the shredded spring onion. Serve with a green salad, if liked.

LEMON RICOTTA CHEESECAKE WITH BLUEBERRIES

This cheesecake recipe is low in fat because ricotta cheese is used instead of the usual high-fat cream and cream cheese. There are many low-fat types of ricotta cheese available, but it's a good idea to read the label and choose the variety with the lowest fat content.

1 For the crust, mix together the biscuits, sugar, cinnamon and spread in a bowl. In a separate bowl, whisk the egg white until frothy. Stir into the crumb mixture. Press into the bottom of a 23 cm (9 in) spring-form tin. Bake in a preheated oven, 190°C (375°F), Gas Mark 5, for 7–10 minutes until lightly browned. Allow to cool.

2 For the filling, place the ricotta and whole eggs in a food processor or blender and process until smooth. Transfer to a bowl and beat together with the sugar, yogurt, lemon juice and rind, flour and vanilla essence until well mixed.

3 In a separate bowl, beat the egg whites until soft peaks form, then fold into the cheese mixture. Spread over the biscuit crust. Bake in the oven for 50–55 minutes until the centre is firm to the touch.

4 Run a knife around the edge of the cake to loosen and allow to cool. Remove the sides of the tin, cover the cheesecake and refrigerate for at least 2 hours or up to a day. Just before serving, spread the top with fromage frais and cover with blueberries or other fruit.

500 g (1 lb) skimmed ricotta cheese

2 large eggs

75 g (3 oz) sugar

150 g (5 oz) natural yogurt

4 tablespoons lemon juice

grated rind of 2 lemons

2 tablespoons plain flour

2 teaspoons vanilla essence

2 egg whites

150 g (5 oz) natural fromage frais

300 g (10 oz) fresh, frozen and thawed or canned blueberries or other soft fruit

CRUST

125 g (4 oz) plain digestive-type biscuits, crushed

2 tablespoons sugar

1 teaspoon ground cinnamon

15 g (½ oz) unsaturated spread

1 egg white

Serves 10

Preparation time 30 minutes

Cooking time about 1 hour

177 kcal • 8 g fat • 4 g saturated fat • 124 mg sodium

MANGO AND PINEAPPLE PAVLOVA

3 egg whites

175 g (6 oz) caster sugar

1 teaspoon strong black coffee

250 g (8 oz) natural fromage frais

125 g (4 oz) mango, diced

125 g (4 oz) fresh pineapple, cut into chunks

1–2 passion fruits

Pavlova, a much-loved dessert, is surprisingly very low in fat. Meringue is naturally a very low-fat choice since it is made from egg white. You can replace a whole egg with two egg whites in most recipes or use dried egg white powder.

1 Whisk the egg whites in a bowl until they are stiff. Fold in 1 tablespoon of the sugar, then gradually whisk in the remainder. The meringue must be glossy and form peaks when spoonfuls are dropped into the bowl. Fold in the black coffee.

2 Spread the meringue mixture over a large sheet of baking paper to form a 20 cm (8 in) diameter round. Make a slight hollow in the centre of the meringue and cook in a preheated oven, 120°C (250°F), Gas Mark ½, for 1 hour until the meringue is crisp. Remove from the oven and leave to cool on the paper for about 10 minutes before peeling off.

3 When the meringue is cold, fill the hollow in the top with fromage frais. Arrange the mango and pineapple on top, then drizzle the passion fruit seeds and juice over the fruit.

Serves 4

Preparation time 20 minutes

Cooking time 1 hour

245 kcal • less than 1 g fat • negligible saturated fat • 77 mg sodium

CHAPTER 7
BREAST WATCH

Whether we like it or not, as we get older our chances of developing a serious illness increase. Keeping fit, eating a healthy diet and living an active life all play a major role in preventing disease, particularly cancer and heart disease, and that is why listening to lifestyle advice is so important.

Breast cancer is the most common cancer in women, affecting one in 10 worldwide. This is disheartening, but there is hope. We are highly aware of this condition. Treatment is improving all the time. If diagnosed early, many breast cancers are curable. This chapter guides you from the first distress of finding a lump, through treatment, then on to rebuilding life after surgery.

UNDERSTANDING NORMAL BREAST CHANGES

Breasts come in all shapes and sizes – it is actually quite normal for a woman to have one breast bigger than the other. Some women have lumpy breasts and others don't, but above all it is important to remember that all these 'differences' are perfectly normal.

'Remember that breasts come in all shapes and sizes, and are often lumpy. Through regular self-checks get to know what your breasts feel like so that you will notice when something feels different or unusual.'

PUBERTY, PREGNANCY AND MENOPAUSE

A girl's body begins to develop in preparation for childbirth and motherhood usually between the ages of 11 and 15. Part of this complex process is the development of the breasts. Each breast contains clusters of milk-producing glands, and each of these has its own drainage system. Fatty tissue provides support for the glands, ducts and the numerous blood vessels and nerves.

Most women experience quite marked changes to their breasts during a menstrual cycle, particularly just before a period, when they become tender (sometimes painful) and swollen. These changes are due to the actions of female hormones in readiness for a possible pregnancy. Breasts usually increase dramatically in size during a pregnancy, often doubling in volume as the glands enlarge.

After the menopause, hormone levels drop and the breasts begin to shrink and lose their elasticity. The skin over the breasts, much like

BE BREAST AWARE

Breast awareness is particularly important for women after the menopause, as the majority of cancers develop over the age of 50. The earlier a cancer is discovered and treated, the better the chances of recovery. But don't let a regular, rigid, breast examination become a stressful chore: let it be a natural part of your normal routine. As long as you are aware of the usual look and feel of your breasts, and can detect any obvious changes, you are on the right track. Here are a few guidelines to help you.

Look at your breasts in a mirror. It is perfectly normal for breasts to differ in shape and size, so look for what is not right for you. This might be a dimpled or 'puckered' area, an inverted nipple, an obvious swelling, discharge from the nipple, or a swelling in the armpit.

skin in the other areas of the body, can become thinner and drier than usual. For some women who choose to take hormone replacement therapy (HRT), such symptoms may be delayed.

BENIGN LUMPS AND BUMPS

There are some common benign (non-cancerous) breast lumps, which are not usually defined as normal breast changes but which are harmless. Usually, they are one of the following conditions.

Cysts are small lumps or swellings filled with fluid or semi-solid material that you can move easily with your fingers and which may feel tender to the touch. About one in 10 women have a problem with recurrent cysts. It is possible to have the fluid removed with a needle and syringe (aspiration) (see page 219).

Fibroadenomas can develop at any age but are reasonably common in women in their 20s. They are made up of fibrous and gland tissue, are often quite large and easily moved around under the skin. In some cases, doctors advise removal of the lump, especially if it is painful.

Fibrocystic disease affects nearly half of all middle-aged women. Fluctuations in hormone levels during the menstrual cycle normally cause the milk glands and ducts to become swollen and tender, but after a period these changes usually subside. In some women, however, the ducts become blocked and surrounding tissue becomes lumpy. Fibrocystic changes usually disappear after the menopause.

See also ▶

Myths and facts about breast cancer, pages 214–215
Minimizing the effects of the menopause, Chapter 4

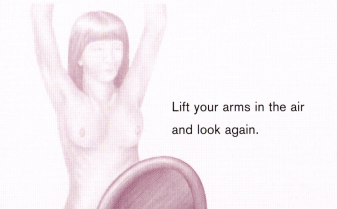

Lift your arms in the air and look again.

Using the length of your fingers, and not the tips, feel across your breasts for any abnormal lumps. If you have large breasts, you may find it easier to lie down and do this. Many women have naturally 'lumpy' breasts, so what you are looking for is something that feels different or unusual.

MYTHS AND FACTS ABOUT BREAST CANCER

You only have to listen to the radio, read the paper or watch the television to be bombarded with 'scare' stories about new cancer-causing agents. If we took heed of all these warnings, we would probably never leave the house. Using common sense and reliable sources of information is the best way to sort out the valuable advice from the nonsense.

'Eating at least five portions of fruit and vegetables each day has been proven to prevent some cancers, including breast cancer.'

RESEARCH AND EVIDENCE

In scientific terms, the results of a single research study are not usually significant. Until there is a large body of evidence – a number of studies with the same findings – experts will rarely advise a change in behaviour. However, if you are concerned that you may be at risk of developing a particular kind of cancer, don't worry unnecessarily. Instead, make an appointment to see your doctor or practice nurse, who will put your mind at rest and clear up any confusion.

Over 40,000 women (three-quarters of whom are over the age of 50) are affected by breast cancer each year in the UK, and over 210,000 new cases were reported in the US in 2003, so it is hardly surprising that a great deal of research into possible causes is continuing all over the world. Despite these statistics, though, it is important to remember that if breast cancer is detected early the outlook is good. Awareness raising has been effective in encouraging women to examine their breasts and improvements in early diagnosis techniques and treatments have meant that more women are surviving breast cancer than ever before.

RISK FACTORS

There are several well-established risk factors for breast cancer, and others that are thought likely to play a role. Many of the risk factors outlined here are related to a long-term exposure to the female hormone oestrogen, which is necessary for some tumours to develop. For example, a woman who started her periods early in adolescence and went through the menopause later than usual will have had high levels of oestrogen in her body for many years. Equally, during pregnancy oestrogen levels plummet, so a woman who has never been pregnant may be at a slightly greater risk.

Other factors are connected to our lifestyles, and the good news about this is that we can actually do something about it.

HEREDITARY BREAST CANCER

A small number of women inherit a gene that puts them at particularly high risk of developing breast cancer. Fewer than one in 20 cancers are caused by this gene, but if a woman is shown to be carrying the culprit she will be very carefully monitored.

ARE YOU LIKELY TO DEVELOP BREAST CANCER?

There are many complex factors involved in the development of cancer. Therefore it is important to bear in mind that, just because you fall into one or more of these categories, it doesn't mean that you will go on to develop breast cancer.

- Women over the age of 50 are more likely to develop breast cancer than younger women. In fact, this is the case with most cancers – the older you are, the more likely you are to become ill. However, breast cancer affects younger women as well.

- Women who have never been pregnant and who have never breast-fed a baby are more at risk.

- An early menarche (first period) and late menopause are associated with a higher risk.

- Obesity and being overweight, particularly after the menopause, increases breast cancer risk. This may be because fat cells are thought to produce hormones similar to oestrogen.

- A close member of the family (mother, daughter or sister) with breast cancer increases your risk.

- An abnormal inherited gene puts you at high risk.

- An excessive intake of alcohol pushes your risk up.

- A diet that is high in saturated fat and red meat increases the risk.

- HRT is thought to increase the risk very slightly. However, it is recommended that women think carefully before discontinuing their HRT therapy.

CURRENT APPROACHES TO CANCER PREVENTION

Keeping in control of your health can be a very positive experience, especially as you grow older. Staying fit and leading a healthy lifestyle have been shown to protect against diseases such as heart disease and some cancers. So, if you want to be proactive in the fight against breast cancer, there are several steps you can take.

SIX STEPS TO HELP PREVENT BREAST CANCER

1 Be breast aware (see pages 212–213).

2 Join any national screening programme available in your country – a mammogram is a fast and efficient test, and the best way to detect early breast cancers.

3 Eat plenty of fruit and vegetables and restrict yourself to small amounts of fatty foods. Try to drink only moderate amounts of alcohol.

4 Keep your weight stable. It is very easy to pile on weight, particularly after the menopause.

5 Take just 30 minutes a day of moderate physical activity, such as brisk walking or gardening, and one hour a week of vigorous activity, such as swimming, jogging or aerobics.

6 Know your family history. A woman whose sister or mother has experienced breast cancer is probably more at risk herself, and should therefore be especially careful to monitor her own health.

NATIONAL BREAST CANCER SCREENING

In the UK, between the ages of 50 and 53, as long as you are registered with a doctor, you will be invited for a mammogram as part of the UK National Screening Programme. You will then have a routine mammogram every year for more than 10 years. The results of the test will be given to you within two weeks. In other countries such as the US and Australia it is recommended that women over the age of 50 should be screened every one to two years.

A HEALTHY BALANCED DIET

We know that eating plenty of fruit and vegetables – at least five portions a day – can help prevent some cancers, including breast cancer. Scientists don't yet fully understand why this is, but they know for certain that there is a link and that some foods protect against cancer. In addition, recent scientific research has shown that women who are overweight, and who regularly eat high-fat foods, are more at risk of developing breast cancer, particularly after the menopause.

HOW DOES FAT INFLUENCE THE RISK?

Many breast cancers are 'hormone-dependent'. This means that in order to grow they need hormones such as oestrogen. One theory as to why overweight women have a higher risk of breast cancer is that fat cells may produce hormone-like substances, which encourage tumours to grow. Sadly, as we grow older, maintaining a healthy weight becomes less easy, but it is all the more important (see pages 74–75).

KEEP MOVING

Many of us find it tricky to get enough exercise but physical activity really does help to keep you in shape, and it also helps in the fight against breast cancer, particularly if you are overweight. Why take the bus or car if you can walk? Or, enlist the help of your family to come up with a personalized physical activity plan that will fit into your daily schedule (see also Chapter 2).

FIVE A DAY

Eating five portions of fruit and vegetables a day isn't as difficult as it sounds. Here are some helpful tips to hit your daily target.

- **Drink** a glass of fresh fruit juice in the morning (one portion).

- **Eat** half a fresh grapefruit with your breakfast cereal (one portion).

- **Snack** on a handful of dried fruit, such as apricots or prunes, instead of a packet of crisps (one portion).

- **Have** a bowlful of crispy mixed salad or a mug of homemade vegetable or tomato soup at lunchtime (one portion).

- **Increase** the vegetable portions in your evening meal and reduce the meat content accordingly. Potatoes don't count, but vegetables such as broccoli, peas, carrots, courgettes or spinach make tasty accompaniments.

IF YOU FIND A LUMP

Discovering a breast lump will inevitably provoke feelings of anxiety, but remember that most breast lumps are harmless, so try not to think the worst at this early stage. A consultation with your doctor will set the ball rolling and, if there is any doubt, an appointment will be made at the hospital for further tests. Women who have not noticed a lump themselves but who have had an abnormal area picked up on a routine screening mammogram will also be asked to attend a breast clinic.

PHYSICAL EXAMINATION

A visit to the breast clinic will always start with a consultation with an experienced doctor, who will ask you about your medical history, examine your breasts, check for enlarged glands in your armpits, and assess the size and texture of the lump. If you have any particular worries, it is a good idea to mention them at this stage.

MAMMOGRAPHY

A mammogram is a low-dose X-ray of the breast that is able to detect an abnormal area of breast glandular tissue before it can be felt with the fingers. During the mammogram, each breast is firmly compressed between a perspex cover and the X-ray plate to make sure that as much of the breast as possible can be clearly seen on the X-ray. To be doubly sure, two X-rays are taken of each breast, from two different angles. Some women find the procedure slightly uncomfortable, but it is very quick and does not cause any discomfort afterwards; nor does it harm the breast tissue.

HINT FOR HEALTH

Why not book yourself in for an aromatherapy body massage, or enrol on a yoga course? Now may be the ideal time to indulge yourself a little.

ULTRASOUND

An ultrasound scan uses high-frequency sound waves to create an image on a monitor. A doctor or radiographer experienced in the procedure moves a device called a transducer backwards and forwards over the breast using gentle pressure. The transducer both emits the soundwaves and receives their echoes as they bounce back. It is usually possible at this stage to tell whether or not the lump is a cyst.

FINE NEEDLE ASPIRATION

The next step is usually a procedure called fine needle aspiration. Often using the ultrasound as a guide, the doctor inserts a small needle through the skin of the breast and into the lump, and withdraws some cells or fluid with a syringe. The samples are then sent to the laboratory and closely examined under a microscope to check whether or not they are malignant (cancerous).

NEEDLE BIOPSY

Sometimes doctors require a larger sample from the lump to be absolutely sure of the diagnosis. Because this procedure is slightly more uncomfortable than the others, local anaesthetic is used to numb the area first. After a biopsy, your breast will probably feel a bit sore but the discomfort should wear off by the following day. You may want to take some mild painkillers.

'Most breast lumps are harmless, so try not to think the worst at this early stage.'

See also ▶
A diagnosis of breast cancer, pages 220–221

RETURNING FOR YOUR RESULTS

Waiting for the results of medical tests, especially if you have a breast lump, can be a very worrying time despite reassurance from medical staff. It could be around a week before you return to the hospital, so here are some tips that may help to relieve the anxiety in the meantime.

- Perhaps the most important fact to remember is that seven out of eight breast lumps are harmless. Although you may feel that you want to prepare yourself for bad news, the likelihood is that your lump is benign.

- Talk to your partner, family or friends. It is always a good idea to express your concerns to a sympathetic loved one.

- Carry on with life as normal. Although you may feel distracted, everyday chores and pleasures will help to keep your mind off your worries.

- Finally, take someone with you when you return to the clinic. If the news is good, there will be someone there to share it with you. If the results are not what you wanted to hear, you will have some much-needed support at hand.

A DIAGNOSIS OF BREAST CANCER

If your doctor tells you that you have breast cancer, you may well feel devastated, and what's more it will trigger an overwhelming variety of emotions and fears, even denial. It is neither unusual nor unreasonable for a woman to want a second opinion, just to make sure that there has not been a mistake. Your doctor will probably understand this and will usually provide you with the details of another specialist. However, it is important to bear in mind that a second appointment could cause a delay in treatment.

TREATMENT OPTIONS

You will almost certainly have plenty of questions to ask, but at the same time you will probably be feeling frightened and confused. You may feel that you can't take in any more information, so it is important to involve a partner or friend who can provide an extra pair of ears. It can be helpful to allow a day or two to let the news sink in before you start thinking about your treatment. During this time, keep a pen and paper to hand and jot down questions as they come to you.

The team of specialists looking after you will take time to explain all the treatment options to you and your family, but it is important to establish a support system during this time. It may be particularly helpful to talk to a woman who has been through a similar experience; the breast-care nurse at the hospital will be able to arrange this. You may also want to do some research of your own, either by reading or by using support groups and other relevant organizations.

The treatment for breast cancer varies from woman to woman and depends on the type and size of the tumour, whether she has been through the menopause and whether the cancer has spread to other parts of her body. All cancers are different, so treatment is carefully planned for each individual patient. The surgeon will make recommendations, but it is important that you and your partner or family are involved in the final decision-making process.

SURGICAL PROCEDURES

If the lump is small and has been detected early, it may be possible to remove it, plus an area of tissue around it, and leave the majority of the breast intact. The surgeon will often remove a number of the lymph nodes in the armpit (axilla) at the same time. This type of breast-saving

'If you have been diagnosed with breast cancer then you may find it helpful to consult a counsellor or support group so you can speak to other women who have been through a similar experience.'

surgery is known by different names, including 'lumpectomy', 'excision surgery' or 'partial mastectomy'.

The area of breast tissue that has been removed, as well as the lymph nodes, are carefully examined in the laboratory. Analysis will reveal whether or not all the cancerous cells have been successfully removed. A wide excision of the lump sometimes progresses to a mastectomy if there are still tumour cells detected in the margins of the tissue that has been removed.

A mastectomy involves removing the whole breast, and sometimes lymph nodes. This type of surgery is carried out if the tumour is larger than about 10 cm (4 in) or if breast-saving surgery has been unsuccessful in clearing all the cancerous cells.

RECONSTRUCTIVE SURGERY

At this stage, you may want to discuss the possibility of reconstructive surgery. In other words, the breast could be reconstructed using implants or tissue from another area of your body. Reconstructive surgery can be done at a later date and no decisions need to be made at an early stage. In fact, many women decide against reconstruction, and instead use a 'prosthesis', or false breast, that is inserted into the bra cup. You may also feel that there is already enough to think about and that this is one decision that can be delayed for the present.

PAIN CONTROL

Before any surgery, a universal concern is whether there will be any pain. You will almost certainly experience some discomfort after the operation, but the team looking after you have a great deal of experience in controlling pain and will make every effort to make your recovery as pain-free as possible.

Injections Immediately after surgery, depending on the extent of your operation, you may have some quick-acting strong painkillers, often given directly into your bloodstream or into a muscle in your thigh or bottom. These may make you feel a bit woozy, but will help to relax you and will numb the pain completely.

Tablets Once you are fully awake and start moving around, you will be offered painkillers in tablet form. Painkilling tablets are available in several strengths, so as the discomfort starts to lessen you can step down the dose, as necessary.

See also ▶
After surgery, pages 222–223

AFTER SURGERY

A woman who has recently been diagnosed with breast cancer faces two challenges – dealing with a serious illness and learning to cope with the physical loss of a breast. Naturally, every woman will be different in how she perceives her body image after a mastectomy, but common feelings are a sense of loss or bereavement on losing a part of oneself, a loss of femininity and a loss of confidence and self-esteem.

IMMEDIATE POSTSURGICAL TREATMENTS

During the operation, and for a short period afterwards, you will probably have a 'drip' or intravenous infusion. This allows fluids to be given directly into your bloodstream, via a small tube in your vein, during the immediate postoperative period when you are not drinking very much, and prevents you becoming dehydrated. As soon as you are able to drink – usually the day after the operation – the drip will be stopped.

Following an operation, body fluids can collect in the area that has been operated on. The surgeon will therefore use a 'drain' (narrow tube), one end of which is left inside your body and the other brought out on to the surface of the skin and attached to a small plastic bottle. Usually the bottle contains a vacuum to gently 'suck' the fluid out. The drain will be removed by a nurse on the ward when the fluid 'dries up', usually 2–3 days after the operation.

HELP AND SUPPORT

On a positive note, feelings of loss and low self-esteem are familiar ones to the staff working in the breast unit and they will be able to make useful suggestions as to how to cope with them. Often, talking to someone who has already been through a mastectomy is very helpful. For some women, it can be extremely beneficial to see exactly what the physical results of the surgery will be, while others may choose to wait until afterwards.

There have been numerous advances in surgical techniques in recent years and, while the priority is to ensure that the tumour is removed completely, serious consideration is also given to the visual effects of the surgery.

GETTING READY TO GO HOME

A hospital stay for breast surgery varies from a few days to over a week, depending on how quickly you recover. But, most women are up and about very quickly after the operation. It is important during the postoperative period to keep as active as possible. A physiotherapist will give you guidance on regular exercises to do to prevent your arm and shoulder becoming stiff – and the sooner you start doing these exercises regularly, the less likely you are to get swelling and soreness in the area affected by the surgery.

After the operation, you may find that certain areas of your skin will have reduced sensation or may even feel completely numb. This is because some of the small nerves that supply your skin will have been cut during the operation. Many women find that the feeling returns in these areas in the weeks after surgery, but in some cases the numbness is permanent.

HOW DO I LOOK?

The first time you look at your body after a mastectomy will be an emotional moment. You can choose whether to cross this hurdle on your own or with a trusted friend or partner. Remember, though, that it is up to you when and where to share your reshaped body with your loved ones.

For the time being, especially if you are feeling self-conscious, you may want to wear light, loose-fitting, cool clothes. There is plenty of time to make decisions about your wardrobe as your confidence builds.

Numerous organizations specialize in making bras for women who have had a breast removed. The breast-care nurse will talk to you about the kind of prosthesis and underwear that will best suit you.

By the time you go home, your drainage tube will have been removed and your wound, or incision, will be covered with a light dressing. Just before you are discharged, you will be given an appointment to return to the clinic – if you have non-dissolvable stitches, they will be removed during this visit. The doctors and staff at the breast unit will also prepare you for the next phase of your treatment, which may involve chemotherapy or radiotherapy, or both.

'Looking after your emotional as well as your physical wellbeing is a very important part of both your immediate and ongoing care.'

See also ▶
Enjoy life's changes, Chapter 8
The feel-good factor, Chapter 9

RADIOTHERAPY

The team of health professionals looking after you will want to be absolutely sure that they have removed all the cancerous cells. Surgery may therefore be carried out in combination with other treatments. One of these is radiotherapy, or radiation treatment, which uses high-intensity X-rays to destroy cancer cells or to slow down their growth. Nowadays, advanced technology means that the rays can be focused very accurately on the area being treated, avoiding damage to healthy tissue. This type of treatment can be used on the affected breast after a partial mastectomy, and occasionally to treat lymph nodes in the armpit, or above the collarbone. Radiotherapy is sometimes used after a total mastectomy if the tumour was large.

HINT FOR HEALTH

After surgery and during the first phase of treatment, your appetite will almost certainly diminish. Small, frequent healthy snacks can give you the nutrients you need for a good recovery. Try fruit salads, smoothies or light homemade soups to boost your energy.

WHAT DOES RADIOTHERAPY INVOLVE?

Your oncologist, who specializes in cancer treatment, will carefully plan a radiotherapy schedule tailored to your individual needs. Unless you are particularly unwell, you will not be admitted to hospital for the treatment, but will visit the radiotherapy department at your nearest hospital on a regular basis.

On the initial visit, the area to be treated will be very accurately mapped out and marked with a pen – don't worry, the markings are not permanent, but act as an important guide. Radiotherapy usually takes place five times a week for a few weeks, although some women are only treated on alternate days.

The procedure is very like having an X-ray, lasts a few minutes only, and does not cause any discomfort at all. You will be carefully positioned and asked to lie very still during the treatments, while the radiographers (health professionals skilled in X-ray techniques) treat the outlined area.

WHAT ARE THE SIDE EFFECTS?

Most of the side effects of radiotherapy are associated with damage to healthy cells. Although treatment is carefully targeted at the cancer cells, healthy cells are inevitably affected. It is important to note that many women experience very few side effects from radiotherapy, and those that do are often only mildly affected. In any event, the staff in

the radiotherapy unit are able to offer advice on, and solutions for, any of the following symptoms.

- **Tiredness** You may feel more tired than usual and have much less energy. Make sure that during your course of treatment you get plenty of rest. Try having a nap during the day and enlist the help of friends or family with running the household.

- **Irritation of the skin over the area being treated** Healthy skin may become damaged during radiotherapy (see 'Looking after your skin', right).

- **Soreness in the breast or chest** This may last for weeks or even longer, but usually disappears over time. You may wish to take some painkilling drugs for this.

- **Loss of appetite** If the treatment affects your oesophagus, you may feel slightly nauseous, although this is unusual.

LOOKING AFTER YOUR SKIN

As the rays pass through the skin, they can damage the cells. This damage may occur as a reddening or darkening of the skin (as occurs in sunburn), dryness or peeling. Although this damage is not permanent, and the cells can effectively repair themselves once the treatment is over, there are several steps you can take to look after your skin.

- **Keep** your skin supple with a gentle, non-perfumed moisturizing cream.

- **Try not to use** any perfumed products at all, including soap, as these may irritate the skin further.

- **Avoid** lying in a hot bath. Instead take a shower, or gently sponge the area with tepid water. Don't rub your skin with a flannel or towel. Instead gently pat your skin dry with a soft towel.

- **Don't apply** a hot water bottle or ice pack to the area.

- **Keep** your skin protected from the sun. Skin that has been irradiated is much more sensitive to sunlight.

- **Wear** loose-fitting clothes, preferably made from natural fibres such as cotton. During this period, you may find that a bra is uncomfortable and rubs the tender skin. Try wearing a cotton vest instead.

CHEMOTHERAPY

The treatment of cancer using chemotherapy (cancer-killing drugs) has advanced rapidly in recent years and there is now a wide range of drugs that are used in various combinations to treat specific cancers. Whether you have chemotherapy after surgery is dependent on the type and size of cancer and whether it has spread to other parts of the body. Treatment with a combination of these drugs usually starts about two to three weeks after surgery, and may last for up to about six months; usually, the treatment is broken up by periods of rest to allow your body to recover. Some women have chemotherapy before surgery, especially if the tumour is very large and there is a danger that it might spread.

HINT FOR HEALTH

There are many complementary therapies, such as massage, aromatherapy and reflexology, which can help to combat the unpleasant side effects of chemotherapy. Always check with your doctor, however, before you take advantage of these options.

HOW DO THE DRUGS WORK?

Cancer forms when cells in the body become damaged and start to multiply uncontrollably. The drugs used in chemotherapy find and attack these cells, preventing them from forming new ones. Most of the side effects associated with chemotherapy drugs are due to the fact that they specifically target cells that multiply at a very fast rate. This explains, for example, why some women lose their hair during treatment, as normal hair cells reproduce very quickly.

HOW ARE THEY ADMINISTERED?

Usually, the drugs are given directly into a vein in your arm – this way they act quickly and are more effective. As some of the drugs are very strong, they can irritate the walls of the veins and cause inflammation. Your doctor may then decide to insert a tube into a more robust vein just above your clavicle, under local anaesthetic. This tube remains in place for the duration of treatment, but is easily covered with clothing.

WHAT ARE THE SIDE EFFECTS?

The side effects you experience depend on the exact drugs you are receiving – you will not necessarily experience all those listed below, and some women feel well during treatment. Remember that your medical team are used to solving these problems and that most of the side effects go away once the treatment has finished.

- **Nausea and vomiting** Not everyone will feel sick during chemotherapy, but it is a common problem. There are, however, several anti-sickness drugs that can provide relief.

- **Diarrhoea or constipation** If you experience any changes in your bowel habit, the nurses will give you advice on ways of dealing with them.

- **Mouth ulcers** You may find that the lining of your mouth becomes sore during treatment. Avoid spicy or sour foods, which will probably cause discomfort, and keep your mouth and teeth clean and moist. Antiseptic mouthwashes will help.

- **General tiredness** Some women feel 'washed out' and lethargic during the treatment. This is not surprising as there is a battle raging in your body. Try to get plenty of rest.

- **Hair loss** Many women experience varying degrees of hair loss (see box, right).

- **Bone marrow suppression** There is a possibility that the drugs will damage the healthy cells of the bone marrow, which are responsible for producing the red and white blood cells and platelets. Low levels of these cells can lead to anaemia, susceptibility to infection and difficulty in stopping bleeding. Your doctor will take regular blood tests to detect early signs of any of these complications.

COPING WITH THE TREATMENT

It is quite usual to feel low during chemotherapy, especially as by now you will have had plenty of time to think about your diagnosis. If you are feeling particularly down, it may help to talk to your breast-care nurse or to some of the other women receiving chemotherapy. As most women do not have to be in hospital to have chemotherapy treatment, you can also share your concerns with friends and relatives at home.

HAIR LOSS

Hair loss during chemotherapy is a common fear. Often, the hair simply becomes thinner, but some women lose their hair (including eyebrows, eyelashes and pubic hair) completely. You may be content simply to wear a scarf or a light turban until the treatment is over, or you may want to invest in a wig. Your breast-care nurse will be able to advise you on all the resources that are available. The most important fact to bear in mind at this stage is that your hair will grow back, although it may be patchy at first.

LIVING WITH BREAST CANCER

When the treatment is over and you have time to look back over the previous months, you will probably wonder how you ever got through it. As well as the physical stress of surgery and chemotherapy, you will also be left feeling emotionally battered. Now is the time to focus on regaining your strength, befriending your body and doing all you can to keep healthy.

'You may find that you view life with a new perspective – this is a positive transition, as it will help you to reassess your priorities and make the most out of your life.'

HORMONE (ENDOCRINE) TREATMENT

Many women have a cancer that is hormone-dependent, meaning that the tumour cells need oestrogen to grow and develop. These women will usually be prescribed hormone therapy (also called endocrine therapy), which either prevents oestrogen coming into contact with the tumour cells or reduces the amount of oestrogen the body produces. Tamoxifen is a commonly used 'oestrogen-blocking' drug that has a good track record in preventing cancer recurrence. It does, however, need to be taken for five years or more.

Like any drug, tamoxifen has side effects and these vary from woman to woman – many have only very mild effects and others none at all. Some women experience symptoms similar to those of the menopause, such as hot flushes. Others may have some vaginal discharge or bleeding. Your doctor will also advise you that if you are taking tamoxifen you have a slightly increased risk of developing a deep vein thrombosis and cancer of the endometrium (lining of the uterus), but that the benefits of taking the drug far outweigh the risks.

LOOKING GOOD

As your confidence grows, you may become more ambitious with clothing, and your breast-care nurse or staff at the clinic can help with this. There are many organizations that provide 'prostheses' in a range of sizes, shapes and colours, and experienced fitters can help you make the right choices and will guided you to specialist retail outlets.

FEELING GOOD

Make sure you take strength from close friends, or a trusted partner, in whom you can confide. You may find that you view life with a new

perspective and that different things matter (or don't matter) to you. This is a positive transition, as it will help you to reassess your priorities and make the most out of your life.

KEEPING PHYSICALLY ACTIVE

Research studies suggest that physical exercise improves the quality of life for breast cancer survivors. Set yourself goals – short-term ones at first and then more ambitious ones as and when you feel able.

- **Swimming** is excellent exercise, both in terms of fitness and as a stretching exercise for your arm and shoulder. Even a few lengths of your local pool will help.

- **Walking** is a popular activity and can be tailored to the way you feel – brisk walking if you are feeling energetic, and a gentle stroll if you are not.

- **Yoga and tai chi** are both excellent for gentle stretching that can keep the area of surgery and the affected arm, as well as the rest of your body, supple. Don't be talked into stretching beyond your capabilities, and do get advice from your teacher.

EATING FOR GOOD HEALTH

Now is the time to start thinking about the health-enhancing properties of food and making sure that your diet fits the bill. Follow the advice about healthy eating given in Chapter 3.

MAKING LOVE AFTER A MASTECTOMY

There are no hard and fast rules about when you can resume your sex life again after a mastectomy. The decision is yours. Many women lose their libido (sex drive) during treatment and it may take a while before sex is high on the priority list. It is also common to have a strong sense of loss of femininity after a mastectomy. Discuss these feelings with your partner rather than keep them bottled up so you can deal with it together. If your concerns continue, your doctor or breast-care nurse at the hospital can give you advice and support. Or, you could ring one of the telephone helplines provided by breast cancer organizations.

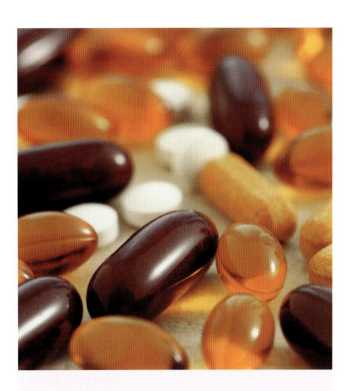

HINT FOR HEALTH

Oil of evening primrose can be bought over the counter and in many health food shops. This natural product is a good source of essential fatty acids and may help to relieve breast discomfort in some women.

See also ▶

Instant beauty boosters, Chapter 1

Loosen up and shape up, Chapter 2

Healthy eating for a longer life, Chapter 3

Enjoy life's changes, Chapter 8

The feel-good factor, Chapter 9

Brain boosters, Chapter 10

PART 3
A NEW YOU

CHAPTER 8
ENJOY LIFE'S CHANGES 232

Many women find that their lifestyle changes enormously around the time of the menopause. You may be retiring or reducing your workload, and your children may have left home or even started their own families. This chapter helps you to make the most of these changes. It includes an invaluable re-energizing plan, plus useful advice on socializing with confidence and being more assertive in your everyday interactions.

CHAPTER 9
THE FEEL-GOOD FACTOR 256

This chapter focuses on ways in which you can optimize your health and wellbeing by relaxing and calming mind and body. Giving your body time to renew and repair itself is vital, and meditation, yoga and massage can all help you to do this. There is also a helpful stress-busting plan to help you combat the tensions of everyday life and indispensable tips for getting a good night's sleep.

CHAPTER 10
BRAIN BOOSTERS 296

It is very important to exercise your brain along with the rest of your body. As you age you may find that your recall is not as good as it was, and you may struggle to remember people's names or telephone numbers, or where you left your keys. This chapter contains numerous useful strategies to maximize your memory, as well as great suggestions on what foods to eat to boost your brain power.

CHAPTER 8
ENJOY LIFE'S CHANGES

This can be a very exciting – or a very disconcerting – time of life as everything seems to be changing and the future may seem slightly daunting. From socializing with ease to revitalizing your energy levels, this chapter shows you how to make the most of your changing lifestyle by minimizing the negative aspects and maximizing your confidence.

NEW OPPORTUNITIES

Your 50s are likely to bring you plenty of life-altering challenges. The menopause aside, this can be a period of great transition – your children leaving home, becoming a grandmother and retirement are all events that might occur during this decade. It may take you time to adjust but you should view this period as exciting and appreciate the chances to do as *you* wish, rather than fulfilling the obligations of a family and/or paid employment.

'EMPTY NEST' SYNDROME

Some parents look forward to their offspring leaving home while others dread the day when they have to redefine their own roles in life and are left in a family home alone. Even those who are not alone might well have forgotten how to relate to their partner over the years of raising and supporting a family.

If this is you, you mustn't forget the fact that, although your children have left the nest, you are still their mother. Your role may have shifted slightly but they will still need your support and advice from time to time – probably more often than you think! You are still a valuable person with plenty to offer and it's time now to concentrate on you – and your partner. Renew your relationship as a couple rather than seeing yourselves in the 'mother' and 'father' roles. Talk to each other, take up new interests as a twosome, reinvent your sex life if necessary and sit down and make plans for the future together. You can still be very much a part of your children's – and later their children's – lives, but at the same time enjoying your newly regained independence, leading your own life and pursuing your own interests.

BEING GRANDPARENTS

Grandparenting generally means you can enjoy the children without taking on as much of the hard work of being a parent – because you've already done that! Rather than get bogged down in everyday routines, enforcing discipline and overseeing homework, you can simply spend time having fun with your grandchildren. You can play with them, tell them stories, teach them your own interests or skills, spoil them and listen to them. Your grandchildren will adore being with you and will certainly help keep you young!

As far as your son or daughter is concerned, try to respect the decisions they make about raising their children. Don't interfere, however much you may want to, and offer advice only when it is sought. Remember that attitudes and practices will have changed since you brought up your children.

If a son or daughter ask you to help with childcare, make sure you set the boundaries at the outset. After all, you do have your own life to lead now and, however much you love your grandchildren, looking after little ones can be extremely tiring!

PLANNING TO RETIRE

The number of people in the world over the age of 100 is increasing. It's estimated that by the year 2030, there will be 30,000 centenarians in the UK alone, and by 2050, 1 million in the USA. The fact that we're living longer and healthier lives means that our retirement years could number almost as many as those of our working life. In general we are fitter and wealthier than previous generations so we are in a good position to enjoy retirement. But with this new-found free time, what are we to do with ourselves?

SUCCESSFUL RETIREMENT

- **Stay in control** One of the biggest challenges of retirement is maintaining your sense of control and worth once you no longer have a paid position in society that defines what you are/do. Loss of control can result in frustration and stress, neither of which are good for health and longevity. The solution is to manage your leisure time wisely and continually achieve goals you set yourself.

- **Look after your health** Your health is the key to living longer, and you now have even more time to devote to it. Continue to eat healthily (see Chapter 3) and stay active – concentrate on your favourite sports or take up a new one.

- **Seize new opportunities** Retirement from full-time employment could bring you another 35–40 hours of extra time a week. Use this new-found time to do something that is meaningful to you. If you don't already have any hobbies and interests, cultivate some before you retire so that you can make the adjustment to retirement more smoothly. Try things you have always wanted to do – take up a musical instrument for example, learn a second language, write that book that has been in your head for years or redesign your garden.

- **Spend more time with your grandchildren** With more and more mums working outside the home and professional childcare costs so high any regular help you can offer looking after the grandchildren is likely to be welcome. If this is not possible, just having them to stay over for the odd night or for a few days usually pleases all three generations!

- **Consider voluntary or part-time work** If you want to involve yourself more with your community think about offering your skills and time to a charity, primary school or local conservation project. Alternatively, you could earn some extra money by working a few hours a week to boost both your finances and self-esteem, and keep yourself mentally and physically fit.

- **Start studying** Brains as well as bodies need to stay active. Retirement brings more time and fewer distractions so consider studying, be it purely for interest or to gain a qualification.

- **Go travelling** You don't have to go far, but travelling is fun and keeps the brain cells ticking. Some travel companies are geared solely towards the older traveller and offer the chance to travel with like-minded retirees. In addition, travel concessions are often available at off-peak times or seasons.

- **Consider moving** Once a job no longer dictates where you live you may wish to move house to be nearer family, take advantage of another climate or pursue a hobby – for example, if you like sailing why not move to the coast? Alternatively, you may simply want to downsize once the children have left home.

- **Take advantage of your senior status!** Many venues, transport companies, colleges and sports centres offer discounts to senior citizens. Don't be proud – enjoy reduced rates for films, concerts, study courses, swimming and exercise classes – after all, you've earned the perks of retirement.

The priority is to make plans for your retirement. Otherwise, it can be an abrupt and stressful culture shock, bringing changes in your finances, responsibilities, position in society and availability of time. Perhaps the two most important considerations are to make sure you do everything you can in advance to ensure you will be financially secure when the time comes and to plan how you will spend your time. Some people find they lack a sense of purpose to each day once the well-worn routine of going out to work has gone. Without planning you could be overwhelmed by this new 'freedom', and end up doing nothing useful and feeling depressed.

Ensuring you have interests and activities that you enjoy is an important part of planning for a successful retirement. They help to facilitate the transition from busy, structured working days to a slower pace of life. The alternative, if you are unprepared for leisure time, is spending hours watching television which could easily become an unfulfilling way of occupying yourself.

The best way forward is to consider retirement as a beginning rather than an ending, with the possibility for you to follow up all manner of opportunities, be it studying for a degree, travelling or simply spending more time with your family. If you really are stuck as to what to do you may want to act upon your answers to the following questions:

* What did you want to be when you were growing up?

* What were you good at that you later had neither time nor energy for?

* What did you enjoy doing as a child?

* What do you want to accomplish in your life?

Life can sometimes sweep us up like a fast-flowing river, and dreams can get left behind. Once you are retired you have the time to follow up any past dreams you may have forgotten or postponed.

HALF-EMPTY OR HALF-FULL?

Whether you consider that oft-quoted glass as half-full or half-empty helps determine your attitude to life. If you have a tendency towards pessimism be aware that you can use your mental powers to reverse this attitude – something that is well worth cultivating since research has shown that people with an optimistic outlook enjoy better health and are likely to lead longer, and happier, lives.

CLEAR OUT YOUR CLUTTER

If you want to ring the changes, a good place to start is your immediate surroundings – your home. Now is the ideal time to get rid of some of the clutter that you and your family have probably acquired over the years. With a decisive approach and a bit of imagination, you can give your home a new lease of life and enjoy a sense of achievement as well.

EFFECTIVE CLUTTER CONTROL

- **Be selective** about possessions.

- **Display** or store possessions astutely.

- **Adopt** clear-thinking, anti-clutter habits.

Our homes are under constant attack from clutter. There is the stuff that accumulates daily almost like dust (newspapers, magazines, bills and laundry) and there are things that you acquire gradually over the years (books, clothes, photographs and furniture). The first group simply needs to be dealt with regularly to keep it under control. The second is more of a problem because it invades your home slowly and imperceptibly, so that you do not realize how much of it you have until your space actually becomes less usable because of it.

BE SELECTIVE

The secret is to take control of your surroundings and choose your possessions – do not let them choose you. That means throwing out anything you have not used or worn in the last 12 months. If it has been waiting to be cleaned or mended, then get it done, have it recycled into something useful or get rid of it.

Eliminate duplicate items, too. You will probably have a favourite you use out of choice, whether it is a stepladder or hairdryer, so ditch the seconds instead of hoarding them. The same goes for books and CDs: weed out spare copies and take them to a charity shop.

Do not hoard packs of old photographs that you are never going to look at. Select the ones you want to keep and put them into albums or frames. Be ruthless about throwing away the ones you do not really like or want. You can always keep the negatives and have reprints made if you suffer nostalgia pangs later.

Work through all your possessions like this, deciding whether you really want things or if they have just attached themselves to you. Tackle one area at a time so that it does not feel too brutal: clothes one week, kitchen gadgets another, books and CDs the next, and so on. Remember, if you have too much stuff you will find that it just gets

in the way. It is far easier to be relaxed and comfortable if your surroundings are calm and organized, so be proactive and get rid of things that you don't use any more.

ORGANIZED STORAGE

What you do decide to keep needs to be stored safely, where you can find it again. Do not just throw things in a cupboard and shut the door on them: if you are prepared to abandon them to this fate, you might as well have thrown them away completely. If they are not needed immediately, create filing systems for them with boxes, bags and crates, and label things clearly so that you know what is what. Avoid cardboard boxes, which are susceptible to damp and rot.

Create organized storage wherever possible, and look for furniture that provides hidden storage space in tables and stools and under beds.

NEAT THINKING

Keep the hallway clear to start off on the right footing, and the rest of the house will follow in the same vein. Store coats, keys and post neatly. Deal with bills, letters and other paperwork as it arrives, and then file it away. And do not let messages, addresses and phone numbers loiter on untidy scraps of paper – transfer the information to your diary or address book and throw away the notes.

Do not hang on to old newspapers and magazines: clear your newspapers at the end of each day. Cut out any features you want to keep and file them, then put out the remains for rubbish or recycling.

If you know you haven't really got the time to deal with everything on a day-to-day basis, invest in some boxes and baskets to hold papers, bills and anything else left lying around – at least, then, it will look tidy. Do a regular collection around each room and sort them out as soon as the container is full. Then have a throw-away day once a month to get rid of anything you do not need to keep.

THROWING OUT FURNITURE

Furniture is particularly difficult to say goodbye to because there is an inevitable sense that it is useful. But getting rid of it will become easier as you clear out other clutter. Extra cupboards and chests of drawers will simply become redundant as you clear out unused things.

CLUTTER-CLEARING BASICS

- **Throw out** anything you have not used for 12 months or more, or recycle it into something that you will use.

- **Get rid of** any items of furniture that are taking up space without adding to the look or practicality of the room.

- **Invest in** storage boxes and baskets.

- **Reclaim** surfaces. You do not have to use every shelf and tabletop – leave some of them empty and spacious.

- **Put things away** as soon as you have finished with them: books back on shelves, tools in their box, clothes in cupboards or laundry baskets.

- **Look for** furniture with hidden storage assets – beds fitted with drawers or coffee tables with lift-up lids.

- **Avoid** glass-fronted cabinets if you cannot keep the contents tidy.

ENERGIZING PLAN

You may find that you simply can't summon up the energy to get up and go, you feel tired and lethargic all the time, or you don't feel able to face the world. If so, this revitalizing plan is for you. In as few as three days, you can reinvigorate your body, improve your energy levels and bring back that enthusiasm for life that seemed lost.

THE ENERGY PROCESS

Energy is created in the body from food. When we eat, our bodies break down the ingested food into glucose, which is the main sugar that we use for fuel. It can do this from any food: doughnuts, rare steaks, plates of spinach topped with lemon juice. Healthy or unhealthy, the body can use food as energy. However, its favourite sources are carbohydrate foods like fruit, vegetables, bread, pasta and rice, because these are easy to convert into energy. When the food has been broken down, it is combined with oxygen. This 'burns' the sugar and turns it into a unit of energy called adenosine triphosphate, which the cells then store and use as they need it.

In a healthy, fatigue-free body, this process works without any problems and, as a result, we spend each day fully functioning and raring to go. Sometimes the energy process breaks down, however, and this is when we start to feel tired.

WHAT GOES WRONG?

Many things can interfere with the energy process, but these are the four main problems:
1 You don't have enough nutrients to trigger energy conversion.
2 You don't have enough blood-sugar to produce energy quickly and cleanly.
3 You don't have enough oxygen in the system.
4 You don't have enough mitochondria – the constituents of cells that turn glucose into fuel.

THE SOLUTION

By following this energizing plan you will boost your body and feel reinvigorated. Although it is given here as a daily plan, you should follow the plan for at least three days. Doing this will double your energy levels in a long weekend. To get the best results, however, one week is the optimum time to follow the programme.

07:20 **Time to wake up** In an energy-boosting world you shouldn't get up before 7.20am, as this creates higher than normal levels of the energy-sapping hormone cortisol in your body. If work pressures mean 7.20am is a lie-in, then at least wake your body more gently by using a daylight alarm clock, which slowly raises the levels of light in the room, waking you slowly and calmly.

07:30 **Take supplements** One multivitamin supplement, one probiotic supplement and one capsule of fish oil (or if you are vegetarian one of evening primrose oil) with a large glass of water. This is the first of eight glasses of water you will drink over the entire day – aim roughly for one glass an hour. The supplements will not only provide nutrients but will also aid your digestion, maximizing what you can absorb from food. Leave half an hour between taking these and eating.

07:40 **Carry out the 'Adapted salute to the sun' exercise** (see pages 268–271). It takes about 5 minutes, and should be done outside or at least facing a window, which adds to your energy banks because sunlight stops production of the sleep-inducing hormone melatonin.

07:50 **Body-brush** Using a natural-bristled brush with medium–hard bristles, brush each area of your body with long, firm (but not hard) strokes. Always start with the soles of your feet, because stimulating these actually starts the lymph flowing. Brush smoothly 4–5 times, always in the direction of the heart, moving around the whole body part. Do this around your calves, then your thighs and hips. Now do your arms, chest, torso and back. Finally, brush your stomach. Once you've finished, shower or at least rinse yourself well. As well as obviously cleaning the skin, the repeated motion of brushing or scrubbing the body causes the speed of the circulation to increase (helping flush toxins out of the system faster), and this is also believed to promote lymph flow.

OXYGEN JUICE

6 slices of pineapple (fresh or tinned)
1 banana
6 fresh strawberries
1 handful of wheatgrass

Put each item through the juicer, then mix together and shake well. Drink immediately.

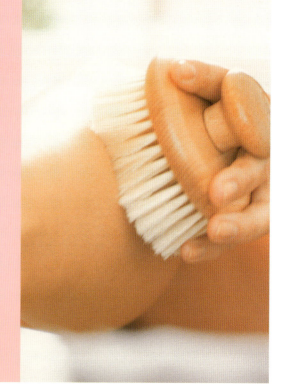

SUGGESTED LUNCH MENU

- A glass of oxygen juice.

- One of the following energizing vegetable bases, using as much of each vegetable as you like.

  Fluid fuel: cucumber, lettuce, celery, chopped apple and a few slices of pear.

  Quick cleanse: asparagus, cherry tomatoes and yellow peppers on a bed of alfalfa.

  Steamed and simple: steamed green cabbage, carrot, mushrooms, asparagus and mangetout.

  Sunshine salad: watercress, carrot, beetroot and pink grapefruit.

- A 50 g (2 oz) portion of one (or a mix) of the following: salmon, anchovies, mackerel, herring, trout, sardines, sunflower, pumpkin or sesame seeds, walnuts or cashews, or tahini. These protein foods create a slowly burned form of energy and provide high levels of essential fatty acids.

08:00 Get your breakfast B vitamins B vitamins are vital to the energy levels of your body, and breakfast foods are an excellent source. For best results, choose a bowl of bran cereal with skimmed milk, and two pieces of wholewheat toast with a little honey and some fruit. If you normally have coffee in the morning, have it; if you are used to having a morning coffee, skipping it will leave you more tired.

10:00 'Dejunk' your day Energy is not just sapped physically from our bodies, it is also sapped mentally by stress, worry and feelings of being overwhelmed. Whether you work in an office or are busy at home, clearing physical and mental clutter should be your first job. Tidy your desk, sort out the bills, or first tackle the one task you really don't want to do. When this is finished, it will feel like a weight has been lifted from you and your energy will start to soar.

11:20 Time for a healthy snack Not only does eating little and often keep the blood-sugar levels of the body stable, but it also boosts energy in other ways. Digesting foods uses energy, and meals that are too large can fatigue the body. Healthy snacks, such as fruit, take the edge off your appetite and stop you overeating at main meals.

13:00 Eat a good lunch This meal should be used to boost oxygen and fluid levels in the body, giving you energy to face the afternoon when energy levels naturally dip. Good oxygen-boosting foods are wheatgrass, watercress, spinach, dark cabbage, lettuce, alfalfa and other sprouts. Also fill up on fluid-heavy foods like celery, cucumber, fennel, apples, pears, watermelon, grapefruit and grapes. Finally, include some asparagus, since this (along with alfalfa) helps neutralize the natural toxin ammonia produced within our body, a common cause of fatigue.

15:00 Head outside By now, the air in your office, or even at home, is likely to be low in oxygen, boosting your feelings of fatigue. Go for a quick walk, or try the following yoga technique, which oxygenates the entire body. Stand up straight and clench your fists. Breathe in quickly through your nose and out through your mouth. As you do this, pump your arms to get blood circulating around your body. Repeat this process for 1 minute, but listen to your body as you do this. The sudden flood of oxygen can make you feel light-headed and, if this happens, you should stop and

simply breathe normally for a while until you feel 'normal' again. It is also a good idea to have some more fruit at this time.

18:00 **Do some exercise** Toxins have the ability to sap our energy by acting negatively on the mitochondria within the body. If you build muscle through exercise, you also increase the number of mitochondria. Take 30 minutes every other day on the plan to do some kind of aerobic or strength training, and ideally do it between 4pm and 7pm.

20:00 **Eat your evening meal** Overnight the body regenerates and naturally detoxes, so the focus of your evening meal should be to provide an ample supply of detoxing foods (see pages 82–83) to boost this process. You should combine these with carbohydrates; while these are primarily energy-givers, in doses of more than 75 g (3 oz) at one time they can calm the body and promote sleep.

21:00 **Blend yourself a bedtime bath** Bathing stimulates the natural cooling process the body uses to trigger sleep hormones. Increase the soporific and calming effects of your bath by adding some essential oils (see pages 282–285). One of the best bathtime oils is marjoram, which has a sedative effect, but also fortifying to the body, helping create strength for the next day. Add 3 drops of marjoram and 3 drops of calming mandarin to your bath, lie back and relax.

22:30 **Go to bed** Getting a good night's sleep is essential as it is how the body recharges.

See also ▶

Instant beauty boosters, Chapter 1

Loosen up and shape up, Chapter 2

Healthy eating for a longer life, Chapter 3

The feel-good factor, Chapter 9

SUGGESTED EVENING MEAL MENU

- A cup of vegetable soup.

- One of these four vegetable bases, using as much of each vegetable as you like.

    Detox salad: watercress, celery, cucumber, cherry tomato, artichoke hearts.

    Cleansing coleslaw: white cabbage, onion, grated carrot, sliced beetroot.

    Roast energy: grilled or oven-baked slices of red or yellow pepper, aubergine, onion and mushrooms.

    Steamed and simple: steamed carrot, mangetout, cauliflower, spinach and asparagus.

- A 75 g (3 oz) serving of one (or a mix) of the following to your chosen vegetable base: brown rice, jacket potato, new potatoes, mashed potatoes, wholewheat pasta, couscous, mashed swede, roast parsnips, corn on the cob, sweetcorn, rye, pumpernickel bread or wholegrain bread.

BOOST YOUR SOCIAL LIFE

It is important to make new friends at every stage of life – so don't just rely on your old friends. Many of us find it difficult to talk to new people in a social situation, because we lack the confidence to chat to 'strangers' and perceive ourselves as 'shy'. Making 'small talk' is easier than you might think, and this section will show you how to develop your social skills and overcome any shyness you might have, by taking you through eight simple stages.

HOW GOOD ARE YOU AT SMALL TALK?

To assess how good you are at small talk, for each of the 10 statements below rate yourself on a scale of 1–10 (where 1 means you agree strongly with the statement, and 10 means you disagree strongly with it).

1 I dry up in social situations.
2 I forget people's names easily.
3 I find it hard to initiate conversations.
4 I find small talk superficial.
5 I worry that people will find me intrusive if I ask them questions.
6 I worry what others will think of me.
7 I feel awkward in the presence of people I don't know.
8 I have lost my sense of curiosity about people.
9 I feel awkward about sharing my interests with others.
10 I have stopped keeping abreast of current affairs.

Score under 30 your inability to make small talk is really holding you back.
30–70 you need to work on overcoming your fear of small talk.
Over 70 your fear of small talk is not really having a detrimental effect on your confidence.

THE ROOTS OF SHYNESS

A feeling of not being able to make effective small talk can cripple the social lives of many people and it can also prevent business people from 'networking' effectively. Poor social skills can prevent shy people from being able to ask someone out for a date and can also make the workplace a misery for new members of staff who find it difficult to make acquaintances, who will often naturally develop into friends. The inability to make small talk has its roots in our early conditioning.

'DON'T TALK TO STRANGERS'

This warning is given to us from an early age. It is an understandable warning to a child to keep them from harm, but can become a permanent mindset, meaning that an adult does not talk to strangers because these are still regarded as people to avoid. The adult will only initiate conversations with someone they already know and trust.

'DON'T PRY'

Children are educated, in the best interests of respect, not to pry into other people's business, because this is considered rude. Again, we take this attitude forward into our adult years, meaning that we dare not ask people questions in case they think we are prying into their personal lives or are being intrusive.

'CURIOSITY KILLED THE CAT'

If, as children, we ask genuine questions of our parents or teachers out of a natural curiosity to learn and discover, then, if the parent or teacher is too busy or simply does not know the answer, we are told not to ask so many questions. This educates us not to be inquisitive and to stifle our natural curiosity.

'DON'T INTERRUPT'

When, as children, in our enthusiasm to speak and make ourselves heard, we are admonished and told not to interrupt, or to speak only when we are spoken to, again this builds a mindset that makes it difficult to be spontaneous in conversation. It introduces a formal code of behaviour based on 'don't' rather than 'do', so that you end up needing permission to speak.

WHAT IS 'SMALL TALK'?

'Small talk' focuses on the small details of life rather than the bigger picture. It is noticeable that those people who excel at making small talk generally have a keen sense of curiosity about people and life. The ability to make good small talk comes from having an 'overspill' of references, facts and information that you want to share with others.

EIGHT STAGES TO EFFECTIVE SMALL TALK

To improve your ability to talk to new people in social situations, here are eight stages for you to work through.

1 IMPROVE YOUR REFERENCE BASE

If you find small talk difficult, then set out to improve your cultural reference base. What you are looking for when starting a conversation are points of connection. In order to be conversant, you must be well informed. Try to learn something new each week about any of these areas:
- World events.
- Sport.
- Trends in fashion.
- The state of the financial markets.
- New developments in science.
- Business trends.
- Recent films and books.
- Developments in health and wellbeing.
- Celebrity behaviour.

2 START A CONVERSATION

The best way to start a conversation is with simple, non-controversial observations. When you share your opinions and observations, other people are more inclined to do the same. You could, for example:
- Comment on the news headlines.
- Discuss the local traffic situations.
- Point out peculiarities and trends in the weather.
- Talk about how your children are wearing the same fashions you once did.

3 ASK QUESTIONS

Many people believe that the best way to keep a conversation going is to ask questions. However, the key is learning how to use questions to start a conversation, not to control it. Don't ask too many questions and avoid those that sound too probing or aggressive. Try asking someone:
- Whether they like going to the cinema or the theatre.
- What they thought about last night's big match or soap episode.
- Where they grew up.
- How long they have been in their profession.

4 REVEAL SOMETHING OF YOURSELF

Although it is risky, when you reveal something about yourself the level of conversation can become deeper. Once you start sharing more with other people, they will start sharing more with you. Obviously, you don't want to air your 'dirty laundry' or give people more information than they can handle. If your instinct tells you a subject is inappropriate, it probably is. Appropriate topics might be:

- Your opinion on a recent film.
- Where you went to college or university.
- What pets you have.
- Your favourite sports team.
- Your experiences at a new restaurant.

5 DEAL WITH AWKWARD SILENCES

One of the fears that many people have about making small talk is the awkward silence – that moment when conversation dries up and neither of you is able to find anything with which to restart the chat. The awkwardness seems to last for ever, until one of you makes a suitable excuse and the agony is over.

What can you do to prevent that occasional awkward silence when the conversation just runs out of steam? The worst time to be inspired to come up with something to talk about is at the very moment when conversation has dried up, so try thinking in advance of two or three things to bring up during a lull. They could involve current events, sports or music, for example.

6 REMEMBER NAMES

Many people forget the names of new people to whom they are introduced, because they are not listening properly or there is too much background noise for the information to be properly processed.

When you are introduced to someone, listen carefully. If it seems appropriate, you can say: 'Would you say your name again? I'm not sure I got it'; 'That's a nice name. Would you pronounce it again?'; or 'How do you spell your name?' You could also repeat the person's name once or twice in the conversation; this will help you remember it as well as letting the other person know that you know it. Be careful not to overdo this, however, since constant repetition of someone's name can be seen as a sign of over-familiarity and become irritating.

- Thanks, Gerald, for that information.
- Charlene, I really appreciate your sharing that.
- Helen, that was a charming story.
- Good to meet you, Will.

7 MAKE AN IMPRESSION

What you say accounts for about 20 per cent of the first impression you create. The sound of your voice accounts for about 30 per cent, and 50 per cent is related to non-verbal messages, such as body language. Here are some ways to create a good first impression.

- **Pretend you are meeting an old friend** Imagine that the person you are meeting for the first time, or are trying to impress, is an old friend you have not seen for many years. You are pleased and excited to see that person again. Adopt this attitude and the rest will come naturally.

- **Mirror body language** When the person you are meeting folds their arms, do the same. If they lightly touch your arm, do the same to them, or cross your legs in the same direction as theirs. These actions may seem obvious to you, but are rarely noticed by the other person, who will subconsciously feel that you are sympathetic towards them.

- **Echo their language** If the person calls their newborn son their 'boy', don't call it a baby, child or infant. Call it a 'boy'. If the person refers to their work as a profession, don't call it their job. Using their special language tells the person you are on the same wavelength.

- **Lean forward** A slight forward lean indicates that you are interested in what the person is saying, are listening intently and don't want to miss a word. Leaning back says that you want to be somewhere else.

- **Make eye contact** Letting the other person know that they are the most important person in the room begins with how you think about them. Tell yourself that they are the most important person in the room. Give them your complete attention, because that is how you would want others to treat you. Don't look vaguely into the distance or keep looking over their shoulder to see if someone more important has just arrived. Try to make frequent eye contact, lasting no more than 2 or 3 seconds each time. Never stare continuously and intensely into the other person's eyes, however, since this may well make them feel very uncomfortable.

- **Use touch and body language** A firm handshake on meeting someone can work wonders. To assist in developing a positive handshake, try imagining that

PUTTING THE THEORY INTO ACTION

Remember that small talk is anything but trivial. People do business with people they know, like and trust. There is no better way for people to get to know you than by you talking to them. Although engaging a person you don't know in conversation may be difficult, don't give up. The art of small talk takes practice, as the eight stages here have demonstrated.

you are a powerful and successful business person. The former US President Bill Clinton always radiates positive body language and one of his hallmarks is the two-arm handshake. This is accomplished by shaking the other person's right hand, while lightly grabbing their arm with your left hand. The higher up their arm you place your left hand the greater the warmth you are felt to be radiating towards them. Another of his tricks is biting his lip to indicate sympathy. If a person is telling you a hard-luck story, gently bite your lip to let them know that you feel for them.

- **Vary your tone of voice** Make sure your voice is not a monotonous drone. Vary the pitch of your voice to accentuate key points. Also try to vary your speeds; a quicker speed is useful if you want to create some excitement in the conversation, and a slower speed helps if you want to create some calm and reflection. If you want to create some intimacy, speak in a quiet voice, almost a whisper.

- **Involve your listener** Some people try to cover up their nerves by talking continuously. They fear that their audience will not find them interesting, so don't risk leaving a pause in the conversation. Check that the listener is still with you by asking them what they think about what you are saying. Invite them into the conversation rather than excluding them.

8 DEVELOP YOUR LISTENING SKILLS

If you know you have a poor attention or listening span, then small talk is probably going to be hard work for you. The ability to create space for others is as important a skill in small talk as asking starter questions. It can be difficult being quiet enough inside oneself to be able to listen. When you listen, conversation is easy. When your head is full of wondering what to say next, then you miss the flow of the conversation, and it does not get out of first gear.

To develop your listening skills, spend 1 minute a day doing nothing but listening. Listen to the sounds around you and learn to analyse what you hear. This will lead to increased stillness and enable you to hear the words of others much better. Ask yourself the following questions:

- How many sounds do you hear?
- Which are close to you and which are far away?
- Are the sounds deep or shrill?
- Are they harsh sounds or soft sounds?

See also ▶
Be confident, pages 250–253
Act positively, pages 254–255

BE CONFIDENT

Many people suffer from low self-esteem or self-confidence, and changes in lifestyle and health can compound and exacerbate these problems. You may find it extremely difficult to say no to others when they ask you to do something, even if doing it will cause you great inconvenience. You believe that a refusal will seem unfriendly or even hostile, and that people will not like you as a person if you say no to them. Yet this is quite untrue – saying no in the right situation may not only alleviate stress on you but also command respect from other people.

CAN YOU SAY NO?

For each of the 10 statements below, rate yourself on a scale of 1–10 (where 1 means you agree strongly with the statement, and 10 means you disagree strongly with it).

1 I worry about hurting others' feelings.
2 I say yes when I really mean no.
3 I dare not speak the truth to others.
4 I want to be liked and approved of.
5 People treat me like a doormat and walk all over me.
6 I worry what others will think of me.
7 I agree to do things because I think that is what others expect of me.
8 I fear saying no to others in case they dislike me.
9 I have to build up my confidence before I can say no to someone.
10 I think that people will get mad with me if I say no.

Score under 30 you need to develop the confidence to say no.
30–70 you need to continue to work on your ability to say no.
Over 70 the ability to say no is not a problem for you.

UNDERSTANDING NO

Many people have a fear of saying no to others, but no is an influence that you can – and should – use to your advantage. It is nothing to be afraid of. No exists to be used for the purposes of enabling a human to have choice. This is one of the features and beauties of being human. Without this choice we become like robots, with no will, and this is not the nature of the human design or purpose. No is a valuable tool that enables us to exercise this choice.

Such a power exists so that we do not become subject to any influences that will divert us from our natural course of development and growth. However, we have to win this power, as part of our development, as part of the struggle to exercise our choice about what we will have and what we won't have.

People who say no are perceived as being cold. This is because the nature of the no influence is cold. No anaesthetizes things. It is like a cold shaft of power that prevents things from growing. No is a vital ally.

WHY IS IT DIFFICULT TO SAY NO?

If you find it difficult to say no, you are not alone. It is probably the most common reason behind the fact that many people have difficulty in rebuilding their confidence. Those who find it hard to say no often do because they don't want to hurt other people's feelings. They worry that if they say no the other person will take offence and a friendship will be lost. There are several reasons why this might happen.

BEING PERCEIVED AS COLD

If you are a warm-hearted, generous and giving person, you will probably worry that others will perceive you as being cold if you say no. Warm-hearted people can find it difficult to say no simply because to be able to say no effectively means that you have to become a little bit cool. The quality of no by nature is a cold influence, because the function of an effective no is to be able to neutralize those things that you personally don't want to process.

PLAYING THE VICTIM

If you have a history of being bullied or victimized, it is possible that you will find it difficult to say no to others. The reason for this is that bullying causes you to take on the role of the victim. You become someone who accepts the blame for everything. Bullying leaves a lot of

WHY DO PEOPLE FIND IT DIFFICULT TO SAY NO?

- **Warm-hearted people** are afraid of seeming cold.

- **Victims** don't believe they can say no.

- **Sensitive people** are worried about how others feel.

See also ▶
Boost your social life, pages 244–249
Act positively, pages 254–255

SAYING NO TO FRIENDS

In order for your no to be received well and not thrown back in your face, you need to nurture the right feelings in the other person. The way to do this is to enable them to feel understood. Try using expressions like these:

- This isn't the answer that you want to hear, but…
- I know you may not like this, but…
- I really appreciate you asking me to help, but…
- I understand your situation, but…
- I would dearly love to help, but…

wounds and scars in the victim; if these wounds have not healed, it becomes difficult to say no because of the fear of being wounded by the person you are rejecting. Your assumed role is the victim, so that people walk all over you. You expect others to have more power than you do, or you simply don't use the power that you have at your disposal because it is not in your role to do so.

BEING SENSITIVE TO OTHERS' NEEDS

If you are sensitive and a friend asks you to do something for them that you don't want to do, your sensitivity will make you aware of your friend's need and also your own need. So you feel both, which means that you become caught in an emotional tug-of-war between ensuring that your needs are met and trying to help your friend. It is very difficult to say no when you are caught in this situation.

YEARNING FOR INCLUSION

One of the psychological anxieties that comes with the struggle to say no is the uncertainty of what will come back to us from others when we do. How will the person to whom we are saying no react?

- Will they explode?
- Will they get angry?
- Will they make us feel bad?
- Will they make us feel a lesser person?

If we are sensitive in some way, we do not want to hurt another's feelings, but neither do we want to do things that are not right for us. This psychological uncertainty is born from the potential hurt and pain that may come from rejecting others, and if we have been hurt before this may be something that we certainly want to avoid. So we end up saying yes to avoid this potential conflict and confrontation. This means that the 'gate' remains open for this other person to include us in their world, even if it is on their terms rather than ours. As we seek security in our lives, we will often seek it from whatever source is available to us, even when it is to our own detriment.

SAYING NO ASSERTIVELY

If you wish your no to be taken seriously, the method of delivering it is very important. First of all, you need to believe it yourself, and to do

this you will need to overcome all the common fallacies that usually get in the way and concentrate on your own rights instead. Getting your message across clearly and calmly is vital – don't forget that other people have a right to make requests of you, so you should not just respond aggressively when they do.

HOW TO BE ASSERTIVE

1 Breathe deeply.
2 Be firm in your vocal tone and body language.
3 Start your answer with the word no.
4 Keep the reply short and clear, but not abrupt.
5 Give the real reason for refusing; don't invent excuses.
6 Avoid 'I can't' phrases; use 'I'd prefer not' or 'I'd rather not'.
7 Don't apologize profusely, if at all (one 'I'm sorry, but ...' will suffice).
8 Acknowledge the requester by name.
9 Ask for more information if needed.
10 Ask for more time if needed.

If the other person repeats their request or persists in assuming that you will comply, calmly employ the following techniques.

1 Repeat your refusal.
2 Slow down and emphasize the words you are repeating.
3 State your reason, if you did not state it the first time.
4 Don't search for better reasons.

DON'T THINK:

- If I refuse, others will feel hurt or angry.
- If I refuse, others won't like or love me.
- It's rude or selfish to refuse.
- If I refuse, I won't be able to make any requests of others.
- Their needs are more important than mine.

THINK:

- I have the right to say yes or no for myself.
- I have the right to set my own priorities.
- I have the right to state the difficulties that others' requests of me will cause.

ACT POSITIVELY

You may find that there are a number of occasions every day when you worry that you won't be able to manage something. This could range from travelling on your own to sorting out a DIY problem, from making a complaint to meeting new people. It is natural that you will worry when facing something new, but it is rarely as difficult as you think it will be, and by having a positive frame of mind and by being confident you are likely to succeed in your novel task. Use the following suggestions to help you redefine how you think about yourself, your capabilities and your opportunities, and you will find that by being positive you will be able to achieve things that you may have previously not tried.

SEEING THINGS DIFFERENTLY

Imagine that a new, difficult assignment is given to you at work. You could think: 'I can't do this. It's too difficult. I don't know how to do this job.' However, why not talk to yourself differently about the task? For example, you could say to yourself: 'Look at the challenge. This task, regardless of how difficult it may seem at the moment, gives me an opportunity to learn new skills.' Here are some examples of negative and positive self-talk.

PROBLEM	NEGATIVE MESSAGE	POSITIVE MESSAGE
Rejection	'What if they say no?'	'What if they say yes?'
Comparison	'I'm not as good as ...'	'What can I learn from ...?'
Obstacles	'It's a problem.'	'There is a way around this.'
Perfectionism	'I did OK but ...'	'I'm satisfied that I did my best.'
Others	'What will others think of me if I do that?'	'I'm my own person.'
Results	'What if I make a mistake?'	'I wonder what the experience will be like?'
Age	'I'm too old to do that.'	'I'd love to try.'
Defeatism	'I can't do it.'	'I don't have to do it perfectly.'

USING POSITIVE AFFIRMATIONS

Positive affirmations have been utilized by the self-development industry for a long time, as a surefire way of programming your mind to help you attract to yourself the things that you want. For example, if you want to pursue wealth, the affirmation might be: 'I am wealthy.' The problem with this is that, if you are not wealthy, the subconscious mind can easily dismiss the suggestion, as it is not your current reality. It is rather like affirming that you are 2 metres tall, when you are in fact 1.85 metres. When you use the words 'I am' to yourself, then you open yourself up to dismissal from the subconscious.

USING POWER WORDS

A more effective way to programme yourself is with the use of power words. Say, for example, that you wish to acquire wealth. You may have been using the affirmation 'I am wealthy.' When using power words, however, the word to focus on is 'wealth'. In quiet consideration, think about the concepts of wealth and what it means to you. What kind of lifestyle changes would you have to make to attract wealth?

By thinking about wealth as a concept, you are instructing your conscious mind to tell your subconscious mind to personalize what the word means to you. You create in your subconscious your own reality of the word and you leave no doubt as to what this word encompasses, without having to try to fool your subconscious mind into believing that you already have it.

Practise the concept of power words. Choose a new word each week and, during quiet time, contemplate what the word means to you. Here are some examples.

'Train yourself to think positively, using power words and positive self-talk, and you will find that your confidence and self-esteem increase enormously.'

- Wealth
- Inspiration
- Health
- Energy
- Wisdom
- Intelligence
- Strength
- Belief

See also ▶

Boost your social life, pages 244–249

Be confident, pages 250–253

CHAPTER 9
THE FEEL-GOOD FACTOR

It is vital to take time to unwind, de-stress and calm the mind. Yoga, massage and meditation can help you do this and can also be used to revitalize mind and body, depending on what you want to achieve. Combined with advice for combating stress and getting great sleep, the exercises in this chapter will ensure that you are functioning at your optimum level.

STRESS-BUSTING

Stress is not only ageing in itself, but it can also make us feel tense and uncomfortable, even out of control. It comes in many different forms – for example you may simply have too much to do, you may have difficulties in a relationship or there may be a specific event that has happened. It can be short term, for example being stuck in a traffic jam, or longer term, for example when chronic back pain makes sleeping difficult. Although stress is a natural reaction and some degree of stress is good for us, we've all had points in our life when stress has overwhelmed us and become 'toxic'.

FIGHT OR FLIGHT RESPONSE

Back in our primitive days when we encountered stress it tended to be something dangerous. We had two ways to handle it: stay and fight or run away. The physical activity involved burned up all the chemicals the stress reaction released so when the fight or the running was over, the stress was gone and there were no after effects. This is why exercise is a very effective way today to reduce stress levels.

WHY WE GET STRESSED

When something stresses us, the hypothalamus gland in the brain tells glands called the adrenals to start producing stress hormones. There are many of these hormones and they lead to a cascade of reactions in the body. For example, the pupils dilate, the immune system starts to release white blood cells and the heart begins to pump more rapidly, sending blood surging to the arms and legs. You breathe faster in order to flood the blood with oxygen, and your muscles tense up.

Often what happens in modern life is that as soon as we tackle one stressful thing another one hits us. Sometimes we don't even have the time to tackle the original stressor, and others build up on top of it. Over and over again, we trigger the stress reaction without letting it settle down. When this happens, stress becomes a toxin.

WHY STRESS IS TOXIC

Too much stress means that all those positive actions that fire us up to deal with our stressors start to turn on our body. Our increased heart rate begins to put pressure on the heart, fatiguing it and potentially increasing the risk of a heart attack. The muscles that have tensed begin to spasm, which leads to problems like backache and headache. The white blood cells that were released in case we got wounded have nowhere to go, and they can trigger allergies and aggravate autoimmune diseases like arthritis. Finally, the adrenal glands start to fatigue, and so do we. Beating stress is therefore a vital way to help our health.

TOP 10 STRESS FIGHTERS

1 PLAN YOUR LIFE

The most important way to decrease your stress levels is to manage your time effectively. At the start of each day spend 10 minutes deciding what needs doing, and in what order. You will find that you manage to do much more if you plan ahead.

2 LEARN TO SAY NO

It is vital to say no to things you don't have time to do: nothing creates stress more than overloading yourself, and learning to say no is a vital aid to beating its effects. (See also pages 250–253.)

3 CUT DOWN ON CAFFEINE

Caffeine stimulates the adrenal glands to produce stress hormones. Research at the USA's Duke University showed that 4–5 cups of coffee a day boosted levels of stress hormones by up to a third. Stick to 1–2 cups a day, or get a lift from peppermint or ginger teas, which boost energy and mental clarity without creating stress reactions.

4 PRACTISE YOGA

Studies have shown that yoga can decrease tension and blood pressure, which makes yoga an important part of stress management. There are many yoga postures that help to relieve stress, but, when it comes to an all-round stress-busting package, 'Adapted salute to the sun' (see pages 268–271) can't be beaten. It's an instant energizer – so much so that it should only be done in the morning. It releases tension in the muscles, it stimulates the circulation and lymphatic system and, by allowing you to focus on your body and take time out, it helps reduce the mental toll of stress. Finally, through using upward and downward movements, it aims to strengthen and balance the adrenal glands.

5 GET YOUR DIET RIGHT

What you eat is vital. Increase the amount of fruit and vegetables in your diet and avoid junk foods. When it comes to fighting stress, focus on the B vitamins that help support the adrenal glands and give you energy. Good sources of B vitamins include breakfast cereals, wholegrain bread, milk, meat, yogurt, eggs, bananas and dried fruits. You should therefore try to include some of these in every meal.

HAVE A HIGH-CARB LUNCH

Carbohydrate foods are known to boost levels of the mood-lifting hormone serotonin in the brain, so eat 40–50 g (1½–2 oz) of a starchy carbohydrate like bread, pasta, rice or potato (note that eating too many carbohydrates in one go can actually make you lethargic). Serve this with a big side salad or some steamed vegetables to fill you up.

6 EXERCISE

If you want to reduce your stress symptoms by a third, exercise when you're under pressure. Clinical trials have found that exercise reduces stress by burning off the excess adrenaline produced by the adrenal glands. It takes just 10 minutes of activity to start this process, and even just brisk walking can have the desired effect.

7 RELEASE TENSION BY STRETCHING

When we're under stress, many of us hold our body in unusual or uncomfortable positions without realizing that we are doing so. This can cause a lot of muscular tension, and result in aches in the head or back. Doing some simple stretching exercises at your desk can therefore help.

8 HAVE A SCENTED DE-STRESSING MASSAGE

Beating stress is one of the major uses for aromatherapy (see pages 282–287). The oils calm us psychologically, reduce tension in the muscles and can strengthen the adrenal glands. A great stress-beating blend is two drops of lavender, two drops of mandarin and one drop of jasmine oil. Add these to 10 ml (⅓ fl oz) of carrier oil and ask someone to apply them via a massage (see pages 274–281).

9 PRACTISE MEDITATION

Meditation is a great way to clear the mind and to calm yourself. It helps you to rationalize any problems that may be worrying you, and may help to provide solutions to problems that have been stressing you. (See also pages 288–291).

10 PLAN FOR A GOOD NIGHT'S SLEEP

If you are tired, your ability to handle stress is compromised. When you're stressed, however, it can be hard to switch off and go to sleep, which is why you should start preparing for sleep about two hours before you go to bed, with your evening meal. Include the following soporific ingredients in your evening meals:

- **Lettuce** contains lactucarium, which is a natural sedative.
- **Red onions** contain a calming antioxidant called quercetin.
- **Dairy products** contain natural opiates called casomorphins.
- **Starchy carbohydrates**, such as brown rice, pasta or potatoes, create serotonin.
- **A little protein** contains tryptophan, which is used to create serotonin.

SELF-MASSAGE

Care Make sure you are comfortable and are sitting straight.

Repetitions Repeat as many times as you want to.

One of the best ways of combating stress is to take regular breaks during your day. Here is a simple routine that can be done while you are at work. All you need is a stable surface, such as a desk, and a little time – whether you spend 5 minutes or 20 minutes working on yourself, you will definitely feel the benefit and will have more energy for the rest of the day. This routine is particularly good for neck tension, which often causes headaches or a feeling of stiffness.

1 With your elbows on the desk, place your fingers at the back of your neck behind your ears, leaning your head forward slightly in a comfortable position. With the pads of your fingers work the length of your neck on either side of the vertebrae by rotating your fingers and applying pressure.

2 Place one hand on the desk with the palm facing down and the other on the opposite shoulder. Tilting your head slightly away from the area you are massaging, squeeze the muscle between your fingers and the heel of your hand, working from the base of the neck to the edge of the shoulder.

3 In the same position as for step 2, place your fingers on the top of the shoulder muscle and rotate the pads of your fingers while applying pressure, again working from the base of the neck to the edge of the shoulder. Move to the other side and repeat steps 2 and 3.

4 Take the lobe of your ears between your thumb and index finger, close your eyes and visualize a calming scene, such as a beach or a garden. Take a deep breath, and on the out breath pull down-wards and off very slowly. Have a drink of water and you will now feel ready to carry on.

REDUCING STRESS

Wherever possible, it's best to try to reduce stress at the source. The following will help you to tackle the first signs of stress:

- **Do a stress audit** For a month look at the most common things that stress you in your life and find ways to tackle them.

- **Keep your arousal level low** If you start feeling stressed, don't panic – tackle simple things that are adding to the problem, such as a phone call you need to make.

- **Write down your worries** This will help you to get things in perspective. Prioritize those that you can tackle now and start to think about ways to solve them.

5-MINUTE FIXES

If you feel yourself starting to tense up, it's good to try to get things under control as quickly as possible. Here are some 5-minute fixes that will lower your stress levels.

- Calm your breath. Inhaling through your nose to a count of 5 and exhaling through your mouth to a count of 10 instantly calms the body.

- Suck half a teaspoon of honey. This takes just 5 minutes to stimulate serotonin in the brain.

- Warm your hands. When we are stressed, our hands cool, but warming them (simply try sitting on them) lowers stress.

- Stimulate the de-stress points in your feet. Find the furrow on the top of your foot where the bones of your first and second toes meet. Then gently press this 10 times.

ONE-DAY DE-STRESS PLAN

It is actually very easy to fit this into your usual daily routine if you just plan ahead a little.

07:00 **Start the day with some yoga** Practise the 'Adapted salute to the sun' yoga exercise. (See page 268–271).

07:30 **Have breakfast** Use this as a time to boost your B vitamins. A bowl of breakfast cereal with milk, a chopped banana and a handful of raisins is a good choice. Alternatively try poached eggs on toast with a glass of milk and a handful of dried apricots.

09:00 **Make a plan** Spend 10 minutes planning what you need to do in the day.

11:00 **Have a snack** Choose a calming carbohydrate snack, such as fruit.

13:00 **Have lunch** Remember to focus on carbohydrates at this point in the day. A jacket potato and salad or brown rice with steamed vegetables are good choices.

13:30 **Go for a half-hour walk** The activity and fresh air will help reduce tension and energize you.

19:00 **Eat your evening meal** Conjure up a calming evening meal.

21:00 **Unwind before bed** Have a calming detox bath or massage.

22:00 **Go to bed** Have an early bedtime for a great night's sleep.

HINT FOR HEALTH

Avoid toxins, as these will just increase the effects of stress. Cut out alcohol, cigarettes, caffeine and junk food, and instead increase the amount of nutrient-rich foods that you eat, for example fresh fruit and vegetables.

See also ▶

YOGA FOR BODY AND SOUL

In yoga, the ancient Indian 'science of life', ill health is regarded as the product of imbalances or blockages in the flow of energy *(prana)* through the body. By practising yoga positions *(asanas)*, breathing exercises *(pranayama)* and meditation you can improve your physical, mental and spiritual health, helping to release tension and stress, as well as stretching the muscles and making them more flexible, toned and supple. Yoga also helps to open the chest, strengthen the respiratory muscles and stretch the lungs as well as improving the circulation and making the body's immune system more efficient. Yoga is therefore especially beneficial for people with respiratory problems, such as asthma, as well as chronic back pain, migraines, arthritis or rheumatism.

FOCUS ON YOUR BREATHING

Concentrate on your breathing while you are practising yoga positions. By consciously controlling your breathing and taking deep breaths that use the full capacity of your lungs, you can improve your oxygen intake and therefore your blood and lymph circulation, as well as boost your concentration and mental alertness.

PREPARATION

When practising yoga exercises you should wear loose clothing and make sure the room is warm before you start exercising – cold is not beneficial to stretching muscles.

As with all yoga exercises, do them slowly, and do not put any unnecessary strain on your body. If you feel at all uncomfortable or have any pain, come out of the posture, rest and then move on to something else. If you have any health problems or concerns then talk to your doctor before starting yoga.

YOGA SESSION

Although you can practise the following exercises at any time of the day, it can be beneficial to start the day with them, even before you breakfast or shower. These exercises will wake up your body and help to focus your mind. However, you may find it easier to practise yoga at the end of the day when your body is less stiff. Remember to leave at least three hours after a main meal before exercising.

For your first few sessions start with one of the more simple exercises, such as the 'Adapted triangle' (see opposite), 'Cat' (see pages 266–267) or 'Sphinx' (see page 272). As your flexibility and fitness increase, perform the 'Adapted salute to the sun' (see pages 268–271). Relax at the end of your routine with the 'Child pose' or the 'Corpse pose' (both on page 273).

ADAPTED TRIANGLE

This is a modified version of a traditional yoga exercise. The sideways bend is beneficial to the spine and balances muscle groups.

2 **Exhale** and slide your left hand down your thigh as you bend from the hips. Look up at your hand. Don't allow your hips to twist.

1 Stand with your feet about 60 cm (2 feet) apart, toes pointing forwards and look ahead. Place your left hand on the outside of your left thigh. **Inhale** and raise your right arm above your head so it is alongside your right ear.

3 **Inhale** as you come upright. Repeat the same movement on the other side.

CAT

This posture improves the flexibility of the shoulders, neck and spine and tones the upper arms. The moves are performed very gently, to coax rather than force.

Care Take care doing step 4 if you have any back problems.

Repetitions 5

1 Start on all fours with your hands placed under your shoulders and your knees under your hips. You should start with a flat back with your head in line with your spine.

2 **Inhale**, then as you **exhale** arch your back towards the ceiling. Keep your shoulders down and allow your head and tailbone to relax down towards the floor.

3 **Inhale** as you release the posture and reverse the movement to a flat back.

4 **Exhale** as you lift your tailbone towards the ceiling, lower your back down and raise your head up so that you are looking straight ahead.

5 To rest, fold back so that you are sitting on your heels with your arms stretched out in front of you. Relax your head on to the mat and breathe deeply.

ADAPTED SALUTE TO THE SUN

Care Keep your back straight.

Repetitions 2 or 3 times

This is a modified version of a more strenuous exercise traditionally performed in the morning. It wakes up your body and helps to focus your mind. When you have finished, relax in the Child pose or Corpse pose (see page 273).

1 Stand up straight, look straight ahead and **inhale**. As you **exhale**, bring your palms together in the prayer position with thumbs touching your breastbone. Balance your weight equally on both feet.

2 **Inhale** as you take your arms above your head while bending your knees. Look up slightly without letting the weight of your head drop back.

3 **Exhale** as you take your arms out to the sides and hinge forwards from your hips, keeping your back straight and your legs slightly bent.

4 Continue to fold over your thighs and take your hands to the floor or to the backs of your calves. Lift the tailbone as high as you can, stretching the backs of the legs.

5 **Inhale** as you place both hands on the floor, bend your left knee as you take your right foot behind you and lower your knee to the ground. Lower your shoulders and lengthen through your spine. Keep your head in line with your spine.

6 **Exhale** as you take your left leg back so that you are now kneeling on all fours, while keeping your head in line with your spine.

7 **Inhale** and then **exhale** as you fold your body back so that you are sitting back on your heels with your arms stretched out in front of you.

8 **Inhale** and come back to all fours.

9 Take your weight forwards through your hands, lowering yourself down to the floor. Keep your arms bent and shoulders down, lift at the chest. Look at the floor slightly ahead. **Exhale**.

10 **Inhale** and return to all fours, curling your toes under as you do so.

11 **Exhale** as you lift your tailbone towards the ceiling. Keep your knees bent, stretch throughout your back and allow your head to hang down.

12 Slowly lower your knees to the floor so that you are on all fours. **Inhale** and bring your right foot between your hands, bending at the knee. Lower your shoulders and lengthen through your spine. Keep your head in line with your spine.

13 **Exhale** and bring your left foot up underneath you so that it's next to your right foot, keeping your knees bent and your palms flat on the floor.

14 As you **inhale**, take your arms out to the sides and with a flat back lift yourself up to standing.

15 Reach your arms towards the ceiling while keeping your knees slightly bent. Look up without letting the weight of your head drop back.

16 **Exhale** and return to the prayer position with the palms of your hands together in front of your chest, looking straight ahead.

SPHINX

This exercise opens the chest and increases mobility in the spine. It also tones the internal organs and helps to strengthen the arms and shoulders.

Care Don't come too far off the floor as you lift your head and shoulders.

Repetitions 3

1 Lie on the floor, face down with your forehead resting on the mat or a folded towel. Your arms should be resting on the floor bent at the elbow with palms facing down.

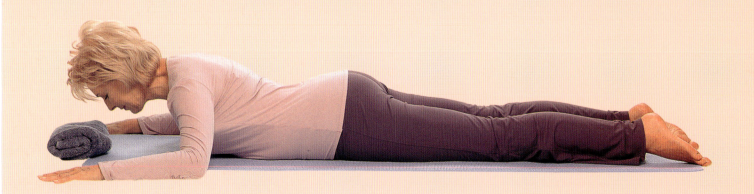

2 **Inhale** as you lift your head and peel your chest away from the floor. Keep your head in line with your spine. Hold this position for a few moments, then **exhale** as you lower yourself back to the floor.

CHILD POSE

This is a very good position to rest in, particularly if your back is not used to stretching.

Care If you find kneeling uncomfortable, place a cushion behind your knees.

Repetitions Once only

1 Sit on your heels with a cushion for support and fold forwards so that you are resting on your thighs. Allow your arms to rest alongside your legs, palms uppermost. Rest your forehead on a cushion or folded towel.

CORPSE POSE

This is so relaxing that you might even fall asleep. Make sure you have something to cover yourself with in this position as otherwise you may begin to feel cold.

Care Make sure your head is in alignment with your body.

Repetitions Once only

1 Lie on your back with your arms slightly out from your sides with the palms facing upwards and the fingers softly curled. Tuck your chin slightly down towards your chest. The legs should be apart with relaxed feet.

2 Allow yourself at least 20 minutes to relax and enjoy the peace and quiet.

MASSAGE TECHNIQUES

Massage has been practised for thousands of years, and its effects have been well-documented – regular massage sessions mean we become healthier and happier. Massage is very versatile and can be effective working at both the superficial and the deeper muscle levels. It can also be used to either relax or stimulate, depending on the kind of massage given.

HANDY TIP

Transfer your massage oil into a handy spout-topped bottle. This will make it easier to oil your hands before – and during – a massage thus avoiding any spillage.

WHAT YOU NEED

Create an atmosphere that is conducive to emotional and physical relaxation. Make sure that the lighting is low and relaxing, that you are in a quiet and warm room (warmer than you would normally have it), and that there is a pleasant aroma, for example from essential oils (see pages 282–287). For working on the floor, a futon is ideal, but a thick duvet or blankets make excellent substitutes. Cover the base with one large towel and use the other to cover your partner, only ever exposing the area of their body being worked upon. Before you start, check that you have everything, so that you do not break your concentration:

- Your chosen oil.
- Box of tissues or kitchen roll.
- Two large bath towels or sheets and one smaller hand towel.
- Small cushions or pillow.
- Blanket or lightweight throw if the weather is cold.
- Water to drink following the massage.

GETTING STARTED

Massage is very easy to learn, and if you work with a friend or partner then you can take turns to practise on each other. You will soon discover the amount of pressure required, which will depend on the part of the body you are working on and the person receiving the massage. As you develop a sense of rhythm and flow, you will find that the strokes will come more naturally.

There are a number of different techniques that you can use. The simplest one is effleurage. You can then use petrissage, percussion or other techniques depending on which part of the body you are massaging and what muscles you want to work on.

EFFLEURAGE

This gentle stroking technique can be used everywhere on the body. It is a rhythmic movement that helps you to spread massage oil, enables you to sense areas of tension and relaxes your partner. It also warms the muscles for deeper work and helps to improve blood and lymph flows.

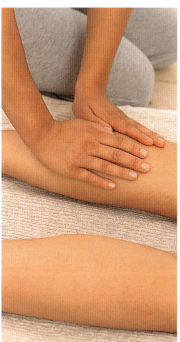

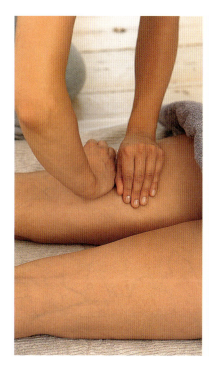
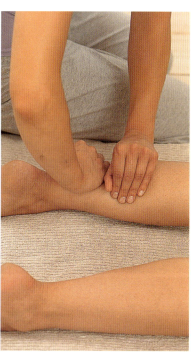

1&2 **Flat-handed effleurage:** Oil the flat of your hands and, with your fingers together and wrists relaxed, make contact with your partner and glide both hands simultaneously with pressure and momentum upwards to your natural reach, then separate and return along the sides of the limb or torso in a breaststroke-like movement. Repeat several times. For extra pressure, place one hand on top of the other when administering the stroke. Pressure can also be applied by the thumb only. If you are working on the back then you can make broad circular movements instead, spiralling up to the shoulders and returning flat-handed down the sides.

3&4 **Cupped effleurage:** Oil your hands, then make contact with you partner and glide up the limb using cupped hands to your natural reach, turn and use the flat-handed stroke to return. Cupped effleurage is a very soothing stroke for the calf and arm muscles. Both flat-handed and cupped effleurage can be done in reverse, where you work in the opposite direction. This stroke will feel quite different to the receiver.

Caution Always remember to lift pressure over joint areas, and when you work on the back place your hands on either side of the spine – do not work directly on it.

PETRISSAGE

Petrissage includes any stroke that presses and rolls the muscles under the skin. It is a medium-depth stroke that is used after effleurage, and breaks up specific knots of tension as well as squeezing the tension, toxins and tiredness out of the body. It also stretches and relaxes the muscles and stimulates circulation.

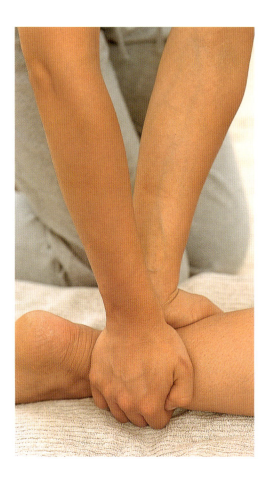

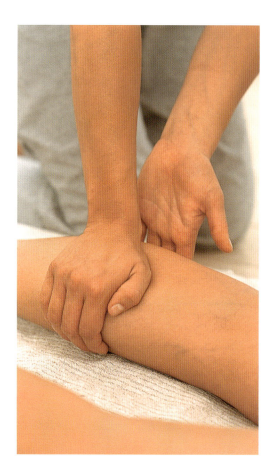

1 With your hands on top of the muscle and supporting the underside with your fingertips, squeeze the heel of your hands downwards, each hand mirroring the other, and then bring your fingers upwards so that you have a handful of flesh between the two. Slide the heel of your hands back and repeat in a continuous rhythm of squeezing and releasing, working upwards over the muscle.

2 Using the same procedure, you can work your hands alternately – one hand squeezing downwards and stretching upwards, followed by the other.

3 For strong pressure, rest one hand on the limb or torso, and repeat the petrissage action with the other, sweeping over the muscle and adjusting the pressure according to your partner's tension. This is particularly good on either side of the spine, along the back or on the shoulders.

THUMB ROLLING

The thumb rolling stroke uses the lengths of the thumbs, applying pressure with the sides. It can be applied on small or large areas of the body to smooth out knotty muscles and is especially useful in releasing tension between the spine and the shoulder blades. It should always be followed by soft, smoothing strokes.

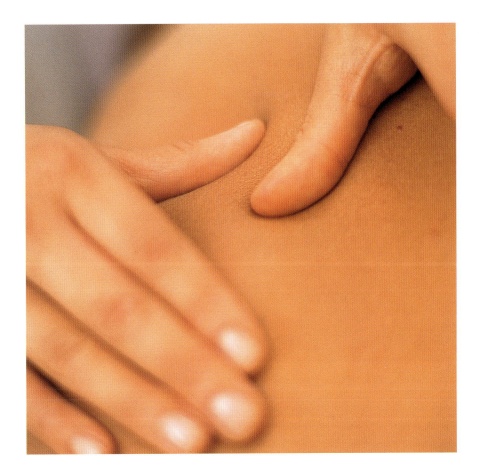

1   Using the length of your thumbs and leaning into your partner's skin with your whole bodyweight, bring one thumb down behind the other, pushing away with short, deep strokes in a rhythmic motion.

'Ensure that your hands are warm and well oiled and keep them relaxed while you massage.'

OTHER MASSAGE STROKES

There are a number of other massage strokes that you can use. These include:

- **Percussion** or **tapping**, where brisk strokes – such as pummelling, cupping or flicking – are made by both hands alternately in a rhythmic motion.

- **Friction**, where the fingertips, thumbs and heel of the hand are used to knuckle, roll or circle the tissue.

See also ▶

Loosen up and shape up, Chapter 2
Aromatherapy healing, pages 282–287

BACK MASSAGE

Your back is vulnerable because it is the body's main supportive structure and it stores enormous amounts of tension in its large muscles. Backache is usually caused by poor posture. The back is often the best place to start a massage, as it enables your partner to relax. With your partner lying on a mat or towel on the floor, position yourself at her head with her arms placed out to the side. Make sure that you are comfortable and reserve your energy by moving your whole body from the hips rather than just using your arms and upper body. With warm hands and warmed oil, place your hands gently on each shoulder blade and hold for 10 to 20 seconds in order to put your partner at ease. At this stage you may observe some tightness and rigidity or even notice the muscles twitching as they start to relax. You can add the back routine to others that treat the head or legs and buttocks, but it is just as effective on its own.

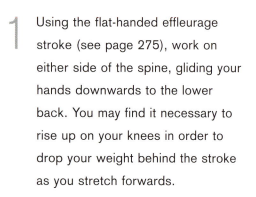

1 Using the flat-handed effleurage stroke (see page 275), work on either side of the spine, gliding your hands downwards to the lower back. You may find it necessary to rise up on your knees in order to drop your weight behind the stroke as you stretch forwards.

2 At the lower back, glide your hands outwards in opposite directions to the sides of the torso and then bring them up the sides with a slight pull, so that you finish level with the armpit.

3 Bring your hands inwards towards the spine, gliding over the tops of the shoulder blades. At this stage you can either repeat the first three, four or five times or continue with the sequence.

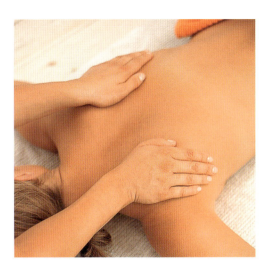

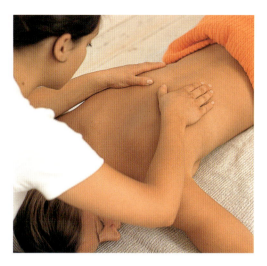

4 At the shoulder blades turn your hands outwards and bring them over the top of the shoulders, so that the flat of your hands are now turned upwards with the fingers resting on the front of the shoulders. Scoop your hands inwards towards the neck area.

5 Repeat the movements from step 2 to step 5 three or four times. On the final stroke, you may wish to bring your hands further up the neck, finishing at the hairline.

6 Place the flats of your thumbs on either side of the spine and, using the effleurage stroke, glide each thumb simultaneously downwards to the lower back. You may feel nodules and observe a change of skin tone in particularly tense areas. Repeat three or four times.

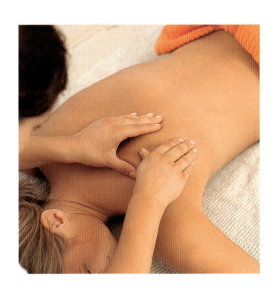

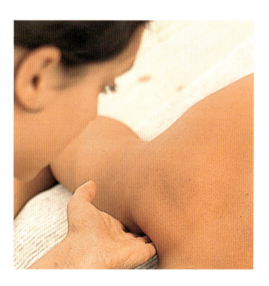

7 In the triangle between the spine, the shoulder blade and the base of the neck, and working on one side and then the other, apply the thumb rolling stroke (see page 277). Spend a little time working on any knots of tension, then soothe with lighter, broader strokes.

8 Rest one hand on the upper back. Make a fist with the other and using the flat part, glide outwards from the base of the neck to the shoulder. Ease off the pressure at the end of the stroke, lift the hand and return to the base of the neck. Repeat three or four times then do the other side.

9 Support your partner's head, which should be facing away from the side being massaged. With the palm and fingers on the underside, glide your hand down the neck to the top of the arm, applying gentle pressure. Repeat several times. Repeat steps 7 and 8 on the other side.

NECK AND SHOULDER MASSAGE

You can use this routine on its own, or it can be a natural progression from the back massage. It is said that we suppress anger and sorrow by tightening the throat and shoulder muscles, so it is important to devote special care and attention to both the back and the front of these areas. Position your partner on a mat or towel on the floor on her back and make sure she is comfortable. Place a rolled-up towel under her knees for support and position yourself at her head.

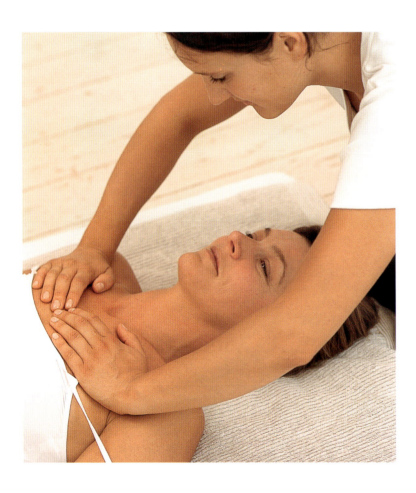

1 Apply oil to your hands and place them gently on the upper chest, just below the collarbone, with your fingers pointing towards each other. Hold this contact for 10 seconds and then effleurage (see page 275) by gliding your hands away from each other towards the shoulders in long, sweeping strokes. Do not lean into the chest and apply pressure only on the outward stroke.

2 On reaching the shoulders, increase the pressure and push them downwards, scooping your hands underneath ready for the return stroke. This gives the neck and shoulders a good frontal stretch.

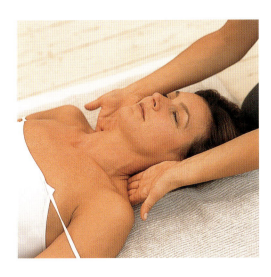

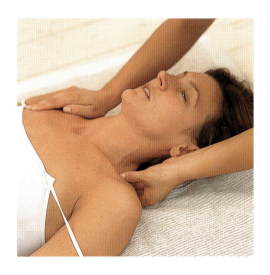

3 With the palms of your hands now facing upwards, continue the stroke, bringing them up underneath the neck until they overlap.

4 Cup your hands under the neck, close to the base of the skull. Pull them towards you slowly, at the same time leaning back slightly to facilitate a very gentle neck stretch without lifting the head. Release slowly. Repeat the first four steps three or four times.

5 Ensure that your partner's head is not facing being worked on. Make a fist and, using the flat part, glide along the back of the shoulder from the base of the neck to the top of the arm. Ease off the pressure at the end of the stroke. Repeat three or four times.

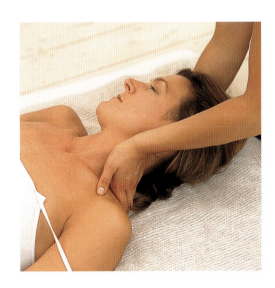

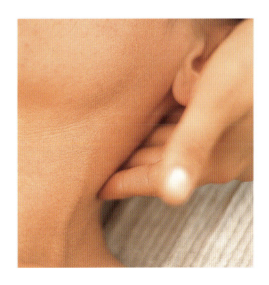

6 Support your partner's head, which should be facing away from the side being massaged. With the palm and fingers on the underside, glide your hand down the neck to the top of the arm, applying gentle pressure. Repeat several times. Repeat steps 5 and 6 on the other side.

7 Place your hands on your partner's shoulders and, using a firm pressure, alternately push down and then release in a continuous movement. One hand should be pushing while the other releases. Repeat several times.

8 Move the pads of your fingers up either side of the neck until they rest on the ridge at the base of the skull. Lean back gently and apply pressure in a circular motion, at the same time rotating your fingers. On the final stroke, comb your fingers through your partner's hair.

AROMATHERAPY HEALING

Aromatherapy is a gentle but effective method of healing and enhancing the mind, body and spirit through the use of natural oils from aromatic plants, trees and grasses; it provides a valuable alternative to chemical-based medicines. The main ways of using essential oils are massage, bathing, inhalation and vaporizing. You may wish to try some or all of the methods before deciding which is the best for you. Your choice of method may also depend on your reason for using a particular oil or blend of oils.

WHAT ARE ESSENTIAL OILS?

Nature has provided us with a healing agent that can be used to enhance our mind, body and spirit. This healing agent comes in the form of 'essential oils', also sometimes known as 'essences' or 'volatile oils', which are extracted from aromatic plants, trees and grasses. These oils accumulate in the glands or sacs within the fibres of the plant, and it is thought that their function is to aid pollination, help with the survival of the plant and prevent attack from predators.

BLENDING OILS

There are over 400 oils, but a skilled aromatherapist will probably use only 40, blending and mixing to achieve the desired results. This skill takes many years to learn and an aromatherapist will know which oil to substitute for another if the desired effect is not achieved. When using oils at home, you will probably have fewer available. However, try experimenting with them, using different oils and in different combinations until you achieve the desired effects. Don't try blending more than three oils at a time as you may find that you 'confuse' the oils and negate their therapeutic benefits.

When blending, use a dropper to count the number of drops more easily – but use a clean dropper for each oil to avoid cross-contamination.

VEGETABLE 'CARRIER' OILS

Oils for massage need to be diluted in a carrier oil. This can be any odourless vegetable oil, but those such as almond, apricot kernel, peach or grapeseed oils are preferable as these are rich in vitamins A,

WHERE ESSENTIAL OILS COME FROM

Essential oils can be found in different parts of the plant:

- flowers (lavender and rose)
- fruit (lemon)
- leaves (eucalyptus)
- berries (black pepper)
- bark resin (frankincense)
- cones (cypress)
- heartwood (sandalwood)
- rhizomes (ginger)
- roots of grass (vetiver).

The orange tree is unusual as it produces three different essential oils, each with differing medicinal properties:

- **neroli** comes from the blossom, and is bittersweet and sedating
- **petitgrain** comes from the leaves, and is beneficial for the skin
- **bitter orange** is provided by the rind, which can help relieve anxiety and worry.

D and E, which are fat-soluble and so more easily absorbed by the skin. Some oils, such as coconut, walnut, sesame and olive, have their own unique aromas and therapeutic properties and, provided these are sympathetic to your essential oil, they can be used successfully.

MASSAGE OILS

For a body massage, 2–3 drops of essential oil should be diluted into 5 ml (⅙ fl oz) or a teaspoon of base carrier oil. This should be sufficient for one massage – you do not need to be lavish with the oil. If you are using a mix of essential oils, the proportion of drops to the 5 ml (⅙ fl oz) or teaspoon of carrier oil should be maintained. Never put neat essential oils on to the skin; choose oils whose smell you like.

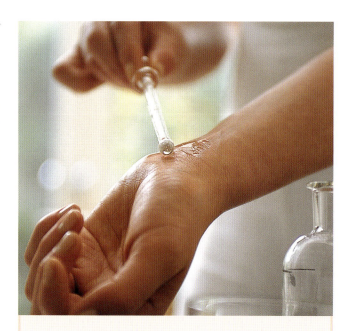

AROMATHERAPY MASSAGE

Massage is an important part of an aromatherapy treatment and is also one of the most effective ways of using essential oils. Touching is a very sensuous and comforting part of human interaction and when touching takes the form of a skilled but sensitive massage, it can relax and revitalize an ailing or tired body. It is also a way of communicating reassurance and a sense of self-worth to another person. When you combine essential oils with massage, you enter a world of healing enhanced with the touch of healing hands and the aroma of healing fragrance. This in itself will help to lift depression and to heal the body.

FRAGRANT BATHING

Bathing is another effective way of using essential oils. Run a warm bath then add 4–6 drops of your favourite essential oil or blend. If you have dry or sensitive skin, add the oil or blend to 10 ml (⅓ fl oz) of unscented foam or milk base (obtainable from all good suppliers of aromatherapy products), which will help disperse the essential oil. Allow yourself to soak in the bath for at least 10 minutes, giving time for the essential oils to penetrate the body and relax and soothe you.

If you prefer to take a shower rather than have a bath, add 6 drops of essential oil or blend to 50 ml (2 fl oz) of unscented shower gel, and use as normal. Don't add essential oils to commercially scented shower or bath preparations, as this can cause a sensitizing reaction on the skin. You can buy unscented bath preparations from any good supplier of aromatherapy products.

For a hand or foot bath, blend 5 drops of essential oil with 10 ml (⅓ fl oz) unscented bath milk base, and add to a bowl of warm water or a spa. Soak the hands or feet for 10 to 20 minutes.

STEAM INHALATION

A simple way of inhaling oils is to put 1–2 drops of neat essential oil on to a handkerchief or tissue and inhale when required. Steam inhalation, in which steam vapours are breathed in through the nose, is very useful for relieving colds, headaches, congestion and catarrh. For a safe and effective steam inhalation, follow these instructions:

1   Put 600 ml to 1 litre (1–1¾ pints) of warm water in a bowl.
2   Add 2–6 drops of essential oil or blend.

WARNING

Always use essential oils with care. There are very few oils that can be used in their undiluted form, so always dilute them unless there is a specific instruction to use them in their neat form.

Before using an oil, always check that it is safe for you. If you have a pre-existing medical condition, are receiving medical treatment, are taking homeopathic remedies or have sensitive skin or a skin condition, don't use the oils until you have checked with your medical adviser and a fully trained aromatherapist.

Always carry out a patch test first, to check that your skin will not react adversely to the oil. Do this by placing a diluted drop on the skin. Leave on for 24 hours. If you see any adverse reaction such as reddening, scaling or any other disturbance of the skin texture do not use.

3 Put a towel over your head and over the bowl, close your eyes and inhale the vapours deeply through your nose for about 1 minute.

4 Don't put your face too close to the steam, as this could burn your skin.

5 Repeat the inhalation several times a day if required.

If you prefer, you can use essential oils with a specifically designed facial steamer instead of a bowl. You should add 2–6 drops of essential oils and inhale for about a minute.

VAPORIZING OILS

There are several ways of vaporizing essential oils to create a perfumed atmosphere in a room.

ESSENTIAL-OIL BURNERS

These usually consist of a ceramic or metal pot with a small reservoir for water at the top to prevent the pot over-heating. A nightlight candle is lit and placed inside the burner. Sprinkle up to 10 drops of essential oil into the water. The heat from the flame vaporizes the aroma from the essential oils in the air. Never put a carrier oil in the reservoir because the oil will heat up and could cause a serious burn if spilt.

DIFFUSERS

These are electric units especially designed for safety and use with essential oils. Up to 12 drops of essential oils may be added to these diffusers, and when plugged in and working they do not over-heat.

HUMIDIFIERS

A saucer of water with up to 12 drops of essential oils placed on top of a radiator will act both as a vaporizer and as a humidifier.

ROOM SPRAYS

Fill a plant-spray bottle with 300 ml (10 fl oz) of warm water and add up to 10 drops of essential oil or blend. Shake before use.

PERFUME

Blend a carrier oil with a blend of essential oils. Pour into a bottle and use it as you would a normal perfume.

CHOOSING AN OIL

Depending on whether you want to calm and soothe or to reinvigorate and revitalize, choose the essence that best suits your requirements.

- **Bergamot** helps to relieve anxiety and depression.
- **Camomile** is a good stress reliever.
- **Frankincense** calms and soothes.
- **Geranium** is a great mood uplifter.
- **Lavender** helps to sharpen the mind.
- **Peppermint** is invigorating and soothing.
- **Rose** is excellent for relieving menopausal complaints.
- **Sandalwood** helps to prevent depression.

AROMATHERAPY RECIPES

Different oils have different effects on your body and mood, so depending on the time of day, how you are feeling and what effects you want to achieve you will need to choose a suitable recipe. Think about how you want to feel, for instance do you want to revitalize yourself in the morning, give your mood a boost for an afternoon pick-me-up or wind down before you go to bed?

SAFETY

Never use more than 10 drops of any oil or combination of oils each day. Using more provides such a clash of aromas that you will negate any positive effects the oils have. You will also risk aggravating your condition rather than improving it.

MORNING WAKE-UP

Start the day off with a bath in this revitalizing blend, which will help perk up the brain and has a fresh, lively aroma.

3 drops basil
3 drops lemon, cypress, neroli or bergamot

Run a warm bath and add the morning wake-up blend.

FACIAL SAUNA

Rehydrate dry skin with this refreshing facial infusion.

4 drops lavender
4 drops geranium
1 drop patchouli

Fill a bowl with hot water, swirl it around and then, placing your face over the steam, make a tent over the bowl and your head with a towel. Linger in this steamy atmosphere for 5 minutes and then wipe your face with a cottonwool ball soaked in toner before applying a rich moisturizer.

ROSEWATER SKIN TONER

Rose oil aids the regeneration of skin cells and this gentle-smelling toner is ideal for dry or normal skin. Use to clean the face after removing make-up or keep the skin clear if you are prone to spots, eczema or dermatitis.

50 ml (2 fl oz) spring or mineral water
15 drops rose

Put the water and rose oil in a glass bottle or jar and shake well. Leave for a minimum of a week in a cool, dark cupboard in order for the oil's aroma to fragrance the water. Filter the water using a coffee filter paper or some kitchen paper. Pour the filtered rosewater into a glass bottle.

CELLULITE MASSAGE OIL

Cellulite usually manifests itself around the bottom, thighs and hips, and gives the skin a crinkly, orange peel look. Massaging the area regularly with this oil will boost the circulation and the lymphatic system, helping to get the blood flowing to the area and feeding the skin.

4 drops fennel
2 drops geranium or juniper
25 ml (1 fl oz) carrier oil

Pour the carrier oil into a small bottle and add the essential oils. Shake well.

REVITALIZING FOOT BATH AND MASSAGE

After a long day on your feet, there is nothing that eases uncomfortable aches and pains quite like a foot bath. Marigold and cypress are both particularly effective in combating odorous feet.

4 drops marigold or cypress
25 ml (1 fl oz) carrier oil
6 drops peppermint

Mix the marigold or cypress oil with the carrier oil in a small bottle and put to one side. Fill a bowl with hot (not too hot) water, add the peppermint oil and swirl the water around. Sit comfortably with both feet in the water and relax or read a book while the peppermint soothes and tones. Pat the feet dry and then gently massage in the marigold or cypress oil.

WINTER REVIVER

Whenever dully and dreary weather has made you feel similarly wet and miserable, use this mix to get the circulation flowing, warm up hands and feet, and impart a relaxing, warming glow to both mind and body.

3 drops ginger
1 drop patchouli
2 drops frankincense
25 ml (1 fl oz) carrier oil

Mix the essential oils with the carrier oil in a small bottle.

SWEET DREAMS BATH RECIPE

To help you unwind after a stressful day, bathe in this relaxing blend. The lavender will help reduce anxiety and depression while the sandalwood will help overcome the potential of insomnia by quietening the brain.

4 drops lavender
4 drops sandalwood

Add the essential oils to the bathwater when the bath is three-quarters full.

MEDITATION

Meditation is the process of entering an altered state of consciousness, one in which you become completely absorbed in contemplation and heightened concentration. When regularly practised it can have a profound effect on mental and emotional wellbeing, enhance self-awareness and promote personal growth, as well as improving and maintaining physical health. It can improve concentration, awareness and memory, as well as decreasing stress and promoting tranquillity.

STARTING OUT

The main thing to remember when learning to meditate is that the intrusion of thoughts is inevitable. Do not try too hard – when any thought enters your mind, observe its presence gently, and do not become irritated by having had it. Recognize the thought, let it go and then re-focus on your breath or the image on which you are meditating.

THE RIGHT ENVIRONMENT

When practising meditation make sure that you won't be disturbed and are comfortable in loose clothing and a quiet room. Either sit in a straight-backed chair or cross-legged on the floor, then close your eyes and focus on your breath, knowing that your body will relax as your conscious mind becomes detached from the outside world.

MEDITATION TECHNIQUES

When you first start meditating try to have each session at the same time and in the same place. Then, when you become more adept, you will be able to meditate at any time in any place. The following three exercises are good to start out with, so that you can learn to focus and cut yourself off from outside distractions.

THE BREATH

Close your eyes and be aware of your breathing. Count each breath, breathing fairly deeply, so that you feel your abdomen rise and fall. Inhale on one, exhale on two, inhale on three, and so on. Your breathing should be even, and you can focus on the counting either on the sensation of air entering through your nose, or the rise and fall of your abdomen. If you lose count, simply start again from one.

THE MANTRA

This is the silent repetition of a word. The word can have a special significance for you, such as 'peace', or a resonant sound, such as 'om'. Your aim is to quietly repeat the word, focusing on it until you reach the point where the sound and its resonance fill your mind.

A REVITALIZING MEDITATION

In many spiritual traditions, the use of water in a ritual is more than symbolic. This exercise is intended to replicate the effect of ritual cleansing using imagery alone, so that it can be practised at any time, anywhere.

THE WATERFALL

Begin by focusing on your breath and when you have quietened the mind, visualize yourself standing at the entrance to a forest. Sense the stillness of this place and the peace that awaits you here. You enter, following a track that leads into the heart of the forest where the carpet of leaves is illuminated by shafts of warm sunlight. Feel the softness of the leaves beneath your feet and listen for the sound of small animals and birds.

Soon you can hear the sound of rushing water growing louder as you move towards the centre. In a while, you come upon a clearing framed by the foliage. In the centre of the clearing is a lake, and on the far side a waterfall. There is not a soul in sight.

Take off your soiled clothes and put your toes in the cool, refreshing water. Feel the revitalizing power of nature soaking into the soles of your feet and saturating every cell of your being. The dirt and dust of the everyday world is washed away in an instant, and so are any aches and pains, mental, emotional and physical. Wade out to the far side of the lake and stand beneath the waterfall which cleanses every particle of your being. Feel the water gushing down the back of your neck and trickling over your face.

Relax and enjoy the invigorating waters until you are ready to return the way you came.

A SERENITY MEDITATION

A certain amount of stress is necessary to galvanize us into action and help us to achieve our aims, but it can become addictive, which can be extremely debilitating. This exercise is designed to alleviate the symptoms and cultivate a sense of detachment and serenity.

THE CLOUD

Lie on a bed or mat with your head supported by a pillow or cushion. Your arms should be by your sides but not touching your body, with your legs slightly apart.

Begin by focusing on your breath and, then, when you feel sufficiently relaxed, scan your body from your toes to your head. Tense each muscle in turn, holding it for a few moments before releasing.

Start to take slightly deeper breaths, pausing at the top of the breath and exhaling in two gradual breaths of equal length. Feel your body becoming lighter as you build a cushion of energy under your body. Continue the breathing.

Visualize yourself supported by a cloud and as the cloud takes form in your mind's eye, feel it rising gently, carrying you up into the sky. Leave your thoughts and your earthbound mind behind, and let go.

Now expand your awareness to take in the view below. Visualize a patchwork of fields and the sea beyond, to which you find yourself drifting. Enjoy the floating sensation. Indulge yourself for as long as you like and explore the skies. Absorb the sunlight, the freshness of the air and the silence.

When you are ready, begin to drift back again, returning gradually to earth, to your home, your room and finally to the bed or mat. Feel the weight of your body being supported and ask yourself to identify the source of the stress in your life, and then ask what you can do to alleviate or resolve this. Consider the matter for a few moments before you return to waking consciousness.

SEEING YOURSELF ANEW MEDITATION

You cannot expect to improve your health, enjoy a better quality of life, nurture fulfilling relationships and increase your prosperity if you harbour an unconscious belief that you are not worthy of the best that life has to offer. This meditation will help you to appreciate yourself.

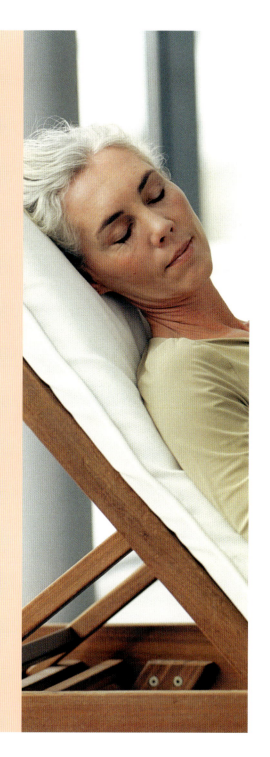

THREE FACES

Make yourself comfortable, close your eyes and focus on your breathing until you have established a steady and regular rhythm.

Now imagine that you are alone in front of a full-length mirror. Study your physical characteristics and consider what you like about yourself and what you could do to enhance these features. What qualities are you particularly proud of? What talents do you possess? How can you develop these further and to what use can you put them? Which abilities would you like to possess and how can you acquire them? Now consider what you don't like about yourself, if anything, and consider what you might be able to change. If it is something that cannot be altered, can you learn to accept it as one of the things that makes you unique? Is it something that you have been conditioned to see as imperfect by others?

Imagine yourself enjoying the company of your friends and family. Visualize yourself as your friends and family see you. What qualities do they see in you? Don't be surprised if you discover that what they perceive as your best qualities are not the same as those you have identified yourself. The physical characteristics that you consider – or have been conditioned to consider – imperfect may well be completely irrelevant to those who love you.

Return to face the mirror, and see yourself as you would like to be in the future. Imagine that you have achieved all your ambitions, fulfilled your potential in every aspect of your life and are enjoying the rewards of your efforts. How have you changed? Again, do not be surprised if the qualities that are now manifest in the mirror are different to those that you believe you possess now.

GETTING GREAT SLEEP

Is any state more natural than sleep? Newborn babies do it for anything up to 23 hours a day and older people find it impossible to resist in the middle of the afternoon. Yet many of us lose that innate ability to drop off somewhere in the intervening decades. This is as much to do with our lifestyle as any physiological changes, so you can change it.

BEDTIME MASSAGE

Massage promotes sleep naturally, which is very important in breaking the cycle of fatigue. Just before going to bed and after a long, warm bath or shower is an ideal time to enjoy a deep, relaxing massage with your partner. As we get older, all the symptoms of adult life – tensions from long, stressful days, overworked muscles or aches and stiffness – rise to the surface and all can benefit from massage. At the same time, massage is also a good channel for communication with your partner and is as therapeutic to give as it is to receive.

THE EFFECTS OF SLEEP DEPRIVATION

Sleep deprivation shows mainly on our faces – in bags or dark circles under the eyes, in saggy eyelids or a drained and pallid complexion. If you possess such undesirable features, follow the sleep hygiene advice below. If your condition has not improved after two weeks, you might be well advised to seek professional help from a specialized sleep clinic.

SLEEP HYGIENE

Sleep allows the body to relax and regenerate damaged and tired cells, so adhere to the following rules to increase your quota.

- Go to bed and get up at roughly the same time each day.
- Avoid alcohol, smoking and drinking any caffeinated drinks before you go to bed.
- Keep all work-related papers or books out of the bedroom.
- Make sure that the room is well ventilated.
- Allow yourself time to wind down before you get into bed.
- Burn a sedative essential oil in your room.
- Avoid very heavy meals in the evening.
- If you cannot sleep, sit up and read until your eyelids begin to droop. Then when you lie down, adopt the yoga corpse pose (see page 273) to help you drop off again.

Sleep abnormalities tend to disappear when a normal sleep pattern is resumed. So, if you are a busy person who needs to stay up late occasionally, don't turn this into a habit. Learn to prioritize better, so that you can get a full night's sleep more often. You will feel better and perform at your optimum level, which in the long run will be more beneficial for you, and those around you.

10 TIPS FOR A GOOD NIGHT'S SLEEP

If you have trouble sleeping, try following these 10 simple rules, and you may well find there is a noticeable improvement in your sleeping patterns.

1 **Get into a regular routine** and go to bed and get up at roughly the same time each day. Get a sense of what your best level of sleep is – maybe 6, 8 or 10 hours. Everyone is different.

2 **Don't be tempted to sleep in**, to 'catch up' on sleep if you want to establish a good routine. Try to start by getting up at the same time and going to bed when you actually feel tired. You should find yourself drifting into sleepiness earlier in the evening. After a few days, you will start to get tired at a regular time.

3 **Avoid caffeinated drinks** in the evenings. Most people know that coffee has a lot of caffeine in it, but people are not usually so aware that tea, cola and other soft drinks also contain caffeine.

4 **Don't drink** excessive amounts of alcohol. Alcohol is a depressant and can therefore put you into a state of low mental arousal, and it also disrupts sleep cycles.

5 **Plan your day** so that you are tackling more taxing and engaging tasks later in the morning and the mid-afternoon, and then do relaxing activities in the evening.

6 **Be aware** that watching television or reading can be over-stimulating, and may cause you to toss and turn, partly depending on the content.

7 **Write down** anything that is racing about your mind before you go to bed. If they become nagging thoughts and refuse to go away, write them down on a pad next to your bed.

8 **Avoid** sleeping during the day.

9 **Get out of bed** and do something relaxing until you feel sleepy if you are not asleep after 15–30 minutes. The point is that you don't want your body to implicitly learn that bed is somewhere where you mull things over restlessly and feel agitated.

10 **Don't work, eat or watch television** in your bedroom – it is not a study, kitchen or living room. Let your body associate it with things that are meant for the bedroom.

See also ▶
Living with the menopause, pages 106–107

SELF-MASSAGE FOR SLEEP

This wonderful self-massage, using the sweet dreams oil (see box, below), will take you only about 5–10 minutes and is a wonderful way to unwind before bed. You can do it after your bath, or even when you are already in bed, although in that case you will need a large pillow to support your back. Take your time and leave the oil on all night.

USING THE SWEET DREAMS OIL

Use half of the mixture (see left) and add to it 25 ml (1 fl oz) of almond oil, grapeseed oil or any cold-pressed vegetable oil. Shake well. Use the oil as you massage your face and neck, and even your scalp if you wish. Take your time, and leave the oil on all night.

SWEET DREAMS OIL

If you have trouble sleeping, put 2 or 3 drops of sweet dreams oil on a tissue and place it on your pillow.

- **12 drops lavender essential oil**
- **8 drops neroli essential oil**
- **5 drops rose essential oil**

Mix the ingredients together and store in a glass bottle.

1 Rest the three central fingers of each hand on each of your eyebrows. Close your eyes lightly and remain in that position for a moment, taking a few deep breaths.

2 Place the middle finger of each hand either side of, and immediately above, the bridge of your nose, between your eyebrows. Now, following the line of the brows, make small circles with your fingers along the length of your brows as far as your temples.

3 When you reach your temples, hold your fingers over them for a moment with a slightly increased pressure. Return to the centre of the forehead, this time with your fingers placed very slightly higher, and trace another line out towards your temples in the same way.

4 Continue to repeat step 2, each time moving your fingers up slightly more until they are following the hairline. Then, follow your hairline with the same circular movements all the way around to the nape of your neck. Repeat this movement several times.

5 Make the same circular movements from the neck hairline down your neck, with your fingers either side of your spine. Do not place them on the spine itself. You may want to use more pressure here.

6 Use the same movements from the centre of your forehead back across your scalp to the nape of your neck. You may want to use two or three fingers here and make the movement cover a larger area.

7 Finally, using the whole hand, cover the whole of your head, as if you are kneading your scalp.

CHAPTER 10
BRAIN BOOSTERS

Your brain is like any other muscle in your body – it needs exercise, as well as a good supply of oxygen and nutrients. This chapter explains which foods contain vital brain-boosting vitamins and minerals. It also shows you how to keep your brain active and challenged by developing new skills and seeking out new experiences and friends.

MEMORY

Memory lapses happen more often as we get older because, just as with our bodies, our brains start to change. Common memory problems may become more frequent. Changes in vision and reduced hearing can also affect memory performance. The speed at which we can process information changes, too, and we become less 'flexible'.

HOW OUR MEMORIES CHANGE

As we age, the ability to take in new information and to recall things is particularly affected. There are lots of differences between individuals, but normal ageing only usually causes mild or occasional difficulties. However, such memory changes can provoke feelings of loss, anxiety and frustration. Understanding such feelings can be an enormous help.

ASSESSING YOUR GENERAL HEALTH

If you feel you are losing your memory and are worried that this might be the result of an illness, the following formal and informal checks should help to reassure you.

- Discuss your changing memory with friends. You will probably find that they worry too.
- Don't panic when you read an article on Alzheimer's disease in the paper – the memory changes associated with disease are very different to those found in ageing.
- Arrange an appointment with an optician for an eye test, and wear glasses if you need to.

- Have a hearing test, and don't be ashamed to wear a hearing aid – it will improve your quality of life markedly, and other people will thank you for it.
- In some areas, there are specialist screening clinics where you don't even need a referral from your doctor. About 90 per cent of people worry unnecessarily, but getting tested can be a huge relief and put your mind at rest.
- If you are still worried, make an appointment to see your doctor for a check-up.

USING STRATEGIES

Try using the following strategies to aid your memory.

- Keep a notepad by the telephone to record all your calls and any messages.
- Put essential information on a notice board.
- Don't be afraid of writing things down to help you to remember them.
- Put items such as keys and glasses in a specific place and keep them only in this place.
- Attach keys or glasses to a neck cord.
- Use a wall calendar to mark appointments and other important information, then get into the habit of looking at this every day.

- Start to keep a diary for recording future appointments, but also for referring back to things you have done in the past.
- Make lists of things that you need to do and tick each one off when you've done them.
- Use a personal tape-recorder to speak into when you think of things you will need to do later. You can then replay the messages to remind yourself.
- When travelling, write down the directions in advance and take them with you.
- If you regularly take medication, buy a pill box marked with the days of the week on it. Prepare the pills for the week in advance on a particular day.

THE BENEFITS OF ROUTINE

Developing habits and routines (see Using strategies, above) will help you to remember and feel organized, and will reduce anxiety. If you do get stressed, try some simple relaxation exercises (see Chapter 9). It is also very important to keep physically healthy by eating sensibly and exercising regularly, and to keep mentally active, by doing crosswords, puzzles and games, or attend discussion groups, for example.

'Don't panic – ageing has only a minor effect on memory.'

THE IMPACT OF INCREASING AGE

Most people notice a change in their memory as they get older. It is natural that just as our bodies start to falter so do our brains, and this particularly affects our short-term memory. Older adults make more memory errors than younger adults. They tend to become worse at working memory and recall first, because the frontal lobes are the first part of the brain to deteriorate. Physical factors can also play a part. Reduced hearing and vision can affect memory function, since they are barriers to taking information in effectively and efficiently.

See also ▶

The feel-good factor, Chapter 9
Test your brain power, pages 300–303
Strategies for improving your memory, pages 304–307
Everyday memory problems, pages 308–309
Fuel for the brain, pages 310–315

TEST YOUR BRAIN POWER

There are different kinds of memory, which means that you need to use different strategies depending on what you are trying to recall – whether numbers, words or when you need to pay bills. Test your memory by working through the exercises below, then use the strategies given on pages 304–307 to improve your recall.

EXERCISE 1 YOUR MEMORY FOR NUMBERS

Ask a friend to read out the following sequences of numbers, starting with just two numbers and progressing to 12.
Don't look at the numbers. Your task is to repeat exactly the same numbers back in the same order. Go as far as you can.

45	12										
6	10	34									
17	99	83	5								
3	68	24	37	12							
19	21	67	82	15	16						
78	55	87	90	23	45	79					
54	7	2	18	48	81	96	33				
11	52	3	89	44	67	28	1	92			
77	46	38	16	8	10	24	26	31	66		
92	6	4	71	85	56	78	94	30	40	13	
67	14	49	46	59	83	12	9	37	93	20	26

Your score is how many numbers you were able to recall in one go.

Less than 5 = poor; 5–9 = average; more than 9 = good.

Most people remember an average of seven 'bits' of information.

'Is your visual memory better than your verbal memory?'

EXERCISE 2 YOUR VERBAL MEMORY

Look at the following list of words and try to remember them – don't write the words down. You have 1 minute.

DOLL	TRAIN	JACKET	RUG
CAR	FOOTBALL	CHAIR	TROUSER
TABLE	MOTORCYCLE	PUZZLE	SOFA
HAT	MARBLES	HELICOPTER	STOCKING

Now cover up the words (don't cheat!) and write down as many of the words as you can.

Score 1 point for each item you recalled correctly (total 16). Less than 5 = poor; 5–9 = average; more than 9 = good. Again, you are likely to have remembered between five and nine items. Did you notice a pattern? If not, look again and you'll notice four categories: toys, transport, furniture and clothing. Grouping items together like this reduces memory load.

EXERCISE 3 YOUR RECOGNITION MEMORY

Look at these words and make a note of which ones were in the list in the exercise above. Don't cheat by looking back. Can you recognize which ones you have seen before?

DOLL	FOOTBALL	DUSTBIN	IRON
CAR	HAT	MOPED	TRAIN
MOTORCYCLE	HOUSE	JACKET	HELICOPTER
RUG	SOFA	PUZZLE	WINDOW

Check back and work out your score. You have seen 11 of these words before. Recognizing less than 9 = poor; 9 = average; 10–11 = good.

Most of us are very good at recognizing words. Recognition tends to act as a natural memory prompt, since the words are all there and you just have to distinguish between those you've seen and those you haven't. A quirk of our memory systems is that, even though it is easier to recall common items, which may come from the same category, it is easier to recognize less common items. The more similar or common items are, the harder it is to distinguish between them.

EXERCISE 4 YOUR EPISODIC MEMORY

This type of memory tends to fall into different categories. Try to answer these questions:

1 What did you have for breakfast this morning?
2 What did you do last weekend?
3 What did you do last Wednesday?
4 If you are married, where were you when you got engaged?
5 Where did you celebrate the millennium?

6 What was the last film you watched?
7 Where were you when you heard that Diana, Princess of Wales, had died?
8 What did you do on your last birthday?
9 What was the last TV programme you watched?
10 What was the last book you read?

Score 1 point for each episode you could recall. Under 7 items = poor; 7 items = average; over 7 = good.

You probably found some of the above were easier to remember than others. It is much easier to recall where you were or what you were doing when there is an important event or when the event has more personal meaning to you. This is because our memories naturally sift information and we forget what we don't need to know.

EXERCISE 5 YOUR SEMANTIC MEMORY

How good is your general knowledge? Semantic memory is our own personal memory for facts.

Try to answer the following questions, and see how good your factual knowledge is.

1 What is the capital of Italy?
2 Who wrote **A Midsummer Night's Dream**?
3 In which direction does the sun set?
4 At what temperature does water boil?
5 Which planet is fifth furthest from the sun?
6 In which year was Nelson Mandela freed?
7 In which year was the Russian Revolution?
8 How many players are there in a soccer team?
9 On which continent is Guyana?
10 In which part of the human body would you find the cornea?

11 Who was the first explorer to reach the North Pole?
12 Who wrote *The Origin of Species*?
13 Which two major oceans border South America?
14 What is the capital of Belgium?
15 Where is the Sea of Tranquillity?
16 What were the dates of the First World War?
17 Which US President was involved in the Watergate scandal?
18 Where was Napoleon Bonaparte's final place of exile?
19 What are the seven colours of the rainbow?
20 Who played the female lead in *Some Like it Hot*?

Under 10 correct answers = poor; 11–15 = average; 16–20 = good.

The answers are given at the bottom of page 303, but if you were to look them up for yourself in books or on the internet you would be more likely to remember them in the future.

EXERCISE 6 YOUR PROSPECTIVE MEMORY

Most of us lead busy lives. How often do you forget each of the following:

1 To pay bills (or whether you have paid them or not)?
 a Often
 b Sometimes
 c Never

2 What time an appointment is scheduled for?
 a Often
 b Sometimes
 c Never

3 To record a television show you will miss because you will be out?
 a Often
 b Sometimes
 c Never

4 What your plans are for the following week?
 a Often
 b Sometimes
 c Never

5 To cancel the newspapers before going on holiday?
 a Often
 b Sometimes
 c Never

6 To draw money out of the ATM before going shopping?
 a Often
 b Sometimes
 c Never

7 To set the alarm clock before turning out the light at night?
 a Often
 b Sometimes
 c Never

8 To take your medications?
 a Often
 b Sometimes
 c Never

9 To send a birthday card to a good friend?
 a Often
 b Sometimes
 c Never

10 To return a phone call?
 a Often
 b Sometimes
 c Never

For each, score 1 point for 'often', 2 points for 'sometimes' and 3 points for 'never'. Add up your scores. 10–15 = poor; 16–25 = average; 26–30 = good.

It can be frustrating when we forget, but the good thing about this type of memory is that it is very easy to improve.

Answers to quiz on page 302
1 Rome; 2 William Shakespeare; 3 The west; 4 100°C (212°F); 5 Jupiter; 6 1990; 7 1917; 8 Eleven; 9 South America; 10 The eye; 11 Robert Edwin Peary; 12 Charles Darwin; 13 Pacific and Atlantic; 14 Brussels; 15 On the moon; 16 1914–1918; 17 Richard Nixon; 18 St Helena; 19 Red, orange, yellow, green, blue, indigo, violet; 20 Marilyn Monroe.

STRATEGIES FOR IMPROVING YOUR MEMORY

We often learn by repetition – for example, by reading things over and over again – and this is called rote learning. This method is not particularly effective, because it is a shallow form of processing. To remember better, you need to learn information more deeply and encode the information in such a way that you are able to recall it effectively a long time later. To do this, you need to add meaning to your learning and utilize extra strategies.

CHOOSE WHAT YOU NEED TO REMEMBER

Although your memory has a huge capacity, you do need to make a choice over what you will need to remember. Trying to remember too many new things can cause interference and overload. This will make older information more difficult to remember. There are often situations

'CHUNKING'

Breaking down information into smaller parts can aid recall, because you are helping your memory by organizing the material. Chunking works well for remembering telephone numbers. You could try to remember the telephone number 0206 411 689 as:

0	2	0	6	4	1	1	6	8	9
zero	two	zero	six	four	one	one	six	eight	nine

That consists of 10 chunks of information, which is too long for your working memory. If you split the number into three manageable parts, it will be easier to remember:

0206 411 689

This is why telephone numbers are normally broken down into several parts, separated by spaces or hyphens.

when you can unburden your memory system by making sure you deal with tasks as soon as they come along, meaning that you do not have to process the item any further. Be selective – you don't need to remember everyone's telephone numbers.

DON'T BE AFRAID TO ASK

One good habit to develop is to discover ways of asking people for information, such as their names, that takes away the need for you to 'carry' or 'process' the information, and that won't make you feel embarrassed. It is probably a good idea to get someone to confirm their name before you make an embarrassing mistake (and run the risk of getting it wrong next time too). In fact, if you were to guess at a name, then next time you meet the same person you could remember your wrong guess rather than the correct version. It helps your memory system to consolidate stronger correct memories by getting things confirmed rather than setting up competing ideas for situations.

MAKING INFORMATION MEANINGFUL

Memory is a product of how well information is perceived and then encoded. 'Effort after meaning' gives rise to a better memory. Attaching meaning to information therefore improves memory by enhancing information traces that are more distinct than items that have only been remembered on a shallower level. The deeper the processing, the better you will remember.

So, if you need to remember information from a lecture, book, talk, TV programme or conversation, a key thing is to be really focused on the meaning. The point is that your memory system is making an effort to make sense of the information, so it is beneficial if you are consciously helping it do this. Asking questions can also aid our understanding (see box, Socratic questions, right).

VISUALIZATION

Learn to associate information with visual images. Difficult material can be converted into pictures and diagrams. Concrete images are more memorable than abstract ideas, and that is why pictures are more memorable. Use your mind's eye. The more silly a visualization is, the better it usually works. Visualization is a particularly useful strategy

SOCRATIC QUESTIONS

One method of making information meaningful, developed by the Greek philosopher Socrates and known as Socratic questioning (and sometimes as 'directed self-discovery'), involves asking some questions about what you are trying to achieve. Socratic questions are ones like 'What do I know already about this?' and 'What might I learn from this?' There is a 'first-letter mnemonic' to help people remember a script of Socratic-type questions to aid their memory: PQRST, which stands for:

- **Preview** Look over the information. What is it generally about?
- **Question** Which questions are you hoping to answer by reading or listening to the information?
- **Read** Read (or listen).
- **Summarize** What was the summary of the information?
- **Test** Have you answered all your questions?

Try **PQRST** on the next documentary TV programme or newspaper article you watch or read, to see if it works for you.

USING AIDE-MEMOIRES

You can help your memory storage system by intentionally pairing something you want to remember with something familiar – that is, you can create an association. Some associations are easy to make, but most things are not so obviously related and you need to be more creative to establish a link. The good news is that if you practise making associations you will get better at it and over time will start to do it without realizing. Aide-memoires include rhymes, memorable sayings or sentences, acronyms and other mnemonics that can be relied upon to jog your memory. You can make them up yourself to help you remember things. Be creative and clever. Be silly. The good thing is that there are already many useful aide-memoires that most of us learnt when we were young:

- **I before E except after C:**
  for remembering how to spell words like 'niece' and 'receive'.
- **Richard Of York Gave Battle In Vain:**
  for remembering the seven colours of the rainbow – red, orange, yellow, green, blue, indigo and violet.
- **Never Eat Shredded Wheat:**
  for remembering the correct order of compass points: north, east, south, west.
- **Spring forward, fall back:**
  for remembering whether to put clocks forward or back.

when trying to remember information about other people, because we learn about others by seeing them.

VISUALIZING PEOPLE'S NAMES

Remembering people's names can be greatly aided by visual images. You may notice that you remember names that are more concrete and visualizable, such as Rowan (berry), Chester (place) or Nat (sounds like an insect). However, most names are far more abstract (John, Peter, Joanna, Rachel), which is why we are all so bad at remembering them. In these instances, it can be helpful to associate the name with a meaningful visual image.

- First, imagine how someone's name is written.
- Then try to link the name with an easily remembered visual tag, for example Michael singing into a microphone (mike).
- For really tricky names, such as Dr Bartoleni, you could try picturing something like a doctor leaning on a bar – as in Dr Bar-to-lean-on.

THE IMAGE-MATCH METHOD

Another type of image strategy is the image-match method. Here, if you need to remember a particular sequence of ideas, link each one with a number and an image. For example, to recall presents you may have received from particular relatives before a party, you could visualize:

1 Jack in slippers.
2 Jon drinking wine.
3 April writing in a diary.

VISUALIZING BY LOCATION

A useful technique is to think of a house with lots of rooms. You have several different types of information to remember, so put each type of information in a different room. When you need to remember something, mentally walk around the house picking up the information as you go.

FINDING YOUR WAY

Many people have a poor sense of direction, but this is easy to improve with practice. If you're one of those who get lost easily, try the following strategies to get you to your destination.

- Visualize a map by looking carefully at a real map and visualizing the route.
- When you are on route, try to see the map in your mind's eye.
- If the route is intricate, add to your visual image by making an ordered list of the directions before you embark on your journey. Take this with you and refer to it if you can't remember which way to turn or the name of a particular street.
- Don't forget that you will probably have to get back afterwards. When you are on the way to your destination, look out for memorable landmarks (make sure that you have paid attention to key landmarks when planning your route). This will help you to get home.

IMAGE STRATEGIES

EVENT	ASSOCIATION	VISUAL IMAGE
You meet someone new.	▶ She has the same name, Polly, as your aunt.	▶ Imagine your new acquaintance and your aunt shaking hands.
You have an appointment on 12 April.	▶ Your mother's birthday is also on 12 April.	▶ Imagine being with your mother on her birthday but having to leave early for your appointment.
You have a new friend who likes to drink tea.	▶ Your new friend is called Theresa.	▶ Imagine Theresa drinking a cup of tea.

MENTAL 'CLUSTERED' REHEARSAL

Imagine you are asked to remember a list of items to buy while you are rushing around trying to do some last-minute Christmas shopping. The list is: greetings cards, tangerines, scarf, beer, wrapping paper, wine, pens, photo frame, socks, sticky tape, toothpaste, chocolate coins, brazil nuts. To remember better, it would help to reorganize the list and repeat it to yourself as:

- **Festive stationery:** greetings cards, pens, wrapping paper, sticky tape
- **Family presents:** scarf, socks, photo frame
- **Drinks:** beer, wine
- **Holiday foods:** chocolate coins, tangerines, brazil nuts
- **Extras:** toothpaste.

This is effectively highlighting and heading the items. The risk is that some things don't cluster well at times – such as toothpaste in this example. So it helps to add on 'Extras' for those kinds of items.

See also ▶

Memory, pages 298–299

Test your brain power, pages 300–303

Everyday memory problems, pages 308–309

Fuel for the brain, pages 310–315

EVERYDAY MEMORY PROBLEMS

This area of difficulty includes forgetting names and numbers, forgetting where you put things, not being able to recall a date or other historical fact, forgetting what you went into a room for, and so on. The good news is that, although just about everyone suffers the same problems, they are actually relatively easy to overcome, with a little practice.

1 REMEMBERING NAMES

Many people find it hard to remember names, because they are often abstract. It is easier to remember unusual names like Brooklyn, Nat and Daisy than ones like Sarah, Peter or John, partly because they are less commonly heard but also because they are more 'imageable' – that is, you can associate them with a place, an insect and a flower. So you need to make associations. Try the following when you are introduced to someone.

1 First, listen carefully to their name.
2 Say their name back to them: 'Nice to meet you, John'.
3 Use their name once again: 'So, John, what do you do?' This helps to cement their name into your memory.
4 Visualize their name in your mind's eye, that is, the individual letters that make up the name – J O H N.
5 Associate their name with something, if that's possible. For example, John is from Scotland, wears glasses, has a prominent brow and has brown hair. This will be particularly useful for when you see them again and need to jog your memory for their name.

2 REMEMBERING NUMBERS AND DATES

This is another everyday difficulty. For dates, keep a diary or calendar and always review a week ahead. For important numbers, try the following techniques.
- Break them down into 'chunks' (see page 304).
- Visualize the numbers written down.
- See the spatial pattern that they make on the keypad (of both telephone and cashpoint machine).

You don't need to remember every number, however, so write less important numbers down in a diary or store them in your mobile phone, if you have one.

3 AVOIDING LOSING EVERYDAY ITEMS

Be organized, and try to form the habit of always putting things back in the same place. If you have lost something and need to find it quickly:

- Think back to where you last had the item.
- Try to visualize what you did with it.
- Look in the all of the usual places you might have left it.

4 REMEMBERING WHAT YOU WENT INTO A ROOM FOR

Work through these steps until you remember:

- Concentrate and try not to be distracted by other thoughts.
- Think back to where you came from and mentally retrace your steps.
- Return to the place you started from. This puts you in the original context and prompts your memory.

5 THE TIP-OF-THE-TONGUE PHENOMENON

We are all familiar with this one – something such as the name of a famous person, a character in a book or a particular place is just on the tip of your tongue, but you can't quite recall it. Try these steps to trigger recall:

- Go through the alphabet and think of words or names beginning with each letter.
- Think of a context or related item as a prompt.
- Relax – stress will stop the word coming.
- Visualize what the person or item looks like and build up a mental picture.

6 FINDING YOUR WAY AROUND

Before you leave for somewhere you have not been before, take time to:

- Plan a route, using a map.
- Visualize the route in your head to create a mental picture so you can get to your destination by memory (rather than having to stop and check).
- Circle the place you are going to on the map, so that if you need to refer to the map you can find it quickly.
- Make a list (using bullet points and large writing) of the main directions to refer to during the journey.

When you are asking for directions to somewhere:

- Listen carefully to what the person is saying. Focus on what they are saying (not what they are wearing, for example).
- Visualize what they are saying.
- Summarize the instructions back to them: 'So I should go left, right, right again, then left', and so on. This will also help to slow them down if they are telling you too fast.
- Before you proceed, run through the instructions, then repeat them to yourself as you go on your way.

FUEL FOR THE BRAIN

The brain has an extensive blood supply. There is a constant flow of blood carrying important neuronutrients, such as amino acids, vitamins and minerals, together with oxygen and glucose to provide energy to the brain. An interruption in the blood flow for just one or two minutes can impair brain function, resulting in confusion or unconsciousness; if the brain cells are deprived of oxygen for four minutes, permanent brain damage may occur. A good circulatory system and strong, healthy blood vessels are therefore vital for keeping the brain well fed and on top form.

HOW THE BRAIN IS PROTECTED

The structure of the brain is so important that the body guards it with several shields against damage. There is not only the physical protection of the skull and underlying membranes but also a system called the blood–brain barrier, which protects against any poisons in the blood. The blood–brain barrier provides a filtration system, which allows only oxygen, glucose and a few selected nutrients to pass through. Unfortunately, this barrier is not foolproof; although it allows essential nutrients and some mood-elevating substances to enter the brain, other chemicals including alcohol, nicotine and caffeine can also pass through to the brain with less beneficial effects.

MAXIMIZING YOUR BRAIN FUNCTION

A vast array of nutrients are needed to keep the brain working in top condition. The neurons (nerve cells) need to be fed to carry strong, clear messages, the supporting structures need to be properly maintained so that the messengers have a smooth, uninterrupted trip, and the whole nervous system needs lots of fuel to power vigorous mental activity. Quality food is therefore essential (see also Chapter 3).

'A vast array of nutrients are needed to keep the brain working in top condition.'

WORKING TOGETHER

It is important to remember that every nutrient is essential for peak brain performance. A deficiency in even just one vitamin or mineral can result in lower IQ, mood changes or even depression. This is because nutrients work together to make things happen in the body and brain.

KEY NUTRIENTS

Each of the following nutrients has a vital role to play in good physical and mental health.

Water makes up 83 per cent of blood and acts as a transport system, delivering nutrients to the brain and carrying away waste products. A good supply of clean water is essential for concentration and alertness.

Protein components provide the structural building materials for most of the body's tissues, nerves and internal organs, including the heart and brain. Proteins are used to manufacture neurotransmitters, chemicals, such as serotonin and endorphins, which facilitate the transmission of messages within the brain. Proteins are essential for maintaining the nerve network, improving mental functions as well as lifting spirits.
Protein is found in: meat, fish, milk, cheese, beans and grains.

Carbohydrates break down into glucose, through digestion, providing the brain with its primary source of energy. It is vital that this level of glucose does not fluctuate too much, otherwise mental confusion, dizziness, convulsions and loss of consciousness could occur.
Carbohydrates are found in: rice, pasta, grains, bread, fruits and vegetables.

Fats come in three forms: saturated, monosaturated and polyunsaturated. The term 'essential fatty acids' refers to two specific polyunsaturated fats called omega-6 and omega-3. Studies of essential fatty acids suggest that these special fats can increase brain size and brain cell numbers, improve vision and aid learning.
Essential fatty acids are found in: salmon, mackerel, sardines, nuts and seeds.

Vitamins are necessary for the growth and function of the brain and body. The body cannot manufacture most vitamins itself, so it is important to get these from food. Vitamins A, C and E are key antioxidants (see pages 312–313), and are particularly important for promoting and preserving memory in the elderly.

The 'B complex' group of vitamins are especially important for the brain and include vitamins B1, B2, B3, B5, B6, B12 and folic acid, which have key roles in producing energy for every cell. When someone isn't getting enough B vitamins, they may lack energy, feel tired and lethargic, and have trouble concentrating. The elderly seem to be particularly prone to vitamin B12 deficiency, and this may be due to inefficient digestion and poor absorption.
B vitamins are found in: brewers' yeast, liver and whole grains such as brown rice, barley and couscous.

Minerals form parts of bones, teeth, muscle, blood and nerve cells. Approximately 17 minerals are thought to be essential to human nutrition. They are important factors in preserving the vigour of the brain, as well as the heart. In particular, the minerals magnesium and manganese are required to convert carbohydrates into brain energy. Sodium, potassium and calcium are important in cell-to-cell communication and maintaining an efficient nerve network to facilitate the transmission of messages. See also pages 78–79 and 144–147.

The term 'synergy' is used to describe the process whereby two nutrients working together have the effect of multiplying their benefits for human health. An example of synergy is the way in which vitamins C and E work. Both are antioxidants, which fight free radicals, but vitamin C also recycles the vitamin E, thus allowing it to carry on the fight even longer. Nature has made it easy by providing the nutrients that work together in the same foods. For example, sweet potatoes contain vitamins A, C and E, while cod, lentils and chickpeas are all good sources of both vitamin B6 and zinc.

FREE RADICALS

As the brain ages, it goes through various changes. Many people feel that they no longer think as clearly or learn as quickly as they did. Most complain of increasing forgetfulness. Researchers now agree that many of the signs of ageing can be put down to the result of free-radical activity. Free radicals are chemicals generated within the body that attack the body's cells and can cause irreparable damage.

Common sources of free radicals are pollution, fried foods, radiation and sunlight, but the body also produces free radicals when fighting infections, exercising and even when breathing. Over time, free-radical damage accumulates and gradually signs of ageing become more apparent. The brain is particularly vulnerable to free-radical damage because these harmful chemicals are attracted to fatty tissues and the brain's structure is primarily fat.

ANTIOXIDANTS

Help is at hand in the form of nutrients called antioxidants, which combat the effects of free radicals. Antioxidants incapacitate free radicals and block their path of destruction. A plentiful supply of antioxidants in the diet can help to slow down the signs of ageing and may boost a failing memory (see also Chapter 3). The key antioxidant vitamins are A, C and E, which are found in abundance in fresh fruits and vegetables; these ACE vitamins protect the brain and body.

Recently, researchers have discovered some very powerful antioxidants called anthocyanidins – thought to be 50 times more powerful than vitamin E, providing strong protection for the brain from the damaging effects of free radicals. Found in abundance in certain fruits and berries (in fruits, stems, bark, seeds, flowers and leaves),

anthocyanidins are interesting because they can provide protection from a wide variety of toxins and free radicals in both watery and fatty parts of the body. This is in contrast to other antioxidants like vitamin C, which protect only watery parts of the body, while vitamins A and E protect fatty tissues. The significance of this dual role becomes apparent when we consider the composition of the human body – most organs have both fatty and watery components.

Colour can give us a clue as to the relative merits of different fruits. Red, purple and blue fruits, in particular berries, are rich in anthocyanidins and will give maximum protection to precious brain cells.

PRE-SENILE DEMENTIA AND DIET

Pre-senile dementia is a brain disorder that begins in middle age and results in progressive memory loss, personality changes and deterioration of mental faculties. It is thought to be caused by hardening of the arteries. The clogged arteries slowly reduce the supply of nutrient-rich blood to the brain and, as the brain is starved of these important nutrients, cognitive function starts to suffer. Eventually the person may suffer a stroke (an interruption of the blood supply to a part of the brain), leading to partial paralysis, coma or death.

A diet rich in essential fatty acids will encourage healthy blood vessels, reduce blood pressure and lower cholesterol levels. High-fibre foods will also lower cholesterol, and lots of dark-green leafy vegetables, nuts, seeds, wheatgerm and whole grains will provide rich sources of vitamin E to improve the body's circulation. For maximum protection, avoid sugar, sweets, fried foods, foods high in fat, processed foods, caffeine and alcohol.

ALZHEIMER'S DISEASE AND DIET

Alzheimer's is characterized by symptoms that include depression, distorted perceptions, inability to concentrate and progressive memory loss. It usually strikes after the age of 60 or 65, although it can be found in younger people. Despite extensive research, the precise cause of the disease is not known. It is believed that genes play a role, but environmental factors are also likely to be significant. Scientists have observed that Alzheimer's sufferers tend to have low levels of B vitamins and zinc, both of which are important in cognitive functioning. Processed foods tend to contain little of these key brain boosters.

HINTS FOR HEALTH

- One reason the ageing body becomes deficient in vitamins and minerals is that it is less efficient at digesting and absorbing nutrients.

- Chewing each mouthful of food 20–30 times can aid the body in extracting nutrients.

- Drinking 2 litres (3½ pints) of still water each day can increase alertness and awareness.

- Stress can inhibit recall at any age. Increasing certain key nutrients, such as vitamins B5 and C, may help to protect against the effects of long-term stress or the stress of a traumatic event.

TOP 10 TIPS FOR INCREASING BRAIN POWER

To maintain a steady supply of glucose flowing to the brain, follow these simple instructions.

1 Always eat breakfast. Choose porridge oats or wholemeal toast with a poached egg rather than a sugary cereal.

2 Eat small frequent meals, which contain protein plus slow-releasing carbohydrates; protein counteracts the effects of carbohydrate.

3 Avoid sugar and sweets.

4 Avoid fast-releasing carbohydrates such as processed breakfast cereals, cakes made with white flour and white rice.

5 Avoid caffeinated drinks, such as coffee, tea and cola.

6 Avoid alcohol.

7 Avoid, or at least reduce, cigarettes.

8 Reduce stress.

9 Eat complex carbohydrates found in wholegrain bread, brown rice and vegetables.

10 Exercise regularly.

Some studies have reported an association between aluminium and Alzheimer's, and high levels of aluminium have been found in the brains of some Alzheimer's patients. This has led experts to recommend that aluminium cookware should be avoided, especially when cooking acidic foods.

Antioxidant-rich foods are particularly important for protecting brain cells from free-radical damage, as is avoiding exposure to free radicals in the first place. Eating whole, unprocessed and unrefined foods may reduce the risk of Alzheimer's disease and will certainly boost the natural protection of the brain and nerve cells.

TOP BRAIN FOODS

The following antioxidant foods can delay the effects of ageing on mental performance. Key antioxidant vitamins A and E protect the fatty parts of the brain and body, including the nerve cell membranes. Vitamin C works with vitamin E for maximum antioxidant power.

BERRIES

New research has declared berries to be the anti-ageing food of the 21st century. They contain anthocyanidins (see pages 312–313), which are powerful antioxidants, and have been found to prevent collagen from breaking down. Collagen is the elastic component in skin, joints and, in particular, veins and arteries, which carry nutrients to the brain. In addition to being rich in anthocyanidins, berries boast high levels of vitamin C and beta-carotene (the precursor of vitamin A). Anthocyanidin-rich fruits include blackberries, blueberries, cranberries, blackcurrants and black grapes. Anthocyanidins survive various food processes, so when fresh berries are not available canned and frozen berries are nutritious alternatives.

CARROTS AND SWEET POTATOES

The rich orange colour of sweet potatoes and carrots indicate that they are loaded with beta-carotene. This carotenoid pigment converts to vitamin A in the body when needed and is a powerful force in the fight against free radicals. Carrots contain more beta-carotene than any other vegetable. Sweet potatoes are also rich in beta-carotene as well as vitamins C and E. Choose the darkest orange specimens for maximum beta-carotene, and avoid shrivelled ones. Beta-carotene is more absorbable when cooked, so baking, steaming or boiling is ideal.

WATERCRESS

This salad leaf is an excellent source of vitamin C. However, vitamin C is particularly vulnerable to degradation, so buy fresh watercress and eat it as soon as possible after purchase. The deep green colour of watercress means that it is rich in beta-carotene.

PEAS

In addition to providing beta-carotene and vitamin C, peas are wonderful antioxidants; plus, they contain more protein than most other vegetables. Pea protein is deficient in the amino acids methionine and cysteine, but these are supplied in ample amounts by cereal grains including rice and wheat. These amino acids supply the brain with the basic building blocks of neurotransmitters.

Peas can be bought fresh, frozen, canned and dried. Cooked dried peas provide about twice as much carbohydrates and proteins as cooked fresh peas, but fresh peas are a much better source of the antioxidant vitamins beta-carotene and vitamin C. As a general rule, fresh peas provide more vitamins and minerals than frozen or canned. However, frozen or canned peas are better than raw peas that have been stored too long and lost much of their nutritional content.

OILY FISH

The omega-3 oils found in certain fish are crucial for protecting the parts of our brain that send messages to the body. Sources of these essential fatty acids include mackerel, sardines and kippers. Fresh salmon and tuna also contain high levels of omega-3 oils, although the canned versions of these fish are poorer sources of these vital fats. A diet rich in these fatty acids will not only protect the function of the nervous system but also enhance your mental abilities.

BREWERS' YEAST

Brewers' yeast is a non-leavening yeast that is rich in virtually all the important brain-boosting nutrients. It is usually sold in powder form for use in cooking or as tablets or capsules. Brewers' yeast is rich in B complex vitamins. Rich in iron, chromium, potassium and magnesium, it also supplies the minerals needed for alertness and concentration.
Caution Brewers' yeast is high in purines and should be avoided by those with gout or kidney stones. Purines are nitrogen-containing chemicals found in many foods and are excreted from the body as uric acid.

See also ▶

Healthy eating for a longer life, Chapter 3
Memory, pages 298–299
Test your brain power, pages 300–303
Strategies for improving your memory,
pages 304–307
Everyday memory problems 308–309

INDEX

ACKNOWLEDGEMENTS

Special Photography:
© Octopus Publishing Group Limited/Mike Prior

Other Photography:
Alamy/Acestock 262; /IPS 84 top; /Stockfolio 253.
Corbis UK Ltd/Anne W. Krause 227; /Will & Deni McIntyre 36; /Jose Luis Pelaez 219; /LWA-Dann Tardif 137. Getty Images 74, 106, 229/Tony Anderson 99;/Robert Daly 218; /J P Fruchet 223; /Deborah Jaffe 240; /Ghislain & Marie David de Lossy 134; /Kevin Mackintosh 235; /Michael Malyszko 136; /Butch Martin 181; /Lori Adamski Peek 184; /Pete Seaward 255; /Piecework Productions 250; /Andreas Pollok 225, 291; /Justin Pumfrey 141; /Marc Romanelli 252, 308; /Stephen Simpson 98; /Paul Thomas 215; /Arthur Tilley 84 bottom; /Bill Truslow 304; /Nick White 234; /Angela Wyant 226. Octopus Publishing Group Limited 228, 285, 289, 290; /Frank Adam 93 right, 98, 110 centre left, 114 picture 3; /Colin Bowling/Organon Laboratories Ltd. 105; /Jean Cazals 79 picture 3; /Stephen Conroy 79 picture 5, 192 top left; /Jerry Harpur 287; /Jeremy Hopley 71; /David Jordan 79 picture 4, 193 centre left top; /Sandra Lane 82 centre, 82 bottom, 85 top, 87, 90 left, 90 right, 93 left, 99 right, 110 bottom left, 165, 286; /Gary Latham 143; /William Lingwood 78 top, 78 centre bottom, 78 bottom, 79 picture 6, 79 picture 2, 89 left, 113, 114 picture 9, 114 picture 7, 114 picture 5, 114 picture 1, 115 picture 4, 115 picture 3, 115 picture 2, 115 picture 1, 115 picture 9, 116, 117, 118, 119, 120, 121, 122, 123, 124, 125, 126, 127, 128, 129, 130, 131, 162, 176, 190 top, 190 bottom, 262 top right, 311; /David Loftus 102; /Tom Mannion 238; /Neil Mersh 177; /Peter Myers 35, 81, 139, 239; /Sean Myers 92 right, 192 centre left top; /Ian O'Leary 72 bottom; /Peter Pugh-Cook 34, 75, 114 picture 6; /William Reavell 18, 22, 37, 72 top, 86 top, 92 left, 112, 114 picture 8, 114 picture 4, 114 picture 2, 115 picture 8, 115 picture 7, 115 picture 6, 115 picture 5, 142, 167, 168, 169, 171, 188, 190 centre, 191, 191 top, 192 centre left, 192 bottom left, 192 centre left bottom, 193 top left, 193 centre left, 193 bottom left, 193 centre left bottom, 194, 195, 196, 197, 198, 199, 200, 201, 202, 203, 204, 205, 206, 207, 208, 209, 214, 217, 248, 283, 284, 298, 310, 314, 315 top, 315 bottom; /Craig Robertson 79 picture 1; /Gareth Sambidge 261, 274, 275, 276, 277, 278-279, 280-281, 282; /Niki Sianni 135, 152, 153, 154, 155, 156, 157, 158, 159, 160, 161;/Simon Smith 170, 172, 174, 175;/Karen Thomas 78 centre top; /Unit Photographic 292; /Ian Wallace 17, 82 top, 91 right, 149, 163, 164, 166, 241, 258, 262 centre, 262 centre right; /Philip Webb 173, 259, 312; /Mark Winwood 186, 216; /Jacqui Wornell 262 top centre; /Polly Wreford 85 bottom. Imagesource 25, 109, 220, 237, 245, 288.
Rubberball Productions 138.

The publishers would like to thank Agoy for providing yoga mats.
www.agoy.com

Executive Editor **Sarah Tomley**
Senior Editor **Rachel Lawrence**
Executive Art Editor **Rozelle Bentheim**
Designers **Martin Topping and Jilly Sitford at 'ome design**
Picture Research **Jennifer Veall**
Production Controller **Manjit Sihra**

Special photography **Mike Prior**
Hair and make-up for Diana Moran **Martin Fletcher**